"It is only through the careful, sensitive interaction between individuals, with an appreciation for community, and with deference to God that a people can grow in understanding, in strength, and in commitment to something bigger than themselves."

Ora Horn Prouser

Contents

Editor's Introduction
Joseph H. Prouser — 1

Your Mother's Torah (Proverbs 1:8)
Ayal Prouser, Eitan Prouser, Shira & Avi Kravitz — 4

Ora Zo Shel Torah: This Light of Torah
A Tribute from *Rabbi Moshe Yaakov Mendelowitz* — 8

Ora Horn Prouser—A Tribute
Shuly Rubin Schwartz — 10

All Shall Be Seen Before Me:
Halakhah Mandates Inclusion & Dignity for those with Special Needs
Bradley Shavit Artson — 12

Triage in the Time of a Pandemic:
The Sanctity of Saving as Many Lives as Possible
Elliot N. Dorff — 29

Moses as Leader in the Eyes of the Tannaim
Matthew Goldstone — 43

May Women Serve as Mohalot?
David Golinkin — 58

The Story of the Story as the Focus of Engagement
Edward L. Greenstein — 64

The Free Exercise Clause and the Challenge to a Civil Society
Debra E. Guston — 81

The Wonder of Trees: Musings in Honor of Tu B'Shevat
Jill Hackell — 90

The Witch of En-dor: Tending the Spring of Generations
Jill Hammer — 96

ראו אור
Ra'u Or

Essays in Honor of Dr. Ora Horn Prouser

"The people who walked in darkness
have seen a brilliant light."
—Isaiah 9:1

Edited by Rabbi Joseph H. Prouser

Ben Yehuda Press
Teaneck, New Jersey

RA'U OR: ESSAYS IN HONOR OF DR. ORA HORN PROUSER ©2021 by the authors of each chapter, who retain ownership over their work. All rights reserved. No part of this book may be used or reproduced in any manner whatsoever without written permission except in the case of brief quotations embodied in critical articles and reviews.

The original artwork adorning the cover was created for this Festschrift by artist and calligrapher Sonia Gordon-Walinsky, of PasukArt, based in Philadelphia, Pennsylvania. Her watercolor is an interpretation of Isaiah 9:1–"The people who walked in darkness have seen a brilliant light." The title of this volume–Ra'u Or ("They have seen a light")–is taken from that Hebrew verse, in reference to our honoree, Dr. Ora Horn Prouser. Those two Hebrew words are mutual anagrams–a fitting tribute to a scholar so adept at approaching the text of the Hebrew Bible from innovative angles and different perspectives, skillfully analyzing its contents, discovering fresh meanings and connections, and providing illuminating new insights to grateful readers and students of Scripture.

Transliteration and notes: The method of rendering Hebrew words and phrases in English characters has been left to each contributing writer as a reflection of personal taste, style, and academic approach. Transliterations thus vary from chapter to chapter. The format of footnotes and annotations embedded within the chapters are, for the same reason, similarly varied.

Published by Ben Yehuda Press
122 Ayers Court #1B
Teaneck, NJ 07666

http://www.BenYehudaPress.com

To subscribe to our monthly book club and support independent Jewish publishing, visit https://www.patreon.com/BenYehudaPress

Ben Yehuda Press books may be purchased at a discount by synagogues, book clubs, and other institutions buying in bulk. For information, please email markets@BenYehudaPress.com

ISBN13 978-1-953829-23-8

21 22 23 / 10 9 8 7 6 5 4 3 2 1   20211107

A Rabbi Muses About "Entering the Zone"
at Grateful Dead Concerts and at Synagogue Worship Services
Jeff Hoffman   109

How Do You Sleep?
A Sermon for Martin Luther King Day
Peter E. Hyman   120

Light and Peace in Our Daily Liturgical Declarations
Michael Kasper   124

Large Issues in Small Spaces:
What Jews Can Learn from Christians about Public Theology
Nancy Fuchs Kreimer   132

Why Did He Die at Half His Days?
The Torah Student Who Wouldn't Touch His Wife
Dov Linzer   140

These Words—A Letter to Ora
Barbara Horkoff Mutch   150

The Day of the Lord and the Book of Esther
Joseph H. Prouser   155

The Politics of Kashrut: Preliminary Observations
Jonathan Rosenbaum   162

Finding the Button and the Buttonhole
Eric George Tosi   181

A TOrah Line
Amy Roth   187

Selected Bibliography: Dr. Ora Horn Prouser   193

Contributors   196

Editor's Introduction

Joseph H. Prouser

Ever since her student days as an aspiring biblicist, Dr. Ora Horn Prouser has identified as her favorite biblical verses—and taken as her guiding light and pedagogical motto—the divine assurance regarding God's Word offered in Deuteronomy 30:12-14.

"It is not in Heaven, that you should say, 'Who shall go up to Heaven for us, and bring it to us, that we may understand it and do it?' Nor is it beyond the sea, that you should say, 'Who shall go across the sea for us, and bring it to us, that we may understand it and do it?' Rather, the Word is very near to you, in your very heart, that you may do it."

Animated by the conviction that the meaning and beauty of Scripture are accessible to all who approach the biblical text with open minds and analytical discipline, Ora has inspired countless students—young and old—to embrace the study of Bible... to find personal meaning in the sacred text while never imposing meanings or interpretations which an intellectually honest, rigorous, scholarly, and critical reading will not sustain. "Where is it in the text?" she will demand. Not in Heaven. Not across the sea. It is in your very heart... but... it must be grounded in the text.

Ora has instilled this approach in adult lay learners as a much sought after scholar-in-residence and through public lectures, classes, and publications. She has trained aspiring rabbis, cantors, and academicians at both the Jewish Theological Seminary of America during her many years on its faculty... and at the Academy for Jewish Religion, which she leads as CEO and Academic Dean, and which she serves as Professor of Bible. She continues to draw devoted and admiring students from among the alumni of these institutions at retreats and conventions and continuing education opportunities. Through the students she has trained and taught among the clergy, Ora has had an immeasurable impact on their religious charges, communities, and congregants across denominational lines.

Ora's faith in the accessibility of Biblical literature—the relevance of the Bible to all people—has also led her to explore how Scripture speaks to—and of—individuals with special needs. In her award-winning *Esau's Blessing: How the Bible Embraces Those with Special Needs*, Ora invites those with physical, emotional, developmental, and educational challenges—the "differently-abled"—to find themselves in the Hebrew Bible... and among its heroes and heroines, its prophets and lawgivers. Not only can we find the

Bible in our own hearts... we can—all—find ourselves in the very heart of the biblical text.

"It is not in Heaven." Yet, among the contributors to this volume are distinguished scholars, accomplished clergy, and renowned academic leaders who have attained dizzying heights in learning, in teaching, and in the service of Heaven. "And it is not across the sea." Yet, among the contributors to this volume are those who have led and taught in institutions "across the sea"—but whose influence is by no means restricted to a single community, country or continent. Among the contributors to this volume are also a physician and an attorney; there are Christians and Jews... an assemblage of writers who represent a diversity of background, approach, experience, and perspective which aptly celebrates a champion of Deuteronomy 30:12-14... and for all of whom "the Word is very near"—and dear—"to you."

The diverse lot of contributors to this volume is also united in gratefully applauding Ora's accomplishments. Thus, the title of this volume, drawn from Isaiah 9:1... *Ra'u Or*: "The people... have seen a brilliant light."

For me personally, it has been a great privilege and joy to coordinate, to curate—and to a modest degree, to edit—this Festschrift in honor of Dr. Ora Horn Prouser... my bride of nearly 40 years... in celebration of her sixtieth birthday. I was never Ora's student in the classroom... although we became study partners soon after we met... and as a still newly married Rabbinical Student, I was, indeed, assigned to her required JTS course in Ketuvim! Seminary leaders—wisely perceiving in such an arrangement both a conflict of interest and an awkwardly fraught dynamic for newlyweds—discreetly allowed me to fulfill the course requirement through rigorous exemption exams administered by Ora's graduate school dean!

For forty years, I have learned with and from Ora. Our sacred literature has been a shared joy... and a shared passion. Our children Ayal, Eitan, and Shira (married to Avi Kravitz)—and now our grandsons Matan and Noam—have all learned and grown and flourished from Ora's loving attention and her personal example as teacher, leader, mentor, parent, daughter, wife, and scholar. They, too, offer a message of tribute and gratitude in these pages.

While Ora's primary area of study has been the Hebrew Bible, she has also illuminated for me the true meaning of a vital rabbinic text... which I could never fully have understood or adequately appreciated without her partnership:

"Rabbi Tanchum said in the name of Rabbi Chanilai: 'A man who has no wife lives without joy, without blessing, and without goodness' ... In the West (that is, in the land of Israel), it was stated further: '...and without Torah.'" (*BT Yevamot 62A*)

Our honoree—Ora—ever since I, at the age of 19, first met her, has been my chief source of joy, blessing, goodness... and an unstinting fount of wise counsel, enlightenment, and Torah.

Or, to borrow from Ora's own motto... she is my "very heart."

Rabbi Joseph H. Prouser
Editor
May 3, 2021

"Your Mother's Torah" (Proverbs 1:8)

Ayal Prouser, Eitan Prouser, Shira & Avi Kravitz

This festschrift, a collection of academics contributing their research to honor our mother, Professor Ora Horn Prouser, is a most fitting gift for her. The works contributed express admiration for the honoree as an individual, while exemplifying the spirit of her work. Ora Horn Prouser has touched so many people as both a person and as a scholar. Moreover, her success in these two realms cannot be separated. We absolutely do not mean to imply that she is one of those academics who cannot step away from their work and navigate real life—except of course at parent-teacher conferences. She had taught some of our teachers (and while defending one of us in a particularly contentious session, made it clear: "Actually it's *Doctor* Prouser"—always the mamma bear!). What we do mean is that her gifts both interpersonal (motherhood and beyond) and academic are driven by the same virtues: a combination of purpose, intention, care, and love.

Between her academic publications, the countless courses she's taught, her many *divrei Torah* both written and presented in person, our mother's Torah has covered a seemingly endless variety of topics. That said, it is always delivered with academic vigor, evincing research, innovative perspectives, and meticulous methodology—a combination of purpose and intention. Quite beautifully, however, her work is often driven by another area of purpose and intention: to do good. Her early work was in the realm of feminist criticism, and her more recent work focuses on studying and embracing those with special needs. In both of these areas, and of course the intersection of the two, there is a deep drive of care and love. Specifically, to help those who may be disenfranchised or distanced with a first glance at the text that means so much to her and to our people. Her work, pursued with care and love, helps others feel guided, elevated, and seen. Remarkably, she also blends her high level of academics and her care for others beautifully in a style of writing that can bring fulfillment both to a novice and to a reader with a deep familiarity and expertise within the field. Purpose. Intent. Care. Love.

Just as in her work, she also navigates the world driven by these ideals. She simply has a way of exuding care and love, with remarkable fluency, that people pick up on within moments of meeting her. For instance, it would not be rare, while grading papers on the side of the gym at her son's trapeze circus lesson, that someone whom she had just met would be crying and venting to her. People simply sense the care and love. This is without a doubt always present in her care as a mother as well. Whether it be in her role as our advocate (as *Doctor* Prouser, of course), a listening ear, a voice of experience, or as a friend. This care extends to our friends as well. Many looked up to our mother and wanted to be close to her, and would turn to her for advice, guidance, and support as if she was their own mother. As we've grown, our friends have started considering our mother as one of their own friends as well.

While she exudes care and love for others with a magnetic pull, she goes out of her way, with intent and purpose, to help them. In addition to being a scholar and an incredible mother, she is also a proud grandmother. Our mother was there to witness the births of both her grandchildren and has been there to love and support her grandchildren every step of the way from that moment (sometimes even their first step!). Her grandsons want to share every success and every booboo with their Savta, knowing it will be met with the exact level of pride or empathy they are looking for. It is not uncommon (almost daily!) that one of her grandsons will want to FaceTime to boast a new trick or skill, sing a song they learned, show a new toy, or even share personal frustrations that can only be understood by their Savta (e.g., "Ima and Aba won't let me have 11 marshmallows"). The parents of those grandchildren could not be more grateful. We love the special connection the kids share with their Savta. Further, while carrying on a rigorous full-time schedule, she manages to help babysit, pick up the kids from school, and provide endless hours of free FaceTime entertainment. Similar dedication is given to her students and colleagues at the Academy for Jewish Religion. To paraphrase one of those colleagues, Hazzan Michael Kasper, our mother is "not tireless, but indefatigable" in her dedication to her work and to all of her students and everyone at AJR. We couldn't agree more, and all of us have been told as much, time and time again, by total strangers.

A little fact that not everyone knows about our mother is that one of her most distinctive gifts is patently non-academic research. We do not mean the aforementioned gift that is her Torah, but research in all its possible expressions. Before there was a circus or aerial school on every other block in urban areas, she had a near encyclopedic knowledge of how to find circus training in the United States (and abroad). If you have lost a file somewhere on the computer, or perhaps your keys in a freezer, she can find them. If you have hesitations about Birthright, she finds the one targeted at musicians like you. If you mention a new fascination with a subject she will come back the next day with new knowledge to offer and conversation to be had. When her grandkids have a new favorite character or favorite book… rest assured that item will be in her grandkids' hands quicker than you can say

"Amazon Prime." Her 5-year-old grandson is already acutely aware of these skills, and will drop not so subtle hints about new interests, suggesting they see what they can find together on her phone. She is always happy to oblige.

She loves research and research is, as we her children have seen, a culmination of all love languages. There are traditionally five love languages: words of affirmation, quality time, physical touch, acts of service and gifting. Our mother puts these all together in both her research on our behalf and in the research that benefits the rest of the world. For her Torah, the subjects of her research, highlighting the other, are words of affirmation. Visibility is fundamental, and, with her words of Torah, she provides a very specific affirmation. Quality time. If anybody knew how much time spent researching does not make it into her work, they would be shocked. In the realm of Disability Studies, she spends significant time learning cultural, medical, pedagogic, and academic nuances impacting this population. She spends quality time immersing herself in this information, with the area of her work, in order most effectively to articulate her words of affirmation. For physical touch, we will simply say touch. We think this festschrift speaks for itself, but her many students over her almost four decades of teaching, whether those who have heard her, or read her work, have all been touched and guided by her Torah. She will never say it publicly, but the plethora of people who have approached her or written to her about the effect that "Esau's Blessing" has had on them is astounding. Lastly, acts of service and gifting are clear. Her work, being accessible to all, and in pursuit of collective betterment, is very clearly both an act of service and a gift to us all.

We recognize this multifaceted love language not merely in her professional efforts, but in her less academically notable research as well. When she's researching to help us with whatever it may be, she is telling us our interests are legitimate, interesting, and that she cares about them: words of affirmation. The time she spends doing this research in her precious little free time makes the quality of that time more notable still. She then, of course, puts her research into practice and finds a way to make it to any event possible in the lives of her children. We do not just mean momentous occasions like a grandchild's first steps, but going to a concert involving her musician son—whether it's an evening of classical music or a metal concert at a bar full of underage drinkers. She does all the research, and meticulously carries through with the application, in order to spend more quality time with us. We also gratefully acknowledge the research she does for us when we are not together in person as a unique form of quality time. Our lives, our careers, our passions, all can be traced back to our mother helping us in some capacity with research. She found a place for us to stay for auditions; carefully investigated different school programs; helped us find the right recreational or professional equipment; and learned to recite her grandkids' favorite book, song, or TV show characters' names by heart. In all of these cases our lives have been touched. There is one telling example of research meeting quality time, figurative touch and physical touch. Only Professor Ora Horn Prouser herself would take the time to read a manual on how to teach unicycle, then (wearing a knee brace) run alongside a novice unicyclist learning to ride over winter break.

These are all, clearly, acts of service and gifts; we do not always know it's happening, but when we find out, we know it's love.

Professor Ora Horn Prouser, we love you, too.

Ora Zo Shel Torah: This Light of Torah

A Tribute from
Rabbi Moshe Yaakov Mendelowitz

1939

(*translated from the Hebrew*)

"As I see them from the mountain tops, gaze upon them from the heights, there is a people that dwells apart, not reckoned among the nations... They crouch, they lie down like a lion. Like a lioness, who can rouse them? Blessed are they who bless you, accursed they who curse you!"
- *Numbers 23:9, 24:9*

At this difficult and bitter hour, when the Jewish People is convulsed in terrible suffering, and hardly a day goes by in which the maelstrom of brutal attacks does not grow more intense,

At this hour when the heart is seized by pain, and the head spins like a wheel, and despair mounts,

At this hour, we must thank God Who Dwells on High, who has bestowed upon us the great privilege of this light of Torah—***Ora Zo Shel Torah***—which invigorates us and gives us heart. So long as the voice of Jacob rings out in our synagogues and in our academies of Jewish learning... So long as the voice of the Torah has not ceased in our Minor Sanctuary here in the Diaspora... the Torah gives us every hope and expectation that we shall prevail over all those who arise against us intent on our destruction.

On the occasion of this gala celebration... I invoke my most heartfelt and expansive blessings upon all members of our holy community, blessings particularly befitting each and every individual, all of whom are dear and beloved to me....

May you be sustained by blessing, and may you be privileged to enjoy utter success in all your endeavors. May you derive happiness from your household; and may you soon witness the Salvation of our People, and vindication and ascendant honor in the cause of our Holy Torah!

אוֹרָה זוֹ שֶׁל תּוֹרָה

מַשָּׂאת מֵאֵת
הרב משה יעקב מענדעלאוויץ שליט"א

תרצ"ט

כִּי־מֵרֹאשׁ צֻרִים אֶרְאֶנּוּ וּמִגְּבָעוֹת אֲשׁוּרֶנּוּ הֶן־עָם לְבָדָד יִשְׁכֹּן וּבַגּוֹיִם לֹא יִתְחַשָּׁב:
כָּרַע שָׁכַב כַּאֲרִי וּכְלָבִיא מִי יְקִימֶנּוּ מְבָרְכֶיךָ בָרוּךְ וְאֹרְרֶיךָ אָרוּר:

בשעה קשה ומרה זו כאשר עם ישראל מפרפר ביסורים נוראים וכמעט שאין לך יום שלא יהי' נחשול הפגעים גובר והולך,
בשעה שהלב מתכווץ מכאב והראש סובב כגלגל והיאוש גובר,
בשעה זו אנו צריכים להודות לשוכן במרומים שזכה אותנו
באורה זו של תורה
המעודדת אותנו. וכל עוד שקול יעקב מצלצל בבתי כנסיות ובבתי מדרשות, כל עוד שקול התורה לא פסק ממקדש מעט בגלותנו, נותנת לנו התורה תוחלת ותקוה להתגבר על כל אלו שקמו עלינו לכלותנו.

לרגל הנשף... הריני מאחל מקרב לבבי ברכות מאליפות לכל בני עדתי הק', איש איש כפי ערכו, כלם אהובים וחבבים לי...

כלם יעמדו על הברכה ויזכו להצלחה גמורה בכל מעשיהם, לאושר רב מבתיהם ולחזות עמנו בקרוב והרמת קרן תורה"ק בכבוד.

[Editor's note: Rabbi Moshe Yaakov Mendelowitz (1897–1940) was ordained at the renowned Slobodka Yeshiva in Lithuania, and later pursued university studies in philosophy in Berlin. He served as spiritual leader of Brooklyn's Congregation B'nai Jacob Joseph and directed Talmud Torah E. & A.J. Grau. Rabbi Moshe Yaakov and Rachel Mendelowitz were the parents of Dena Horn... and the maternal grandparents of Dr. Ora Horn Prouser.]

Ora Horn Prouser—A Tribute

Shuly Rubin Schwartz

"At age sixty—old age," Pirkei Avot states. Perhaps, for the rabbis, selecting sixty as the point of "old age" invoked the midpoint of Moses' ideal 120 years, with the assumption that after that all must be downhill. Thankfully, in our era, that is no longer the case for those fortunate to reach this age. On the contrary, this moment presents an opportunity to celebrate a milestone in the life of AJR's CEO and Academic Dean. In so doing, we lift up the outstanding career of our colleague, friend, mentor, and teacher, Ora Horn Prouser, and offer our blessings for her continued inspired leadership in the years to come.

Jill Ker Conway, an American historian and the first woman president of Smith College, lamented how frequently women's achievements were described through passive language, often in the passive voice. Their life's work "found them" or they "fell into their job." Similarly, in my own study of rabbis' wives, I discovered that more often than not, rabbis' wives' prodigious efforts were depicted as being derivative and undervalued—that is, if they were depicted at all. Rebbetzins themselves internalized this perspective, often understanding their roles as "simply" helping out or pitching in. Rare was the rebbetzin who recognized—and who achieved recognition for—the tremendous impact she had as a religious leader. While this accurately reflects the reality that rebbetzins' power derived solely from the fact that they had married rabbis, it obscures the erudition, expertise, and sense of calling that so many brought to the role and the impact that they had on their local communities and beyond.

Thankfully, by the time I, and then Ora, came of age, the opportunities for women's leadership were beginning to broaden. Moreover, the significance of second-wave feminism lay not only in the expansion of opportunities for women's education, careers, and leadership but also in the reframing of our understanding and appreciation of women's agency in achieving them. I find it no accident that both Ora and I grew up in rabbinic homes with two parents who devoted themselves to serving the Jewish community. Our parents were committed Hebraists, Zionists, and educators who instilled in us a love of Jewish learning, Judaism, and the Jewish people. Despite our upbringings, neither Ora nor I chose the newly-possible women's ordination route but we each felt called to service on behalf of the Jewish people through scholarship. Our parents had clearly modeled how a life of service to our people could be immensely fulfilling.

I feel privileged to have worked with Ora at JTS for so many years. When we began our careers, female colleagues were a rarity and it meant so much to have a colleague with similar goals, priorities, and experiences. Though we were at different stages in our journeys in different fields of Jewish studies, we were both young professionals aiming to strike the right career equilibrium between scholarship, writing, teaching, and administration, while also juggling child-rearing, our own rebbetzin roles, and arduous commutes to JTS.

Rare were the moments when we had the luxury of reflecting together on our efforts to balance these variables, on the inevitable frustrations we experienced, or on the pleasure of achieving milestones of accomplishment—who had time for that!—but I always felt that in Ora, I had found a fellow traveler who understood both the challenges and triumphs of those years. As Ora took on ever-increasing responsibility at AJR, I knew how fortunate the institution was to benefit from her talents, and I watched with pleasure as the school flourished under her leadership. Female colleagues who share a level of camaraderie, trust, and mutual admiration are a gift often overlooked historically and still under-acknowledged in the present. I can't imagine my career without it, and for that, I am indebted in large measure to Ora. I look forward to seeing the fruits of her labors in the coming years—the Jewish community will continue to be much enriched as a result.

All Shall Be Seen Before Me[1]

Halakhah Mandates Inclusion & Dignity for those with Special Needs

Bradley Shavit Artson

She'eilah:

In 1992, in response to a question from the Masorti Movement regarding the permissibility of holding Bar/Bar Mitzvah ceremonies for children with special needs, Rabbi Reuven Hammer wrote a teshuvah for the Israeli Committee on Jewish Law delineating the halakhic status of such children regarding their obligation to perform mitzvot and concluding that they are obligated and that such ceremonies are permitted and should be held. In this teshuvah he further indicated the importance and benefits of such ceremonies to the children, their parents and the community. This teshuvah was endorsed by the entire committee and on this basis hundreds of such ceremonies have been held in Israel sponsored by the Movement. A further question has now been asked regarding specific matters considering a renewed halakhic exploration of the basis for bar/bat mitzvah ceremonies for children with special needs. To respond adequately requires considering: What participation does *halakhah* permit or mandate for a person with special needs for counting toward the quorum in a minyan, for leading services (as *shaliach tzibbur*, receiving an *aliyah* to the Torah, chanting Haftarah or Megillah), for observing the mitzvot (learning, performing mitzvot, performing acts of tzedek), and for performing the mitzvot on a level that releases others from their halakhic obligation to perform that same mitzvah? Specifically, what wisdom might Judaism offer for the purpose of attaining the status of בר\בת מצוה (*bar/bat mitzvah*) and for its public celebration?

---

[1] M. *Hagigah* 1:1. This teshuvah builds on the brilliant, courageous, and pioneering writings of Rabbi Reuven Hammer. See his teshuvah at http://www.responsafortoday.com/vol4/2.pdf and *The Other Child in Jewish Education: A Handbook on Learning Disabilities* (New York: United Synagogue Commission on Jewish Education, 1979. Many of this teshuvah's strengths flow from his example, work, and insights. Its flaws are exclusively my own.

Teshuvah:

Context

Jewish law shuttles between two value clusters: (1) an assertion of human dignity and value as among the highest of Torah values[2] (כבוד הבריאות דוחה[3] לאו שבתורה) and (2) the reliance on social status and mental consciousness (as measured behaviorally) to observe the mitzvot with appropriate reverence and intention (מצוות צריכות כוונה[4]). Often these two poles function symbiotically, lifting the practitioner to unanticipated heights of piety and awe—for example, witnessing *kohanim* blessing a congregation on a holy day, hearing a trained *hazzan* chant the seasonal *nusach* for a special reading, participating in a text *shiur* with a master sage. Not infrequently, however, these two poles generate legal tension, as shifting awareness over time expands to include previously excluded people as now having legal status as conscious, self-determining agents. Considerations for conferral of such status is also influenced by changing social norms and the persistent testimony of actual people who defy a priori stigmatization.

Ancient Judaism struggled to integrate the *Erev Rav*, the mixed multitude, and to expand the standing of women beyond that of many surrounding cultures, and the Prophets demanded attentiveness to those marginalized in biblical society: the poor, the orphan, and the widow. Pharisaic and rabbinic Judaism continued that expansion of human dignity to include even greater legal standing for women, allowing Gentiles to convert to Judaism, and creating nearly universal male literacy and focusing rabbinic authority on ameliorating the plight of the poor and those lacking pedigree. In each age, restrictive practice gave way before a growing assertion of the humanity of previously marginalized groups. In recent decades, that expanding circle of dignity advanced to include gendered categories, as Masorti/Conservative Judaism joined the fight for the legal agency and ordination of women, marriage equality and ordination for LGBT Jews within a halakhic framework.

In the reflections which follow, I adhere to the practice of Rabbi Judith Z. Abrams, ז"ל, choosing not to render the Hebrew terms phenomenologically

---

[2] For a lengthy discussion and several examples of this impulse within traditional Judaism, see Artson, "Halakhah and Ethics: The Holy and the Good," *Conservative Judaism*, Spring 1994, 70-88.

[3] *Berakhot* 19b, *Shabbat* 81b and 94b, *Eruvin* 41b, *Menachot* 37b.

[4] *Berakhot* 13a, *Eruvin* 95b, *Pesachim* 114b. I am aware that there are also many instances in which the rabbis rule that particular mitzvot do not require intention.

descriptive of various behaviors or challenges facing people with special needs into hardened English categories or diagnoses. These labels are, she notes, basic-level categories, broader than any specific people. They create legally and culturally self-fulfilling perceptions, modes of interacting and organizing.[5] But in the process of relying on the shorthand of a diagnostic label, the actual people fade into the background. The theoretical category, itself not something real but a generalization based on many actual people and attributed or highlighted commonalities, attains a priority that spills beyond legal conceptualization, erasing the very people it is intended to label. Rather than seek an English equivalent, I will generally let the Hebrew behavioral phenomena stand as their own linguistic marker for clusters of people that we lump together as the result of a cultural or legal legacy, and will provide an approximate English description only at the descriptive term's first use. Labeling people is a political assertion of who has power and who gets to marginalize or be marginalized. This paper is an attempt to put people first and to relegate labels to mere utility.

Far from the tradition's expansion of human dignity constituting simply a contemporary retrojection onto the past, Jewish traditions themselves offer examples where the specific reality of thoughtful individuals with special needs erupts through the smothering stigma of social presumption:

Is this to say that one who cannot speak cannot learn!?! Consider the case of these two אילמים *Elemim*/people with challenges of speech and hearing who were in Rebbe's neighborhood, who were the sons of Rabbi Yohanan ben Gudgeta's daughter (some say they were the sons of Rabbi Yohanan's sister.) Whenever Rebbe would enter the study hall, they would enter and sit down before him, and they would nod their heads and move their lips. Rebbe besought mercy on their behalf, and they were healed. And it was found that they were well versed in *halakhah*, *Sifra*, *Sifri*, and the entire *Shas*.[6]

Notice in this aggadic tale that the two nameless mutes are presumed to lack understanding. They simply wobble their heads and make apparently meaningless motions with their mouths. But with the miracle of Rebbe's prayer, they are revealed as having been learning and synthesizing at a brilliant level all along. The reasons that the law had marginalized them were erroneous, reflecting the society's inability to create modes through which they could communicate the awareness and intentionality they had always possessed. At the end of the story, the "technology" of prayer strips away the barriers and makes their ample mindfulness apparent.

---

[5] See Judith Z. Abrams, *Judaism and Disability: Portrayals in Ancient Texts from the Tanach through the Bavli*, Washington, D.C.: Gallaudet University Press, 1998, 124 - 126.

[6] Hagigah 3a.

There are even halakhic examples where individual opinions dissent and confer legal personhood on the *Shoteh*/a person with psychotic behavior[7]. For example, while the anonymous view of the Mishnah is that one should not steal from a *Cheresh* or *Shoteh*, not because it is theft but for the sake of peace, there is a dissenting view: "Rav Yosi says, It is actual robbery."[8] That judgment is Rav Yosi's recognition of the legal agency of the *Shoteh*. He affirms the fullness of their humanity, even against the consensus of his contemporaries.

In another such story about a local scholar who did not have sight, Rebbe and Rabbi Hiyya were once going on a journey. When they came to a certain town they said: "If there is a rabbinical scholar here, we will go and pay our respects." The inhabitants told them: "There is a rabbinical scholar here, but he is סומא *Suma*/blind." Said Rabbi Hiyya to Rebbe, "You remain here, do not degrade your position of Nasi; I will go and pay my respects." Rebbe bested Rabbi Hiyya and went along with him. When they were departing from the סומא *Suma* scholar, he said to them: "You came to pay your respects to one who is seen but does not see. May you merit to pay your respects to the One who sees but is not seen." Rebbe said to Rabbi Hiyya, "Had I now [listened to you] you would have prevented me from this blessing."[9]

In this second story, we are again confronted with a social stigma, the presumption that a *Suma* scholar would somehow degrade the Office of Rebbe by his presence. Rebbe rebuts this stigma and as a result, what becomes possible is a blessing that would otherwise have never found expression.

The experiences of thousands of Israeli children with special needs who have benefited from the Israeli Masorti Movement's Bar/Bat Mitzvah program since 1995 already have created ample testimony to this new recognition: these children really do bless their communities when they bless, really do lift the community when they chant from the Torah or haftarah. They create a precedent we dare not ignore.

We possess the insight and the tools to extend our recognition of self-determination and human dignity to include people with special needs. That ability and insight creates a duty to re-read our ancient wisdom, *halakhah* included, in the light of what life has taught us and what technology now makes possible (for communication, mobility, and independence). The time

---

[7] For more information, informed by contemporary scientific and psychological literature as well as halakhic texts, see Rael Strous, MD, "The Shoteh and Psychosis in Halakhah with Contemporary Clinical Application," *The Torah U-Madda Journal*, December 2004, 158 - 178.

[8] Gittin 59b.

[9] Hagigah 5b.

is past due to engage in this traditional Jewish dynamic of revising ancient prohibitions that have become maladaptive to their original goals, given the insights and capabilities of our contemporary social capacity and context.

We recognize that *halakhah* functions according to procedural guidelines and precedent. We also insist that Jewish law is not directionless, not simply the mechanistic indifferent application of rules. Traditional halakhic process is constrained by authority, precedent, and aphorisms filtered through the perspectives of individual *poskim* loyal to the fundamental Jewish value-concepts that lure toward greater חסד/*chesed*/love, צדק/*tzedek*/justice, חיים/*chayim*/experience, and מוסר/*mussar*/morality. That means that *halakhah* is more like an organism than a machine. It invokes and adapts rules to allow us to survive and thrive better. In our time, that systemic directionality heeds the Torah's bold assertion that all people are made in God's image[10] (נעשה אדם בצלמנו), that all people are equal under the law [11] משפט אחד יהיה לכם) and that all people are beloved of God (הֲלוֹא אָב אֶחָד לְכֻלָּנוּ)[12], demanding that the halakhot pertaining to people with special needs honor those bedrock commitments just as it would for all people.

The Challenge

Classical Judaism created a legal system of stratified obligation, in which only someone with a similar or stronger level of obligation could fulfill a religious duty for someone else or for a community. In ancient Jewish circles, as in the world at large, free adult men held power, governed, engaged in commerce, and marginalized women, children and slaves in a variety of ways. Like other ancient cultures, Judaism both reflected that privilege and resisted it, as the emotions of some of the men and the humanity of women carved out exceptions and contradictions. That complex mix of theoretical marginalization and compelling exceptions was also the case with children and slaves. With time, the human dignity and legal capacity of actual people—women, slaves, even children—prevailed over the theoretical exclusions of jurisprudence, and the rights of these people expanded to reflect their changing social standing and the larger society's recognition of their capacity.

The excluded group that now demands our attention are those people with special needs. In early rabbinic parlance, those people were known as the חרש/*Cheresh* and the שוטה/*Shoteh*. Along with the קטן/*Katan*/minor,

---

[10] Genesis 1:26.

[11] Leviticus 24:22.

[12] Malachi 2:10.

they were restricted in their self-determination: barred from owning property[13], giving testimony and serving as a witness[14], entering and terminating marriage[15], inheriting, and having the legal standing of one who would be degraded by insult[16], prohibited from participating as agents rather than as objects[17].

In fairness to the ancients, humanity did not have the scientific tools to ascertain whether or not the individuals they encountered were self-aware and intentional, and capable of self-determination. Restricted only to what their eyes could see, and lacking any educational program to elicit communication from these diverse people, the rabbinic presumption was that people with special needs lacked intellectual capacity. For example, a passage in the Mishnah notes that

הכל חייבין בראיה חוץ מחרש שוטה וקטן וטומטום ואנדרוגינוס ונשים ועבדים שאינן משוחררין והחיגר והסומא והחולה והזקן שאינו יכול לעלות ברגליו

All are obligated to appear [at the Jerusalem Temple for the Festivals] except for a Cheresh, a Shoteh, a minor, a Tumtum, an androgyne, women, unemancipated slaves, the Chiger/a person with a limp, the Suma, the ill, and the elderly who cannot ascend the Temple Mount by foot.[18]

At first that passage might be taken simply as an exemption of obligation that is impossible for those categories of people to fulfill in the ancient context. The clarifying expansion in the Talmud affirms exempting their participation even in the mitzvah of rejoicing:

ואת שאינו לא שומע ולא מדבר ושוטה וקטן פטור אף מן השמחה והואיל ופטורים מכל מצות האמורות בתורה

---

[13] *Mishneh Torah, Hil. To'en* 13:2.

[14] T. *Shevuot* 3:8, 5:10, T. *Terumot* 1:1 and 2, and *Mishneh Torah, Hil. Edut* 9:11

[15] *Yevamot* 112b.

[16] *Bava Kama* 86b.

[17] For example, reading the Megillah on behalf of the community (B. *Megillah* 19b, *Mishneh Torah, Hil. Megillah* 1:2, and *Shulhan Arukh, O.H., Hil. Megillah* 689:2), or selling and purchasing (*Mishneh Torah, Hil Mechirah* 29:1).

[18] M. Hagigah 1:1.

> *Those who can neither hear nor speak, those who are Shoteh, or those who are Katan are exempt even from rejoicing since they are exempt from all the mitzvot.*[19]

The reasons for that exemption are made explicit in the words of the Talmud:

חוץ מחרש שוטה וקטן וכו'. קתני חרש דומיא דשוטה וקטן. מה שוטה וקטן דלאו בני דעה, אף חרש דלאו בר דעה הוא

> *"Except the Cheresh, the Shoteh and the Katan, etc." [Our Mishnah] speaks of the Cheresh like the Shoteh and the Katan. Just as the Shoteh and Katan lack intellectual capacity, so the Cheresh lacks intellectual capacity.*[20]

The *Shoteh* and the *Cheresh* are presumed to lack *da'at*, which can mean attentiveness, capacity to learn, mindfulness. An additional category of people, the סומא/*Suma*, and the פסח/*Piseach*/those with ambulatory challenges, also face different levels of exclusion and marginalization, but not as comprehensive or dire as the stigmatization facing the *Shoteh* and *Cheresh*.

In the course of Jewish legal development, what begins as an exemption often hardens into a prohibition: women were exempted from the requirement to wear tefillin, and later authorities construed that exemption as a prohibition[21]. Similarly, the exemption of the *Cheresh* or *Shoteh* often metamorphosed into prohibitions against participating in the legal system as self-directing agents, and against participating in the liturgical life of the community as fully obligated, hence capable of discharging the obligations for other Jews.

Often the objects of pity and compassion, for people with special needs the impact of this legal presumption nonetheless was stigma and marginalization, enforcing the very legal incompetence that the laws presumed from the start.

This conceptualization of people with special needs entered the legal literature, as exemplified by this passage of the Rambam:

---

[19] B. Hagigah 2b.

[20] B. Hagigah 2b.

[21] For a brilliant exploration of the history and implications of this "exemption/exclusion" from tefillin for women, see Ethan Tucker, "Gender and Tefillin: Possibilities and Consequences," *Times of Israel*. http://blogs.timesofitsrael.com/gender-and-tefillin-possibilities-and-consequences/.

הפתאים ביותר שאין מכירין דברים שסותרין זה את זה ולא יבינו עניני הדבר כדרך שמבינים שאר עם הארץ, וכן המבוהלים והנחפזים בדעתם והמשתגעים ביותר הרי אלו בכלל השוטים, ודבר זה לפי (מה) שיראה הדיין שאי אפשר לכוין הדעת בכתב.

> *People who are very feeble-witted, who do not recognize matters which contradict each other and don't understand a concept as it would be comprehended by other common people are among the mentally unstable, continually unsettled, tumultuous, and they are included as Shotim. This matter is dependent on the assessment of the judge; because it is impossible to assess people's awareness through a text.[22]*

While we will argue that Rambam's formulation doesn't extend far enough to suffice in our time, it should be noted that he does reflect the traditional Jewish compassion for human diversity and the attention to the unique dignity of each human being when he insists that such assessment cannot be made by reference to abstracted characteristics and text book theory. Only by seeing the specific human being, can a living human being (in this case, the judge) engage the complex contradictions and nuanced confluences that make up each person. Only in that living relationship can an accurate assessment emerge.

New Information

The ancients applied their legal precedent and principles to the best observations they were capable of making and with the best of intentions, seeking to protect people with special needs from abuse and harm, and to shield them from social pressure and unrealistic demands. If people with special needs appeared to be incapable of thought, lacking in intention, unable to fulfill the functions that the mitzvot required, then the humane response was first to exempt them and later, functionally, to bar them from these obligations. The data and the range of responses possible at the time drove the application of the rules (in this case, the religious rituals of becoming a bar/bat mitzvah).

We retain the traditional obligation, as their heirs, to demonstrate the

---

[22] Rabbi Moses Maimonides, *Mishneh Torah*, Laws of Testimony 9:10. It is worth noting that even the Rambam asserts that a text-driven definition can never capture the complex realities of actual people, so he limits how an assessment can be conducted, requiring a judge to actually get to know the individual being assessed in their specific humanity. He leaves the details of that assessment to each particular judge.

same humane responsiveness, but we must now implement it differently. What has changed in this matter, from antiquity to today, is our scientific capacity to recognize mindfulness, self-awareness, and intentionality in many people with special needs that had previously been presumed to lack those very characteristics, and our technological capacity to create modes of communication previously beyond human attainment[23].

The voluminous scientific documentation[24] of such capacity makes a comprehensive description impossible, but reference to one famous case might provide a useful example. Helen Keller was a woman who overcame her culture's stigmatization of those lacking sight or hearing to be able to communicate, to write books, and to teach a generation the capacity of someone previously viewed as completely disabled to rise to real moral and educational leadership. The limits were not intrinsic to her condition, but were imposed by a toxic blend of low expectations, few pedagogical techniques, and no technological solutions. With the recalibration of those three, her genius could manifest, astound, and benefit the world. Helen Keller is not alone; there are countless others like her.

Until very recently, individuals with autism, Down syndrome, and other conditions were similarly obscured through assumed cultural presumptions, such as lacking the ability to socialize, to desire relationships or to articulate significant thought.[25] Inability to communicate *through conventional channels* was taken as an inability to communicate at all, which was in turn construed as evidence of incapacity to think, discern, or engage. Mobility challenges were seen as unalterable barriers to those who faced them, rather than as challenges for society to overcome.

These assumptions have been revealed as social presumptions and stigma, rather than an accurate measure of the capabilities of these courageous people with special needs. Coalitions of parents, experts, and self-advocates are transforming the expectation of what services and education might make

---

[23] For important documentation of the necessary impact of scientific data on halakhic rulings, see Joel Roth, "Extralegal Sources within Halakhah," *The Halakhic Process* (New York: Jewish Theological Seminary, 1986), 231 - 304; see Daniel Eisenberg, "The Ethics of Smallpox Vaccination," at http://www.aish.com/societyWork/sciencenature/The_Ethics_of_Smallpox_Immunization.asp, Edward Reichman, "Halachic Aspects of Vaccination," *Jewish Action*, https://www.ou.org/jewish_action/12/2008/halachic_aspects_of_vaccination/.

[24] For a compilation of scholarly and medical sources, see Stanley I. Greenspan, M.D. and Serena Wieder, Ph.D., *The Child With Special Needs: Encouraging Intellectual and Emotional Growth* (Reading, MA: Perseus Books, 1998).

[25] See Douglas Biklen, *Autism and the Myth of the Person Alone* (New York: New York University Press, 2005).

possible for people with special needs.[26] And with these transformed expectations, we are witnessing many brave individuals who are now capable of attaining levels of communication and engagement previously held to be impossible.[27]

That new possibility—for a great diversity of special needs— is the reality to which contemporary halakhah must respond. All of this comes to a head with the subject of bar/bat mitzvah celebrations for people with special needs. Once we realize that they can communicate, even in non-typical ways, once it is evident that they discern, have opinions, seek meaning and connection, then the normal Jewish expectations extended to others pertains to those with special needs, too, and Judaism must create possibilities for these people to participate in community as members of the covenant and as active agents for Judaism's advance and the repair of the world.

The Resolution

During antiquity and the Middle Ages, manifesting special needs was taken as evidence of lack of legal standing. Being labelled a *Cheresh* or a *Shoteh* entailed lacking *da'at*, which disqualified the individual from the religious obligations (and privileges) of a full Jewish life.

We now know that assumption not to be true in many instances. Our task at present is to integrate contemporary scientific knowledge (about the mental capacity and physical abilities of individuals with special needs) with halakhic principles of legal opportunity and obligation, so they apply accurately in the case of people with special needs.

The solution we propose is three-fold: First, we presume mindfulness for *all* people as our initial stance. Only when there is unimpeachable proof that mindfulness is lacking would a person be considered to lack *da'at*. Second, we distinguish between a theoretical חיוב/obligation for the mitzvot which applies to all Jews presumed to possess *da'at*, versus the ability to act on that חיוב, which even for some *b'nei da'at* might be precluded for particular

---

[26] See Anne M. Donnellan, PhD and Martha R Leary, MA, CCC-SLP, *Movement Differences and Diversity in Autism/Mental Retardation: Appreciating and Accommodating People with Communication and Behavior Challenges*, (Pacific Beach, CA: DRI Press, 1995) and Martha L. Cole and Jack T. Cole, *Effective Intervention with the Language Impaired Child*, (Rockville, MD: Aspen Publications, 1989).

[27] Two beautiful examples of professionals rising to articulate these new possibilities are Ricki G. Robinson, MD, MPH, *Autism Solutions: How to Create a Healthy and Meaningful Life for Your Child*, (Don Mills, Canada: Harlequin Publishers, 2011) and Barry Prizant PhD, *Uniquely Human: A Different Way of Seeing Autism*, (New York: Simon & Schuster, 2015).

reasons (sensory or proprioceptive issues, for instance). In those moments, when special circumstances prevent the fulfillment of the general obligation to observe the mitzvah, the individual is פטור. A third guideline, emerging from the first two, would recognize that speech is far broader than a set of verbal or written words and syntax, and that for our purposes it includes any content-filled communication, so that individuals with special needs could utilize a range of methods for leading prayers, reading Torah, chanting Haftarah even though they are not commonly utilized by neurotypical people for those purposes.

1. Presumption of mindfulness: All people are presumed to have intellectual capacity (בר דעת), intentionality (כוונה), and agency sufficient to be recognized as מקבלי עול מלכות שמים. Rather than demanding evidence of mindfulness/דעת as the necessary prior condition to confer legal self-determination and agency on a person, we deliberately reverse the burden of proof, and presume mindfulness in each and every person[28]. In recent decades, enough instances have emerged, of people in a so-called 'vegetative coma' who turned out to be tracking conversations about their own euthanasia without being able to demonstrate their own awareness (and terror!), of people presumed unaware who, with the proper training and technology, were able to express sophisticated and nuanced thought. The burden of proof should no longer appease those who demand evidence of mind *before* recognizing legal agency[29]. The risk of erasing someone's dignity and deny-

---

[28] Such an inversion is rare in the annals of Halakhah, but not unheard of, and remains a systemic prerogative for a contemporary *posek*. One ready example that comes to mind is the prohibition on any *melakhah* on Shabbat, which was understood, until the Maccabees, to require allowing an enemy army to attack and to submit to slaughter from them. One such defeat and the Maccabees (I Maccabees 2:29 - 37) created the halakhic principle ultimately recorded in the Talmud that "It is preferable to violate one Shabbat in order to observe many other *Shabbatot (Yoma* 85b*)*." Recall that Shabbat observance is so central that its violation calls for execution; this inversion is as deep systemically as is possible. Yet they—and the rabbis after them—inverted the priority to create a new halakhic norm: surviving alive overturns even Shabbat restrictions. In our time, honoring the humanity of those marginalized should, too, when those two values are in unavoidable conflict.

[29] For example, see Christof Koch, "The Conscious Infant," *Scientific American Mind*, September/October 2013, 24 - 25; Gareth Cook, "Do Plants Think? Scientist Daniel Chamovitz Unveils The Surprising World of Plants that See, Feel, Smell—and Remember," *Scientific American*, Tuesday, June 5, 2012; Kat McGowan, "Back From the Brink," *Discover*, March 2011, 64 - 71; Christof Koch, "What is it Like to Be a Bee?," *Scientific American MIND*, December 2008/January 2009, 18 - 19; Christof Koch, "A Theory of Consciousness," *Scientific American MIND*, July.August 2009, 16 - 19; Saigusa, Tetsu, et al., "Amoebae Anticipate Periodic Events," *Physical Review*

ing their legal agency simply because others can't yet perceive it is so great, and the consequences of presuming mindfulness when it isn't really present is so minor, that common sense, morality, and religious principle all unite around this insistence: Judaism's fallback policy must affirm the biblical imperative of the primacy of human dignity[30] (predicated on mindfulness). The rabbis understood that in a case of doubt regarding a Biblical principle, one decides stringently. Without in any way pretending that countervailing precedent does not exist, we affirm that in our time human dignity is elevated to a First Principle of halakhah, an organizing value of our stream of Jewish life. Masorti/Conservative Judaism today—across a wide swath of rulings and practices—must consistently assert human dignity as a determinative Jewish value which our rules and practices must both exemplify and advance.[31] So we too rule that even for those people for whom we have a hard time creating ways to demonstrate mindfulness, we must assume its presence unless definitively precluded[32].

2. Challenges to demonstrating regular fulfillment of a חיוב: A person

---

Letters, 100 (1): 018101, January 11, 2008, at http://hdl.handle.net/2115/3304; Gerald Edelman, "Naturalizing Consciousness: A Theoretical Frame-work," *PNAS*, April 29, 2003, 100:9, 5520 - 5524, at www.pnas.org/cdi/doi/10.1073/pnas.093149100.

[30] גדול כבוד הבריאות שדוחה את לא תעשה שבתורה - Berakhot 19b, Shabbat 81b, 94b, Eruvin 41b, Megillah 3b, Bava Kama 79b, Menachot 37a, 38a, Mishneh Torah Hilkhot Shabbat 26:23, Shulhan Arukh, Orah Hayyim 13:3, 312:1, 355:3, *Yoreh Deah* 303:1. An example of this in halakhic literature is found in תוספות יום טוב , on M. Bava Kama 4:4, where he distinguishes that if a person can focus and do the action, then they are חייב. For extensive exploration of this central Jewish value, see Hershey H. Friedman, PhD, "Human Dignity and the Jewish Tradition," *Journal of Halacha and Contemporary Society*, www.jlaw.com/articles. In addition to sifting through the halakhic literature, he also provides an extensive bibliography.

[31] Beitza 3b. For more examples see Joel Roth, *The Halakhic Process: A Systemic Analysis* (New York: Jewish Theological Seminary, 1986), 25 - 48. I am aware that there is also a strain within halakhic precedent that does not see כבוד הבריות as דאורייתא. But as these sources and others attest, there is also a robust interpretive tradition that does make precisely that assertion. See, for instance, Hershey H. Friedman, PhD., "Human Dignity and the Jewish Tradition," *Journal of Halakhah and Contemporary Society*, 2008; Rabbi Mark Dratch, *The Divine Honor Roll: Kevod ha-Beriyot (Human Dignity) in Jewish Law and Thought*, http://www.jSafe.org/pdfs/Kevod_Habriyot.pdf; Aharon Barak, *Human Dignity: The Constitutional Value and The Constitutional Right* (Cambridge: Cambridge University Press, 2015), and Nahum Rakover, *Human Dignity in Jewish Law* [in Hebrew] (Jerusalem: The Jewish Legal Heritage Society, 1998).

[32] Lack of communication or bodily control would not suffice to demonstrate a lack of mindfulness or agency.

who is מקבל עול מלכות שמים (and who can focus to mobilize full intentionality at specific moments) might still struggle with sensory, neurological, or biological challenges at a given moment which could occasionally preclude participation in a particular mitzvah or mitzvot, without calling their being categorized as a בר דעת into question.

Even after we establish the presumption of דעת, the question remains whether or not there might be other factors which interfere with an individual observing a mitzvah at a specific moment. One might encounter a problematic physical location (needing to pray, but constrained in an unclean space), or encounter an emotional or bodily impediment to communication and bodily control. The distinction here is between *ad hoc* decision making (is the person capable at this moment?) vs. a status issue (is that person precluded from this mental level?) For example, it might be possible for a person to have the דעת to know the meaning of leading the congregation in prayer, blowing a shofar, chanting from the Torah or Megillah and to have the proper intention, but that person could still struggle with temporary issues that make fulfilling those mitzvot or leading the ritual extremely difficult at that moment. If that person could muster the motivation to perform one or more of those sacred tasks at a particular instant, their דעת would suffice to make them (and others) יוצא. But that their sensitivity issues might preclude implementing them the next day (or most days on a consistent basis) would not constitute a violation of Jewish law or an impermissible omission on subsequent days, precisely because of the specific conditions rendering the behavior impossible at that moment. Similarly, someone who could muster the focus and discipline to have an aliyah, or to lead the prayers for their bar/bat mitzvah ceremony and at future events or times, would be recognized as בר דעת and hence able to fulfill the congregation's obligation when leading the prayers. But the superhuman effort required by some people with special needs might not be possible to sustain on a daily basis, and that level of difficulty would exempt them from the requirement when they were not able to perform these tasks (without obviating their ability to make others יוצא on the days they *are* able to rise to that level of implementation.

What we are calling for, then, is to distinguish between a person's status as בר דעת as a separate consideration from whether or not a person can manifest an ongoing חיוב. It is possible for the answer to the first question to be in the affirmative (the proper intention is always there) while the answer to the second might be in the negative (the capacity to enact that intention in behavior might occasionally be compromised, modified, or sometimes not be possible)[33].

---

[33] This approach would have benefits in other areas of halakhah, too. For example, a

3. Communication is a right. Communication is a right, not a privilege. Therefore, creating possibilities of communication is an obligation binding the community at large and remains a right for each its participants.

Language, (and its many Jewish manifestations, such as "Chanting," "Reading" and "Praying") is hereby understood as any symbol system that communicates content. Language need not be verbal,[34] and it might utilize technology in unprecedented ways unavailable to the Rabbis of previous generations to communicate content to others.

A corollary of our assumption of mindfulness is our recognition that the function of language—communicating content from one individual to another or to a group—while generally manifest by humans through verbal expression, need not be limited to that mode. There are a host of ways of communicating in addition to speech, writing or explicit words. In the diversity of people with special needs, we assert that communication is not a privilege but a birthright. All people have a right to communicate, and the larger Jewish community must recognize that communication is a necessity for human thriving, not a luxury. What that means practically is that most people can chant the Torah or Haftarah verbally, but not all. Most people can sing the prayers and recite blessings verbally, but not all.

In those cases where one's mode of communication is the use of a tool, a symbol set, pictures or movement, we rule that such modes of communication function as language and are to be considered as such. Modes of expression have no bearing on the status of mind or of legal agency.

Recognizing language broadly means that a bar/bat mitzvah child who signs the blessings, or points to pictures corresponding to the blessing's content, or uses a typing-to-speech implement fulfills the halakhic requirement of speech or chanting, both for themselves and for the purpose of making others in the congregation יוצא. A person with special needs who is dependent on using a machine for that purpose is permitted to do so, even on Yom Tov or Shabbat, as פיקוח נפש, as a necessary component of their עונג, and as an expression of their humanity[35].

---

divorcing husband who is intermittently שוטה/*Shoteh* can be examined situationally and is permitted to grant a Get (divorce document) in periods of manifesting דעת. What our approach would permit is recognizing that we are not assessing his possession of דעת, but his ability to manifest that intellectual capacity behaviorally.

[34] Precedent can be found, for example, in the extension of divorce without verbal communication: כשם שהוא כונס ברמיזה כן הוא מוציא ברמיזה / "Just as [a *Cheresh*] can enter marriage with gestures, so he may divorce using gestures (M. Yevamot 14:1)."

[35] For a comparable and already-accepted practice in a related area of halakhah, see Meir, Yair (1990). "The Electric Wheelchair on Shabbat," in Ezra Rosenfeld, ed., Crossroads:

The Ruling

Mindful of the Torah's obligations to love our fellows as ourselves, to honor the divine image in each other, to heighten the blessing of human diversity, to elevate the dignity of the congregation, and to enhance the glory of Torah and God, and to refrain from putting impediments before people with special needs[36], we rule לחומרא stringently in favor of human dignity (הבריות כבוד) that each and every Jew, regardless of ability or special need, is presumed to be a בר דעת who is מקבל עול מלכות שמים. Consequently, we rule that any Jew[37] counts toward a minyan, is eligible to lead prayer services, to recite blessings (to which the congregation must respond with "amen,") to sound the Shofar, to chant from the Torah, Haftarah or Megillah, in the manner of communication which is their normal manner for communicating. For those for whom that primary mode of communication is electronic, we rule that such communication is permissible even on Shabbat or Yom Tov.

Davar Acher: A Last Word

To have only neurotypical people weighing in on the subject of the legal agency and status of people with special needs would be a grievous perpetuation of unconscionable marginalization and stigma. So without in any way claiming that he speaks for all people with special needs, consider the writing of Jacob Artson, a self-advocating young man with severe autism, who testifies as one example of a person who had been dismissed as lacking mind, consciousness, or the capacity to make informed choices:

> *You have probably never met anyone like me who can't speak but can communicate by typing. I am an example of how someone can be impaired in one area but have great strengths in another. That is true of most people, but it is true in the extreme about people with autism. When I was diagnosed at age 3, I couldn't speak or move my body properly, and 15 years later I am still extremely impaired in both areas. But if success is measured by being a mensch and helping make this world a better place, then I would classify myself as a success.... When I turned 6, my family moved to LA in search of opportunities for me. Our journey took us*

Halacha and the Modern World, Vol. III, pp. 97- 107 (Alon Shvut-Gush Etzion: Zomet Institute). See also Jachter, Howard (2001). "Taking Medicine on Shabbat—Part II," http://www.koltorah.org/ravj/medicONshabbat2.htm.

[36] Leviticus 19:14.

[37] Only in a particular case where there was incontrovertible proof that such mindfulness is lacking would this presumption not be affirmed.

to many purported experts, but they all saw me as merely my extremely impaired verbal and motor abilities and assumed my cognitive abilities must be similarly nonexistent. After several months, me and my parents came to the last place on our list—the "autism doctor." I am not really sure what I was expecting, but Dr. Ricki looked nothing like I expected. She wore a fashionable sweater with a colorful necklace. But mostly I noticed her smile. I had been to so many doctors at that point I couldn't even remember all their names or specialties. But not one had ever smiled at me like Dr. Ricki. She kept smiling, watching and waiting for me. For the first time in my life, I was able to smile back. I stayed for an hour and we played with puppets, but mostly I was just watching Dr. Ricki in complete fascination. I had expected that she would have some medicine or treatment to prescribe and that would be the end of the appointment. But she said nothing about any pills or therapies. She just smiled at me for an hour as though I was a person worthy of respect and dignity. I had always thought of myself as a defective human being. It had never occurred to me that a doctor would see me as a person with the potential to be a productive member of society. At that transforming moment, Dr. Ricki taught me that despite my disability, I was as worthy of love and respect as any other child. That smile gave me hope, and hope gave me the motivation to begin the battle to conquer autism before it destroyed me. So I began my journey of millions of small steps. Along the way I found supporters as well as detractors, and the steps sometimes did not appear to be going forward, but I persevered because I had hope and people who believed I could fly.

Jacob testifies that the advent of people who continued to expect him to rise in his humanity, coupled with techniques and technologies that created pathways for communication and connection made it possible for him to progress and to contribute, often despite the consensus of experts and against the resistance of some administrators and teachers in the educational system. Yet his writing is a clear demonstration of intellectual capacity, a passion for life, and a commitment to self-determination. We all need his insights, and those of others who struggle like him.

Conclusion

One consequence of these findings is that it constitutes a meritorious communal practice to support the widest range of individuals counting toward a minyan, leading services, chanting from the Torah and Haftarah. Of particular merit is the practice of people with special needs celebrating becoming bar and bat mitzvah. Celebrating their humanity and their place as self-determining loci of dignity only enhances the dignity of all God's children, and we all benefit from building such a world.

We are all in need of the blessings of those who for too long have been stigmatized as incapable of conferring blessing. Thanks to new possibilities in education and in technology, coupled with a renewed sense of God's image in each person, we are now capable of creating Torah communities in which the harvest of these wondrous blessings will become commonplace, and the circle of human diversity and dignity can expand yet again.

May we merit to publicly celebrate children with special needs as they become bar/bat mitzvah, and to make visible the human dignity of all people with special needs through full inclusion in the observance of mitzvot and the leadership of Jewish worship in public. Such a harvest of blessings elevates the community that makes it real, and extends the circle of covenant in a way that honors God's incomparable potentiality. "Just as you have blessed one who cannot see but is seen, so may you merit to be blessed by One who sees but cannot be seen."

We owe it to all involved to multiply those blessings into the world, for the sake of God's glory and to add to the greatness of Torah.[38]

---

[38] My thanks to those who read drafts of this paper, conversed about its contents, and helped me clarify my thoughts, for which I alone am responsible: Rabbi Aaron Alexander, Barbara Artson, Ph.D., Joshua Buchin, Rabbi Judith Edelman-Green, Rabbi Abe Friedman, Jeremy Markiz, Rabbi Ephraim Pelcovits, Rabbi Cheryl Peretz, Rabbi Andrew Sacks, and Rebecca Walker.

Triage in the Time of a Pandemic:

The Sanctity of Saving as Many Lives as Possible

Elliot N. Dorff

First things first: we all must recognize that in this time of the Covid-19 pandemic, we are all feeling discombobulated and stressed out. We mourn and grieve our normal lives, their routine, and the meaningful tasks and interactions with people that they include. There is no shame in feeling this way; it is just normal. From Genesis 2:18, "It is not good for a person to be alone," through many other classical Jewish texts, the Jewish tradition recognized that although we all need some time alone, we also need interactions with other people. One graphic proof of that is that in a prison environment, short of execution or torture, the harshest penalty is solitary confinement, and we unfortunately have ample evidence that people held in isolation for extended periods of time go insane. The Jewish tradition was also keenly aware that how we think and feel about ourselves affects our physical health, and vice versa (consider B. *Sanhedrin* 90a-90b, M. *Avot* 2:2), so in this new normal existence that we have for the time the pandemic lasts, it is really important to reach out and connect with other people, even if we can safely do that only electronically.

If this is a stressful time for us all, it is even more stressful for doctors, nurses, and other health care workers. The vast majority of them are involved in clinical care, where the object is to do the most you can for the welfare of the patient in front of you. American medicine focuses on that to a greater extent than doctors in most other countries and probably to a fault, for American families often insist on doing everything possible to keep loved ones alive even when the medical prognosis is both clear and hopeless (and that is even before we consider quality of life issues, like dementia). For American medical personnel, then, what the pandemic involves is what philosophers call "*a paradigm shift*," in which they need to shift from a patient-centered focus to a public health perspective. Put more plainly, doctors and nurses now need to think not about whether they can save person X but how can they save as many people as possible, even if that means abandoning the care of person X. As the pandemic gets worse, that may even mean not providing palliative (comfort) care for the dying for lack of human and equipment resources. This is hard for all of us to think about, but most especially for those used to doing all they can for their patients.

The term used for deciding whom to save and whom to ignore is "triage." It comes from the military environment, where medics had to decide which wounded soldiers on the battlefield they should try to save and which ones they unfortunately had to ignore. The general rule of triage that comes out of that environment is this: without regard to rank or other element of social status, pay attention first to those who need immediate attention in order to survive and, among those, treat first the ones who have the best chance of survival so that they can continue to fight if helped to survive now.

Ancient sources in the Jewish tradition also spoke of triage, but not in a medical context. That is because although ancient and medieval medicine was remarkably good at preventive techniques, its curative capabilities were largely ineffective. Thus Leviticus 13-14 already understands that quarantine should be used to contain contagious diseases, and the Talmud tells us to avoid crowds during epidemics[1]—remarkably astute advice for our time. The Sabbath was a significant Jewish contribution to human understanding of what is necessary for physical as well as emotional and spiritual health. Rabbinic sources warn against eating uncooked meat[2] and advocate eating vegetables.[3]

Curative care, though, was a totally different matter. Until the 20th century, the only curative measures that doctors did in an attempt to cure diseases were two things: (1) surgery, but then patients often bled out and died for lack of blood, or they died from infections[4]; or (2) bloodletting,

---

[1] B. *Bava Kamma* 60b.

[2] B. *Sanhedrin* 9a.

[3] B. *Berakhot* 44b.

[4] Herbert Rakatansky, MD, FACP, FACG, Clinical Professor of Medicine Emeritus, Warren Alpert Medical School, Brown University, sent me an email in response to an earlier draft of this responsum, in which I mentioned that it was only in 1865 that Dr. Joseph Lister (after whom Listerine was named) recognized that fewer people died if doctors washed their hands between surgical procedures, and I want to thank him for this information:

The effect of handwashing on post-delivery mortality was observed independently in Boston by Dr. Oliver Wendell Holmes, Sr. and in Vienna by Dr. Ignace Semmelweiss, both in 1845. Their conclusive findings were ignored in both situations. They were never aware of each other. The then current belief in miasmas triumphed over the objective findings.

The germ theory was developed by Pasteur in the 1850's. Joseph Lister practiced surgery in Scotland…His seminal paper was published in 1867. It demonstrated that spraying carbolic acid on the wounds of compound fractures prevented death (100% mortality previously). He was a friend of Pasteur and believed in the germ theory.

because doctors had a sense that many diseases were blood borne. They were right about the blood-borne nature of many diseases but wrong in thinking that taking a pint of blood would cure the disease; the only disease for which that works is one that my mother had, polycythemia (too many red blood cells), for which the treatment still today is to take a pint of blood every once in a while. It was only in the advent of the sulfa drugs in the early 20th century and then antibiotics (Sir Alexander Fleming discovered penicillin in 1928, but it could not be widely produced until the early 1940s) that curative care became effective.

The Jewish sources that deal with triage are therefore not about access to health care, which was ineffective and therefore cheap. The sources instead address two other conditions of scarcity that Jewish communities faced, namely, poverty and redemption from captivity. In Chapter Twelve of my book, *Matters of Life and Death: A Jewish Approach to Modern Medical Ethics*, I review the sources that deal with how to determine who gets the community's limited resources to respond to both poverty and captivity. The following criteria for determining who gets what emerge from the sources (see the book for the sources and a description of how each would be used in context):

Social hierarchy: save those who are most important in society, defined in the same source (M. *Horayot* 3:7-8) as variously dependent on the number of commandments to which a person was subject, or the person's priestly status, or how much Torah the person knows.

Concentric circles: yourself first, then your immediate family, then your extended family, then your local Jewish community, then the larger Jewish community, and then people of other faiths (B. *Bava Metzi'a* 62a, 71a; B. *Nedarim* 80b; T. *Pe'ah* 4:9; T. *Gittin* 3:18; B. *Gittin* 61a; S.A. *Yoreh De'ah* 251:3; 252:9).

A hierarchy of social responsibilities: redeeming captives first, then the sick among the poor, then feeding the poor, then clothing the poor (with women taking precedence over men for both food and clothing), then Jewish education, then building and supporting a synagogue (S.A. *Yoreh De'ah* 249:16; 251:7-8; 252:1, 3).

He got the idea about carbolic acid from reading a newspaper article from Carlisle, Scotland describing the effect of spraying carbolic acid on fields adjacent to a river contaminated with sewage. Those fields had become poisonous to the cows that grazed there. The carbolic acid restored the fields and the cows thrived. Lister put together all these facts and concluded that microorganisms caused the cows to die and might cause the fatal suppuration of compound fractures. He was correct. But even then it took a number of years for antisepsis to be generally accepted, The first patient to survive an operation on the abdomen without dying of sepsis was operated on in Vienna in 1881 by Theodore Billroth.

Greatest needs of the individuals at risk: Save those whose lives are most at risk first, followed by those at lesser degrees of risk for their lives, followed by those at risk for harm (e.g., assault, rape) (S.A. *Yoreh De'ah* 252:8).

Everyone is equal (M. *Sanhedrin* 4:5; B. *Berakhot* 17a; and the difficult case of handing someone over to the enemy in J. *Terumot* 7:20 and *Genesis Rabbah* 94:9).

Although saving people from poverty and captivity may indeed have involved saving lives, the situations our ancestors faced were not usually as overwhelming in the numbers of people in need or in the immediacy of the possibility of death as in the situation that we are now facing in the Covid-19 pandemic. In this context, individual physicians, ethicists, and ethics committees at hospitals, including those who wrote about triage decisions years before the current pandemic and those who are wrestling with formulating hospital policies now, have identified all of the following moral principles that might guide triage decisions:

Treating people equally, either through "first come, first served" or through a lottery.

Favoring the worst-off on the basis of the "rule of rescue."

Maximizing total benefits (utilitarianism), measured either by the number of lives saved or the number of life-years saved.

Promoting and rewarding social usefulness, based either on instrumental value for the future of the society or on reciprocity for past contributions, including those on the front lines of fighting Covid-19.[5]

As the many discussions of triage in a medical context demonstrate beyond any doubt, highly intelligent, thoroughly informed, reasonable, and morally sensitive people both can and do disagree with each other on what is the best policy in the morally and psychologically excruciating decisions front-line doctors must make when they lack the resources to do their best

---

[5] There are many discussions of these principles and how to weigh and balance them, but here are three, for example, that come to different conclusions: Gavind Persad, Alan Wertheimer, Ezekiel J. Emanuel, "Principles for Allocation of Scarce Medical Interventions," *Lancet* 2009: 373: 423-31; E. Lee Daugherty Biddison, Ruth Faden, et. al, "Too Many Patients…A Framework to Guide Statewide Allocation of Scarce Mechanical Ventilation During Disasters," *Chest* (*Contemporary Reviews in Critical Care Medicine*) 155:4 (April 2019): 848-854 (with thanks to Dr. Neil Wenger, Chair of the Ethics Committee of UCLA Medical Center, for alerting me to these and other articles on this topic); and New York State Task Force on Life and the Law, New York State Department of Health, *Ventilator Allocation Guidelines*, 2010, revised 2015 (with thanks to Rabbi Julie Schonfeld for alerting me to this document),
https://www.health.ny.gov/regulations/task_force/reports_publications/docs/ventilator_guidelines.pdf
(accessed 3/27/20).

for every patient needing their care. Furthermore, I have no doubt that people trying to apply the Jewish tradition to these decisions will also disagree with each other. Indeed, although my good friend, Rabbi Daniel Nevins, and I through two months of a wonderful interaction of critiquing each other's earlier drafts have decided to come to the same conclusion, we disagree on how to get there in reading and applying relevant Jewish sources and in some of the nuances of our shared conclusion, and that is fine: friends can disagree, and one might especially expect that on issues like triage that are both as serious and as morally difficult as can be. After all, we are talking about nothing less than decisions that will determine life and death, and the grounds for making these decisions are also as morally murky as can be, as evidenced by the many different and conflicting criteria for making triage decisions affirmed in both Jewish sources and in secular ethical discussions, as described above. Let me say here, at the outset, that I want to thank him for forcing me to sharpen my own thinking on this issue as he developed his.

First, then, with a deep sense of the gravity of what I am about to write and an even deeper sense of humility in even addressing these triage issues, this is what I would say:[6]

Patients who have capably indicated, either verbally or in an advanced care document such as the one created by Rabbi Aaron Mackler for the Committee on Jewish Law and Standards, based on the responsa on end-of-life care by Rabbis Reisner and Dorff,[7] that they do not want their life prolonged by medical means or the clinical circumstances are such that life-sustaining treatment cannot attain their goals should have their preference respected and should not be included in the triage pool, provided that their preference clearly is warranted by their current clinical circumstances. In other words, triage decisions to deny care to a given patient out of medical necessity to treat those most likely to survive to hospital discharge are, by definition, those made against the will of the patient and/or his or her family.

---

[6] I am deeply indebted to discussions of the UCLA Medical Center Ethics Committee, of which I have been a member since the 1980s, for what I write here. Although I am writing here from a Jewish perspective, the UCLA Ethics Committee discussions and the many materials Dr. Neil Wenger, its Chair, had us read in preparation for these discussions, have alerted me to the complications of applying any of the moral principles articulated in Jewish sources and in the general bioethics literature directly, without qualification, and the way in which many of these principles conflict in practice so that painful choices must be made in formulating policy guidelines.

[7] Rabbi Aaron L. Mackler, "Jewish Medical Directives for Health Care,"
    http://www.rabbinicalassembly.org/sites/default/files/assets/public/halakhah/teshuvot/19861990/mackler_care.pdf (accessed 3/27/20)

Similarly, what in some circumstances can be life-sustaining treatment (e.g., a ventilator) should not be initiated on patients who have no reasonable prospect of benefiting from it because of their underlying physical condition, for to do so is simply bad practice of medicine. This is true under normal circumstances and, all the more so, during a time necessitating triage of scarce medical resources.

Because triage will result in patients being denied care that in normal circumstances would be provided and because such denial will possibly lead to adverse medical outcomes for them and maybe even their death, triage protocols should be initiated and maintained only where and when there is evident need to do so because of a shortage of medical personnel and/or materials needed to respond to the demand for them.

Because clinical care physicians are trained to focus on the patient at hand, they cannot be expected to carry the moral burden of treating some patients at the cost of others. Decisions about whether particular patients meet or fail to meet the triage criteria should therefore be made by a triage officer or team not involved in the clinical care of any of the patients under consideration. This not only recognizes the difficulty of clinical care physicians making the necessary paradigm shift to think of their efforts to heal from a public health perspective rather than a clinical care one; it also is at least a plausible reading of the precedent of the Rabbinic story that proclaims that if the residents of a besieged city can be saved by giving up one of their number chosen by the enemy (in our case, death, and thus those in the process of what the medical community calls "active dying"), that person should be given up but it should not be Rabbi Joshua who hands the person over to the enemy but rather people not involved in the case.[8] Furthermore, it must be a person or group representing the public good that requires and justifies physicians to abandon their Jewish duty to care for all patients who seek their aid[9] in favor of treating some and not others when they cannot treat everyone who needs them.

As in the military context, in the medical context the primary goal of triage should be to maximize the number of lives saved. More specifically, the goal is to maximize the number of patients who will survive to hospital discharge in a state of health that makes it probable that they will survive beyond that. Nobody knows, of course, how long anyone is going to sur-

---

[8] J. *Terumot* 8:10; a shorter version of this story appears in T. *Terumot*, end of chapter 7 and in *Genesis Rabbah* 94:9. I discuss this story and the various ways of interpreting its ending in Elliot N. Dorff, *Matters of Life and Death: A Jewish Approach to Modern Medical Ethics* (Philadelphia: Jewish Publication Society, 1998), pp. 291-299.

[9] S.A. Orah Hayyim 339:1.

vive or in what condition, but if the person meets the medical criteria to be stable enough to be discharged from the hospital for further recovery at home, that counts as saving the person's life. This is in accord with the core Jewish value of *pikku'ah nefesh*, saving life.[10] It is also in accord with the principle enunciated in the same Rabbinic story noted above that instructs us to save a group even if it requires giving up a particular person to the enemy for execution—or, in our case, not treating some dying patients who are unlikely to be saved in order to save others whose lives can be saved.[11]

This is also in line with my 1990 responsum on end-of-life care, in which I used the Jewish legal category of *treifah*—that is, a person with a terminal, incurable disease—to determine what kinds of medical care may be withheld or removed from a patient.[12] A person can continue as a *treifah*, though, for months and, in the case of some genetic diseases like Familial Dysautonomia, for years before death, and so the criterion I am invoking here is much narrower than that—namely, that it counts as saving a person's life if he or she can survive to the state of being medically appropriate for discharge from the hospital. Then, of course, we would hope, but never know, that he or she will survive long after being discharged in the state of health that the patient had before contracting Covid-19, or even better.

This is not utilitarianism, for that theory would have us focus on the life years saved, thus favoring young people, and possibly also those who are most useful to society, however that is defined. Saving as many lives as possible, whatever their state of health or ability or age or social or economic status, is rather an articulation of the deep Jewish values of saving life and seeing everyone as of equal worth as created in the image of God as applied to the excruciating decisions required when human and material resources are not sufficient to care for everyone, and so triage is necessary.

This will mean that some patients who would ordinarily receive and benefit from treatment may either not receive treatment at all, have the initiation of treatment postponed, or have treatment discontinued. All of these cases—including those who do not receive necessary treatment at all—are situations in which people may die or suffer some other adverse health-related consequence. This is the tragedy of the necessity to triage.

Triage decisions apply to both withholding and withdrawing limited

---

[10] B. *Yoma* 85a-85b; B. *Sanhedrin* 74a-74b. For an expanded discussion of this principle, see Dorff, *Matters of Life and Death*. pp. 15-18 and note 3 on pp. 328-329.

[11] See note 4 above.

[12] Rabbi Elliot N. Dorff, "A Jewish Approach to End-Stage Medical Care," http://www.rabbinicalassembly.org/sites/default/files/assets/public/halakhah/teshuvot/19861990/dorff_care.pdf (accessed 3/27/20).

medical resources. Life-sustaining treatment need not and should not be continued solely because it was begun. This applies no less to treatment initiated before triage was required. Understanding the considerations justifying withholding or withdrawing medical interventions to be equivalent morally and halakhically is in line with both responsa on end-of-life care approved by the Committee on Jewish Law and Standards, one by Rabbi Avram Reisner and the other by me.[13]

In line with this, in triage conditions the use of scarce medical resources on particular patients must be reevaluated on a timetable supported by the best medical evidence for the patient's condition. This periodic reassessment[14] entails the possibility that a later evaluation will result in the removal of life support from a particular patient for whom continuing care is adjudged by the medical personnel to be futile and transferred to another patient who, if given the treatment, has a reasonable chance of survival to hospital discharge. Such a transfer of medical resources from one person, for whom the use of those resources is now futile, to another who can reasonably be expected to benefit from those resources to the point of hospital discharge should happen even if the patient and/or his or her family wants treatment continued; in fact, hospital futility policies are precisely intended to deal with circumstances when physicians determine that continuing medical interventions cannot achieve the medical goals for which they were initiated and therefore, according to the policy, may and even should be removed despite the patient's or family's opposition to doing so. To remove a medical intervention from one person for whom the intervention is futile to be used by another who may benefit from it is *not* a violation of the Rabbinic principle of *ain dokhin nefesh mipnei nefesh*,[15] that

---

[13] Rabbi Avram Israel Reisner, "A Halakhic Ethic of Care for the Terminally Ill," http://www.rabbinicalassembly.org/sites/default/files/assets/public/halakhah/teshuvot/19861990/reisner_care.pdf (accessed 3/27/20); Rabbi Elliot N. Dorff, "A Jewish Approach to End-Stage Medical Care," http://www.rabbinicalassembly.org/sites/default/files/assets/public/halakhah/teshuvot/19861990/dorff_care.pdf (accessed 3/27/20).

This differs from many authorities in the Orthodox world who permit withholding treatment but not withdrawing it; for very good reason, in my humble opinion, both Rabbi Reisner and I maintain that there is no moral or halakhic difference between withholding or withdrawing treatment, for the appropriate question is whether the treatment is medically appropriate, given the patient's condition, or whether it is instead a prohibited impediment to the patient's natural course of dying.

[14] During a meeting of the Committee on Jewish Law and Standards, Dr. Toby Schonfeld told us that at the Veterans Administration hospitals, the reassessment happens every 48 hours.

[15] As Rabbi Nevins notes, this principle is stated in B. *Pesaḥim* 25b, B. *Yoma* 82b, and

one may not prefer one life over another, because that refers to situations in which it is simply our decision as to whom to save; in triage situations the medical condition of the patients involved is determining which one is more likely to survive, not our voluntary choice.

All patients who require use of limited medical resources, whatever their disease or their need to utilize limited medical resources, should be equally subject to the triaging process. That is, all patients who need a particular, scarce medical resource such as, but not limited to, a ventilator, are subject to the triage process, not just Covid-19 patients or Covid-19 patients in preference to others. It should go without saying that considerations of gender, race, ethnic background, social-economic status, disability, religion, educational background, and ability to pay for care should play no role in deciding who gets what. Age may be considered only insofar as it is clinically relevant to determining a patient's likelihood of survival to hospital discharge. This follows directly from the principle in the Jewish tradition of the equality of every human being.

Health care personnel on the front lines of caring for people infected by Covid-19 should receive preference in triage decisions over others who are not involved directly in saving lives in, for example, providing protective gear and vaccines, when available, to first responders and those treating patients over those in the general population. This preference is based on the underlying principle of trying to maximize the number of lives saved by protecting those in the thick of the process of doing so. Health care personnel who become infected, however, should be part of the general triage process in obtaining treatment.

If none of these principles breaks the tie between two or among three or more patients who have not yet been treated, then the ones to get the scarce resource should be chosen by lottery, invoking the principle in Jewish law that we are each equally created in the image of God. A simple flip of a coin will do, however arbitrary that may seem—but that, of course, is exactly the point: if no medical conditions distinguish potential patients, then fairness requires that everyone have an equal chance to be treated. The alternative egalitarian possibility, "first come first served," suffers from the injustice that it would prefer those who have ready access to care for socioeconomic reasons to those who do not; it is therefore unjust in these circumstances. Using either method to decide whom to treat will clearly not remedy the rampant inequality in society generally or in the delivery of health care in particular. That inequality is especially evident and problematic in the United States, which lacks universal health care for every

---

especially B. *Sanhedrin* 72b-74a.

resident, but it exists even in countries with socialized medicine whose governments provide a basic level of care for every citizen but permit their wealthier members to augment what the government provides with private insurance. The fact that we cannot provide a full remedy for these inequities does not mean that we should fail to do what we can to treat people as fairly as possible. A lottery will do that in choosing whom to treat when two or more people present themselves to the Emergency Room with more or less equal prognoses and not all of them can be treated for lack of personnel and/or equipment.

If possible, palliative care for symptom control should be offered to all patients. This is in accord with the responsa of both Rabbis Reisner and Dorff, and stems from our duty to care for others even when we cannot cure, which, in turn is based ultimately on such verses as "Love your neighbor as yourself" (Leviticus 19:18). In the event that there are inadequate resources to meet the palliative needs of all patients, those patients who have been denied priority access to life-sustaining treatment and are expected to die as a consequence of that denial should have priority access to palliative interventions, if these are necessary.

As I understand Rabbi Nevins' position in comparison to mine, the primary place where we disagree is on my assertion that sometimes an intervention should be removed from Patient A in favor of Patient B because Patient B has a better chance of survival than Patient A does. Several things about this need to be explained. First, as I stated above, this is *not*, in my view, a violation of the Talmud's principle that we may not prefer one life over another because all of those cases are ones in which it is simply a decision based on *the actor's preference to choose one person over another*, for whatever reason the actor has for that choice. In triage situations, in contrast, *it is the underlying medical conditions of the two or more patients before us* that determine who should have access to the machines, medications, and personnel needed.

Second, yes, as Rabbi Nevins says, people involved in making these decisions are going to suffer major stress both psychologically and professionally. Indeed, I would hope that they would be sufficiently attuned to the moral stakes and ambiguities involved to feel such stress and ambivalence. This is exactly why I stated above that front-line physicians should not be asked to bear the moral burden of making these decisions, that such decisions should instead be made by a clear policy and applied by a triage officer or team not involved in the care of any of the patients for whom triage decisions must be made. These are excruciating decisions, and the last thing we would want is that the people who are already overwhelmed in treating patients must additionally bear the moral burden of deciding whom to help when they cannot help everyone. Furthermore, from a Jewish point of view, as also stated above, it needs to be someone who is not involved in particular patients' care that makes this public health decision so as to relieve physicians from their Jewish duty to treat all people who come to them for care and to instead, in line with the Rabbinic story cited in that paragraph, put that burden on someone or some group acting in the name of the public, not Rabbi Joshua who is directly involved in the case.

Third, yes again, as Rabbi Nevins maintains, under normal circumstances we would never remove life support from someone who can benefit from it and who wants to continue to live with whatever its burdens are. But the whole point of this inquiry is to deal with the hopefully very abnormal situation—but the one in which we find ourselves during this Covid-19 pandemic—in which there are not sufficient resources to provide life support for everyone who needs it. In such situations, first having access to, say, a ventilator does not establish the patient's ownership of that ventilator; it belongs to the hospital, and in triage situations the hospital has the duty to try to save as many lives as possible. This will require periodic reassessments of the medical conditions of people using the hospital's resources and decisions to remove them from patients whose medical interventions have proven to be futile in the effort to save their lives to hospital discharge, despite their own desires to continue using such resources or the wishes of their family.

Fourth, yes, in normal times, if one person is in greater danger than another, and if the second person can simply wait or survive with temporary measures while we attend to the first person, then sure, we should treat the person in greater danger first. Hence the precedent of Pri Megadim that Rabbi Nevins cites, followed by others in the twentieth century. That is exactly what emergency medicine is all about and why, in normal circumstances, people with emergencies will get immediate attention while others will have to wait. That presumes, though, that even though by hypothesis all of the people in the Emergency Room are there for true emergencies, some of them are more urgent than others, and so some people can wait while the most serious emergencies are treated. That, though, is not the situation here, when, by definition of triage, we are dealing with cases where we cannot save everyone because everyone has effectively arrived at the emergency room at the same time so that it is overwhelmed and cannot accommodate everyone, and everyone must be treated immediately or die. Then some people will inevitably die—not because we want them to die or choose some over others to die, but because some are in worse shape medically than others and their varying medical conditions will determine who shall live and who shall die—and then, I submit, we must do what we can to save the lives of those we can, even if that means that the patients' varying medical conditions will force us to decide to provide medical support for some patients rather than others or to discontinue life support for those who will die shortly anyway so that we can save others.

Fifth, as stated above, when two or more patients who have not yet been treated have the same diagnosis but not all can be treated because of shortage of medical personnel and/or equipment, then I prefer the lottery system for deciding who will get access to care over "first come, first served" because the latter privileges those who, for socioeconomic reasons, have greater access to health care and is therefore unjust in triage situations as in life in general, while the lottery system is more egalitarian. It is bad enough that we have that inequality in access to medical care in normal times, especially in the United States; we should not extend it to triage as well if we can do otherwise, as we can with a lottery system.

Finally, sixth, it is precisely the story in the Tosefta, Jerusalem Talmud, and Genesis Rabbah that deals exactly with triage when it is immediately and clearly a question of who should live and who should die. It is, in other words, directly on point, the most relevant source for our question. Furthermore, I would suggest that as reluctant as Rambam is to affirm this precedent (and I am too—I would much rather that we never have to face such situations),[16] in the end, it does provide guidance of what we must do in these cases. Specifically, if the enemy—in our case, death—does choose one person over another, then our duty is to save the person whom we have a chance of saving over someone whom we cannot, even if we tried up to this point. To assert that whoever happened to be put on the ventilator first should remain on it even when the chances of saving that person to the point of eligibility for discharge from the hospital are slim to nonexistent and the chances of saving someone else to that point are much better seems to me to be ignoring the medical realities of the cases we are considering, the shortages that are unfortunate but real, and, ultimately, our duty to save lives. Saving lives is what is sacred, so sacred that we are to violate all but three of the other commandments in order to accomplish that.[17]

Again, these criteria of triage are to be instituted only when, in a particular time and place, there is a clear shortage of medical personnel and/or resources, and only for the duration of that condition. Although current conditions portend that at least in some places triage will be necessary for a

---

[16] M.T. *Yesodei Ha-Torah* 5:5.

[17] B. *Sanhedrin* 74a; see also B. *Yoma* 85a-85b. On this issue generally, see Dorff, *Matters of Life and Death*, pp. 15-18 and, especially, note 3 on pp. 328-329; and, more extensively, Immanuel Jakobovits, *Jewish Medical Ethics* (New York: Ktav, 1959, 1972), pp. 45-98.

period of time because of the Covid-19 pandemic, let me express the hope of all of us that it not happen and, if it does, that it be over soon. In the meantime, it is incumbent on all of us to follow the instructions of civil health care authorities to practice social distancing as much as possible in order to stop the spread of the virus. It is also important, in accordance with our tradition's recognition of our need to interact with others, not to reach out and touch someone (!), but to reach out and be there for each other through phone calls and other electronic means of connection.

The Jewish tradition demands that we take care of our own physical and mental health. Thus it is important that we maintain some form of exercise during this pandemic, even if it is not the usual ways we exercise or in the usual places or with the group of people or team we usually are part of. For our own mental health, it is also advisable to engage in new and old ways of learning and social interaction, including reading the books that you intended to read but never got to, learning new things online, playing games online with other people or in person with the members of one's own household, and having conversations with others by phone and online because "it is not good for a person to be alone."

P'sak Din: Consensus Halakhic Conclusion by Rabbis Dorff and Nevins

Our respective responsa addressed many of the medical, logistical, moral and spiritual challenges of medical triage in a crisis such as the Covid-19 pandemic. While our presentations differ in approach and presentation, and we reach some incompatible positions, we agree on the following practical conclusions:

Equal access to medical care is a moral and halakhic imperative. Triage decisions must not be based on criteria other than the best chance to save lives.

Scarce resources used to prevent infection such as personal protective equipment and vaccines may be assigned on a priority basis to medical professionals and other emergency responders in order to support them in their life-saving efforts.

Jewish law differentiates between brief respite (חיי שעה) and recovery (חיי עולם). Scarce medical resources may be directed toward patients who are expected with this therapy to recover over those who are not expected to recover, even with this therapy. Diagnostic tools such as the Sequential Organ Failure Assessment may be used to prioritize allocation of scarce medical resources towards patients who may be rescued, and away from those who are not expected to survive to hospital discharge.

If a patient is already receiving medical therapy and is responding, they may not be removed from the equipment prematurely in order to rescue the life of another person based on comparison of the two patients' age, ability, general health, or social status. The only criterion for removing a person from therapy is the determination that they cannot survive to discharge, or their own request to shift to palliative care.

If the triage officer determines that a patient cannot be saved, and that their medical resources must be reallocated to another patient in urgent need, the basis for this decision must be explained fully and sensitively to the patient or their representative, and the hospital must continue to support the patient with appropriate palliative and pastoral care, maintaining the respect and dignity of the patient until the end.

This responsum was written in June 2020, before vaccines were available, but the same triage decisions about distributing scarce ventilators apply to vaccines. Furthermore, the duty to guard one's own health requires that anyone eligible to be inoculated with any of the vaccines that protect against contracting COVID-19 must do so. See Elliot N. Dorff and Susan Grossman, "Wearing Face Covering, Physical Distancing, and Other Measures to Control the COVID-19 Pandemic," https://www.rabbinicalassembly.org/sites/default/files/2021-07/Dorff%20 Grossman%20Masks%20final%20reclassified%20%281%29.pdf(accessed 8/5/21).

Moses as Leader in the Eyes of the Tannaim

Matthew Goldstone

This volume honors a remarkable leader. A person of grand vision who is able to successfully guide an institution of diverse voices while overseeing innumerable moving pieces in the larger puzzle of daily activities. Such a herculean task is certainly no easy feat and Dr. Ora Horn Prouser's skill and wisdom serve as a model for all who know her. In honor of her accomplishments as a leader, my modest contribution to this volume examines the depiction of one of Judaism's greatest leaders, Moses, through the lens of the tannaitic *midrashim* from the school of Rabbi Akiva—*Sifra* and *Sifrei Devarim*.

As is well-known, the rabbis craft an image of Moses as the primordial rabbi who taught Torah to the Israelites just as the *tannaim* instructed their disciples.[1] But, in casting Moses in their own image, the rabbis refrain from portraying Moses as the flawless ideal of a sage. Rabbinic literature frequently whitewashes the deficiencies of biblical characters, cultivating an aura of moral and ritual perfection.[2] This can result in perfect biblical exemplars to which all may aspire, but no regular mortal can actually attain. Yet, in the case of Moses, the tannaitic *midrashim* refrain from purging all of his imperfections. Rather, these sources simultaneously laud Moses' actions while admitting his failings and faults, constructing an imperfect icon that can actually serve as a realistic role model for imitation. Indeed, some of the shortcomings that the rabbis choose to amplify about Moses are the very areas in which the rabbis themselves recognize their own deficiencies.[3] In

---

[1] Jacob Neusner, *Rabbi Moses: A Documentary Catalogue* (Lanham, Maryland: UPA, 2013).

[2] See, for example, the discussion in Richard Kalmin, "Rabbinic Portrayals of Biblical and Post-Biblical Heroes," in *The Synoptic Problem in Rabbinic Literature*, ed. Shaye J. D. Cohen (Brown Judaic Studies, 2020), 119–20; Richard Kalmin, "Portrayals of Kings in Rabbinic Literature of Late Antiquity," *Jewish Studies Quarterly* 3, no. 4 (1996): 329–38; James Diamond, "King David of the Sages: Rabbinic Rehabilitation or Ironic Parody?," *Prooftexts* 27, no. 3 (Fall 2007): 373–74.

[3] In some ways, this reading is similar to Christine Hayes' argument that "rabbinic authors introduce or exploit the presence of *minim* (i.e., heretics or sectarians) and Romans... in order to voice and thus grapple with their own ambivalence and radical doubt concerning non-contextual methods of exegesis" (Christine Elizabeth Hayes, "Displaced Self-Perceptions: The Deployment of 'Mînîm' and Romans in b. Sanhedrin 90b-91a," *Religious and Ethnic Communities in Later Roman Palestine*, 1998, 250). It also has parallels to Dov Weiss' identification of "protest ventriloquism" in

this essay I examine three such areas—rebuke, judgement, and immortality. I demonstrate that tannaitic sources portray Moses as largely successful in each of these areas up until a certain point. Despite his almost superhuman ability to excel in each of these areas, ultimately Moses reaches a point of fault or failure that returns him to the mortal realm. I suggest that the introduction of Moses' limitations when it comes to these issues expresses the anxiety of the early rabbis who feel that they too fall short of the mark when it comes to rebuke, judgement, and the quest for immortality.

Early *midrashim* place Moses on a pedestal as an active participant in revelation. Contrary to the general tannaitic antipathy towards the idea of people challenging God, in one particularly "stunning" passage found in both *Mekhilta deRabbi Ishmael* and *Mekhilta deRabbi Shimon bar Yochai* (in slightly different versions), Rabbi Yehudah bar Ilai suggests that God actually set up a scene in which Moses would demonstrate to the Israelites his ability to impose changes on the content of revelation: "'In order that the people may hear when I speak with you' [Exod. 19:9]: Rabbi Judah [bar Ilai] says: 'The Holy One, blessed be He, said to Moses, "Behold I will say something to you and you will challenge me, and behold I will retract and accede to your words.""[4] As Steven Fraade explains, in this text,

> God stages a rabbinic-style halakhic dispute with Moses in the hearing of the whole people, in which Moses challenges God's articulation (whether outrightly refuting or simply correcting is not clear), whereupon God retracts and accepts instead Moses' alternative formulation… All of this is done in Israel's hearing so that they will, *in the future and for all time* (לעולם), have confidence in Moses as the divinely authorized transmitter of the commandments,

---

which the rabbis deal with a theological problem by "putting protests into the mouths of biblical heroes" (Dov Weiss, *Pious Irreverence: Confronting God in Rabbinic Judaism* [Philadelphia, PA: University of Pennsylvania Press, 2017], 15). However, while these scholars are primarily looking at the Bavli and later rabbinic literature, in this essay I am interested in the expression of rabbinic concerns through the lens of a biblical figure within tannaitic literature.

[4] Translation from Steven D. Fraade, "Moses and the Commandments: Can Hermeneutics, History, and Rhetoric Be Disentangled?," in *The Idea of Biblical Interpretation: Essays in Honor of James L. Kugel*, ed. Hindy Najman and Judith H. Newman, Supplements to the Journal for the Study of Judaism 83 (Leiden: Brill, 2004), 399–422. On the tannaitic antipathy towards challenging God, see Weiss, *Pious Irreverence*, 22–25.

not simply as unthinking stenographer, but, as it were, as contributor to revelation, with advance divine approval.[5]

Moses is cast as the first rabbi, encouraged by God to engage in "rabbinic-style halakhic dispute" and ultimately to have a formative hand in shaping the direction of divine revelation. The early rabbis likewise saw themselves as active participants in defining the contours of Torah, presenting themselves as the spiritual and religious heirs to Moses. Yet, while Moses stands as the progenitor of the entire rabbinic project, he is not idealized to the point of immaculate perfection. Tannaitic discussions of the three issues discussed below—rebuke, judgement, and immortality—capture the ways in which even in the areas in which he excels, Moses has his limitations, marking his portrayal as an expression of the early rabbis' own anxieties about their limits as aspiring leaders.

Rebuke

Sifrei Devarim portrays Moses as the paradigmatic rebuker. This tannaitic midrash opens by establishing that the words Moses speaks in the Book of Deuteronomy constitute rebuke and that subsequent prophets followed in Moses' footsteps. *Pisqa* 1 begins by asking:

> *These are the words which Moses spoke* ([Deut.] 1:1): Did Moses prophesy nothing but these words? Did he not write the entire Torah, as it is said, *And Moses wrote this Torah* (31:9)? Why then does the verse state, *These are the words which Moses spoke*? Hence we learn that they were words of rebuke, as it is said, *But Jeshurun waxed fat, and kicked* (32:15).[6]

In typical midrashic fashion, *Sifrei Devarim* wonders why the Biblical text must add the ostensibly superfluous term "these" (אלה)—why are "these" words distinct from everything else that has been recorded in the Torah up until this point? The midrash answers that these words are a particular type of speech—specifically, rebuke. Introducing this remark on the very

---

[5] Fraade, "Moses and the Commandments: Can Hermeneutics, History, and Rhetoric Be Disentangled?," 405–6.

[6] Unless otherwise noted, translations from *Sifrei Devarim* follow Reuven Hammer, *Sifre: A Tannaitic Commentary on the Book of Deuteronomy* (New Haven: Yale University Press, 1986).

first verse of Deuteronomy and illustrating the chastising nature of Moses' speech with a quotation from near the end of this Biblical book (Deut. 32:15), the midrash asserts that the entirety of Deuteronomy constitutes Moses' rebuke.

This Mosaic diatribe serves as the model for subsequent prophets and leaders. *Pisqa* 1 continues by enumerating four other figures who follow in Moses' footsteps: Amos, Jeremiah, David and Solomon. In each of these cases, the example is preceded by the connecting phrase "Similarly Scripture states" (כיוצא בו אתה אומר) and the figure is referred to as prophesying—נתנבא. While Moses, Amos, and Jeremiah are all regularly framed as prophets within the Biblical corpus, David and Solomon are more commonly thought of as kings rather than prophets. The usage of the root נ.ב.א for all of these different figures is thus somewhat unusual and attracts our attention. The term conveys exceptional knowledge not available to everyone. Presenting Moses as first in this list establishes him as the exemplar from whom all others learn and the use of the verb נ.ב.א suggests that he has access to knowledge of the optimal way to reprove the Israelites.

Sifrei Devarim proffers a number of ways in which Moses' reproof, perhaps due to his prophetic insight, was particularly well planned and executed. According to the Biblical text, Moses spoke to "all of Israel" (אֶל כָּל יִשְׂרָאֵל). Within the Biblical narrative this is likely a function of the fact that Moses was shepherding the entire people to the Land of Israel. But the midrash understands Moses' speaking to the *entire* people as a conscious strategic move. The midrash imagines what might have happened had Moses only engaged some of the people with his rebuke: "*Unto all Israel* (1:1): Had he rebuked only some of them, those who were in the market place might have said, 'You heard this from the son of Amram, and you did not answer him back? By God, had we been there, we would have had four or five retorts to him for every one of his words!'" Moses' astute sense of the possible repercussions led him to chastise the people together as a whole. Moreover, the midrash presents an alternative gloss on the phrase "unto all Israel" suggesting that Moses actually warned the people "I am about to rebuke you. If anyone has anything to say in a rebuttal, let him come forth and speak," so as to avoid taking them by surprise.

Not all of Moses' clever tactics stem from his own ingenuity, even he had role models from whom he learned. *Sifrei Devarim* picks up on the fact that the speech of Deuteronomy takes place in the fortieth year of wandering in the desert—the final year before the people enter the Land of Israel and Moses passes away. The midrash suggests that from the timing we learn that Moses rebuked the people only when he was about to die. The text then asks: "From whom did he learn this? From Jacob, who rebuked his sons only when he was about to die." Citing the beginning of Jacob's deathbed blessings (or curses) to his sons, *Sifrei Devarim* finds patriarchal precedent for Moses' delay in confronting the Israelites. The midrash goes on to establish several reasons why it is preferable to wait until one is about to die in order to chastise people: "so that A would not be rebuking B over and over again; so that, whenever B sees A, he would not feel ashamed; so that B would not hold a grudge against A." In order to avoid the necessity of constantly repeating rebuke, the shame that accompanies a rebuked person when they encounter their confronter, and the grudge that the rebuked person may carry, the midrashic tradition recommends postponing confrontation until the last possible moment. This is ostensibly what Moses did when he gave his Deuteronomic speech at the end of his life.

Moses serves as the rabbinic exemplar of a consummate rebuker. He learns important lessons from his predecessors, he employs expert tactics when confronting the Israelites in the desert, and he is the model for the prophets and kings who come after him. Yet, when we examine the text carefully, we find hints that perhaps Moses deviated from the ideal course or, at the very least, that even his prodigious skill was not enough to make his actions a complete success.

Deuteronomy opens with a list of places in which Moses spoke to the Israelites throughout their journey: "These are the words that Moses addressed to all Israel on the other side of the Jordan.—Through the wilderness, in the Arabah near Suph, between Paran and Tophel, Laban, Hazeroth, and Di-zahab, it is eleven days from Horeb to Kadesh-barnea by the Mount Seir route" (Deut. 1:1-2). One interpretative strand that we find within the midrash is to understand a few of these place names as metaphors, hinting at the sins the Israelites committed. For example, with regard to Tophel, "This refers to the disparaging words (*tiphlut*) that they spoke concerning the manna." More common, however, is to understand each of these names as actual places in which the Israelites sinned. The text thus asserts with respect to each place: "Hence we learn that Moses rebuked them for what they had done in" that place.

There are two ways of understanding this list of places in which Moses rebuked the people. The first is that this is a compilation of all of the different places in which the people sinned for which Moses is now rebuking them at the end of his life. The second possibility is that Moses actually rebuked the people at each and every stop. While the former interpretation aligns with the idea that Moses learned from Jacob to postpone rebuke until the last possible moment, the latter interpretation breaks from the proper practice Moses inherited from Jacob. In fact, such repeated rebuke is exactly what the midrash suggests one should strive to avoid by waiting to rebuke until the end of one's life. If Moses indeed rebuked the people at each of these locations, then clearly, he did not properly absorb the lesson from his predecessor. Although both readings are certainly possible, the midrash provides support for the latter understanding, in which Moses actually rebuked the people at each stop: "One might think that he rebuked them only at the beginning of a journey. Whence do we learn that (he rebuked them also) between one journey and another? From the statement *between Paran and Tophel*." When read in conjunction with the passage intimating that Moses learned proper rebuke technique from Jacob, this pericope demonstrates the limits of Moses's ability to perform this practice properly. Unable to restrain himself until the people finally reach the land, Moses found himself rebuking the people each time they sinned—precisely what *Sifrei Devarim* warns against.

While the aforementioned passage provides possible evidence that Moses' rebuke of the people was not entirely successful, a passage in *Sifra* presents clearer testimony to the limits of Moses' success. *Sifra* (*Shemini* 1) picks up on the discrepancy between the Pentateuchal passages that describe how the Israelites mourned for Moses and Aaron. According to Numbers 20:29, "All the house of Israel bewailed Aaron thirty days," while Deuteronomy 34:8 records that "the children of Israel wept for Moses." The midrash asks:

> Why did *all* of the children of Israel weep for Aaron for thirty days [after he died] but for Moses only [some of] the children of Israel and not *all* of the children of Israel wept for him? Because Aaron never said to a man or woman "you sinned." But Moses, because he rebuked them, it was said about him that [only some of] "the children of Israel wept for Moses" (Deut. 34:8).

In contrast to the dominant portrait of *Sifrei Devarim*, *Sifra* suggests that Moses' efforts at chastising the people were not entirely successful. His confrontation of the Israelites mostly seems to have left a bitter taste in the mouth of some of them, leading only a portion of the Israelites to mourn Moses after his passing. Despite being the paradigmatic rebuker, even Moses failed to perform this task without negative repercussions.

Telling followers or subordinates that they have erred is a critical, yet incredibly difficult, facet of serving as a leader. While Moses generally excelled at rebuking the Israelites, the tannaitic *midrashim* also reveal the ways in which he was unsuccessful—his repeated chastisement of the people at each new location and the interpretation that only some of the Israelites mourned Moses after he passed away. Moses' limitations in this area reflect the anxieties of the rabbis themselves. In *Sifrei Devarim*, immediately following the various glosses on the phrase "all of the Children of Israel" (Deut. 1:1), the midrash introduces the voices of three prominent *tannaim* who each express the view that rebuke is simply not viable in their day and age:

> R. Tarfon said: "I swear by the Temple service, I doubt if there is anyone in this generation who is fit to rebuke others." R. Eleazar ben Azariah said: "I swear by the Temple service, I doubt if there is anyone in this generation who is able to receive rebuke." R. Akiba said: "I swear by the Temple service, I doubt if there is anyone in this generation who knows how to rebuke."

These emphatic declarations that no one in their generation is equipped to properly perform or accept rebuke suggest that the rabbis themselves felt unable to challenge people for behavior they considered inappropriate.[7] The tannaitic *midrashim* project this hesitancy and anxiety onto the figure of Moses who, despite serving as the prophetic exemplar for rebuke, nevertheless failed in some respects to accomplish the task in an ideal fashion.

Judgement

One of the prominent features of Moses' leadership of the Israelites in the desert was his regular rendering of judgement. According to Exodus, prior to implementing a stratified court system, Moses judged the people from morning to night (Exod. 18:13). The Biblical text has no qualms about recognizing the limits to Moses' leadership acumen when it comes to the realm of judging. His father-in-law Yitro provides a more sustainable framework for judging the entire people by creating a network of different levels of magistrates. Moreover, the Pentateuch describes a number of cases in which Moses did not know the proper judgment and needed to seek guidance from God, such as the case of the man who gathered sticks on Shabbat (Num. 15:32-36) and the daughters of Tzelofchad who desired to inherit from their father (Num. 27:1-11). Although *Mekhilta deRabbi Shimon bar Yochai* endorses Yitro's sagacious advice, *Sifrei Devarim* follows Deuteronomy's lead in marginalizing the role of Yitro in establishing the revamped justice system. Indeed, our Midrash seems almost scandalized by the notion that Moses could not handle the needs of the Israelites on his

---

[7] See my extended discussion in Matthew S. Goldstone, *The Dangerous Duty of Rebuke: Leviticus 19:17 in Early Jewish and Christian Interpretation*, Supplements to the Journal for the Study of Judaism 185 (Leiden; Boston: Brill, 2018), chaps. 5–6.

own. *Pisqa* 9 comments on Deut. 1:9, "Thereupon I said to you, 'I cannot bear the burden of you by myself'":

> Is it possible that Moses could not sit in judgment over Israel, this man who had brought them out of Egypt, who had split the sea asunder for them, who had brought down the manna for them, who had fetched the quails for them, and had performed other signs and miracles for them? Such a man could not sit in judgment over them? Rather, he spoke to them thus: *The Lord your God hath multiplied you* (1:10) upon the backs of your judges.

Given all of Moses' feats during the Exodus and subsequent wandering in the desert, is it possible that such a leader would have been incapable of judging the people? Of course not, the midrash declares! Rather, the people's sinful actions have placed added burden upon those tasked with judging them.[8] Moses is an expert judge and, in fact, the only occurrence of the term "exemplar" (דוגמא) in tannaitic literature, in *Pisqa* 29 of *Sifrei Devarim*, is applied to Moses serving as an example for judges.[9] However, this passage in *Pisqa* 29, which identifies Moses as an example for other judges, actually highlights the way in which Moses went too far in pushing God. This midrash revolves around the exchange in Deut. 3:25-26 in which Moses pleads with God to let him into the Land of Israel. God refuses, saying: "Enough (רַב־לָךְ)! Never speak to Me of this matter again!" (Deut. 3:26). The rabbis understand this dialogue as harking back to the incident in which Moses called the Israelites "rebels" and struck the rock to bring forth water rather than speaking to it (Num. 20:10-11):

> Another interpretation: *And the Lord said unto me, "Let it suffice thee (rab lěka)"*: God said to Moses, "Moses, you are to serve as an example for judges, who will say, 'If Moses, the wisest of the wise and the greatest of the great, was not forgiven for saying *Hear now, ye rebels* (Num. 20:10), for which it was decreed that he was not to enter the land, how much more so those who divert and distort justice.'"

---

[8] Reuven Hammer explains, "The burden of the consequences of judging your actions is too great" (Hammer, *Sifre*, 394 and 14). Also see Finkelstein's comments on this pericope (Louis Finkelstein, *Sifre on Deuteronomy* [New York: Jewish Theological Seminary of America, 1969], 17).

[9] Tzvi Novick, *What Is Good, and What God Demands: Normative Structures in Tannaitic Literature* (Leiden: Brill, 2010), 185.

According to this midrash, Moses sinned by calling the people "rebels," resulting in God prohibiting him from entering the Land of Israel. Yet, through this error Moses actually serves as an important model for others. Tzvi Novick, in his work *What is Good, and What God Demands*, explains the significance of this passage:

> God's words, רב לך "enough of you," are taken in this pericope to mean "a teacher for you," i.e., Moses will serve as a teacher. Through his example, judges will be chastened to judge fairly. Moses judged the people correctly, albeit harshly, in characterizing them as rebels, and, despite his greatness and the triviality of his transgression, received punishment. Surely, then, judges who abuse their office will suffer. While Moses models improper judgment, God serves implicitly as the counter-type. He offers a lesson in honest judgment by refusing to show Moses favor.[10]

Moses not only serves as an exemplar for the people as a fair judge, but also through his mistakes—demonstrating that God favors no one in judgement. While this passage points to Moses' error in the way in which he responded to the Israelites, elsewhere in *Sifrei Devarim* we find that God calls Moses out for his haughtiness in overestimating his own judicial capabilities. Recounting how he set up a system of justice in Deuteronomy 1:17 Moses says, "And any matter that is too difficult for you, you shall bring to me and I will hear it." As the pinnacle of the judicial totem pole this process makes sense. Routine issues are brought to the lower judges while the most challenging cases are for Moses to arbitrate. Yet, the midrash identifies Moses' statement as presumptuous, prompting God to demonstrate the limit of Moses' ability to determine the appropriate law (*Pisqa* 17):

> *And the cause that is too hard for you (ye shall bring unto me)* (1:17): Said the Holy One, blessed is He, to Moses, "You think that you can decide difficult cases—by your life, I shall make you know that you cannot decide difficult cases. I shall bring you a case that your pupil's pupil will be able to judge, but you will not." And what case was that? The case

---

[10] Novick, *What Is Good, and What God Demands*, 185–86.

of the daughters of Zelophehad, of which Scripture says *And Moses brought their cause before the Lord* (Num. 27:5).[11]

The Pentateuch describes Moses as a "very humble man, more so than any other man on earth" (Num. 12:3), a trope generally echoed in tannaitic *midrashim*.[12] However, while passages in early rabbinic sources often assume Moses' humility, the text above from *Sifrei Devarim Pisqa* 17 calls Moses out for his presumptuousness. The fact that the rabbis portray Moses as overstepping the bounds specifically with respect to judging the people may point to another area of rabbinic anxiety. The early rabbis had a limited sphere of judicial authority over the people, but presumably desired greater jurisdiction. As Hayim Lapin argues,

> "Rabbis acted as judges primarily for adherents or associates… For the earlier period, the picture is consistent with a small group of religious experts within a religious association putting that expertise at the service of pious members. For the third and fourth centuries, the picture is more complex. Rabbis hear a broader range of cases, possibly for a broader sector of the population…"[13]

Having a limited scope of judicial authority, primarily confined to their immediate followers and specific areas of law, the *tannaim* may have been self-conscious when it came to their role as communal judges. Portraying Moses as also having some degree of limitation in his judicial capabilities may alleviate some of this anxiety. However, not wanting to diminish their judicial prowess, the midrash notes that while Moses himself might not be able to solve the problem, his later students (תלמיד תלמידך) would. The limit to Moses' judicial capacity is a challenging case, while the limit to early rabbinic judicial authority is the limited number of people who would actually turn to them for arbitration.

---

[11] Hammer, *Sifre*, 41–42.

[12] See, for example, Jacob Zallel Lauterbach, *Mekhilta De-Rabbi Ishmael a Critical Edition, Based on the Manuscripts and Early Editions*, vol. 2 (Philadelphia, PA: Jewish Publication Society, 2004), 273; Menahem Kahana, *Sifre on Numbers: An Annotated Edition*, vol. 1 (Jerusalem: Magnes Press, Hebrew University, 2011), 251.

[13] Hayim Lapin, *Rabbis as Romans: The Rabbinic Movement in Palestine, 100-400 CE* (Oxford: Oxford University Press, 2012), 99. However, as Lapin notes, the relative dearth of early rabbinic evidence of judging could also be related to other factors beyond rabbinic authority, such as the insularity of the community (see Lapin, *Rabbis as Romans*, chap. 4).

Immortality

The third area in which the Akivan *midrashim* present Moses as superior but also flawed is with respect to death and immortality. Recounting the conclusion of Moses' life, Deuteronomy 37:7 announces that "Moses was a hundred and twenty years old when he died; his eyes were undimmed and his vigor unabated." The very end of *Sifrei Devarim* (*Pisqa* 357) comments on the phrase "his vigor unabated" and states in the name of Rabbi Eliezer ben Yaakov: "but 'even now his natural force is still not abated,' for if anyone should touch the flesh of Moses, its natural force would spring out in all directions." The midrash suggests that even in death Moses retained a degree of liveliness.

Beyond supernatural postmortem vitality, the midrash also presents Moses as resisting death itself. In a somewhat extended narrative, *Sifrei Devarim* (*Pisqa* 305) imagines how Moses delayed his demise by dismissing the angel of death who came to take him:[14]

> At that same time the Holy One, blessed be He, said to the angel of death, "Go and fetch Me the soul of Moses." The angel went and stood before Moses, and said to him, "Moses, give me your soul." Moses replied, "You do not even have the right to be in the place where I dwell, and yet you dare say to me, Give me your soul?" Moses thus rebuked him, and the angel left crestfallen. The angel of death then went back and reported to God, whereupon the Holy One, blessed be He, told him once more, "Go and fetch Me his soul." The angel went looking for him at his home but could not find him. He went to the sea and asked it, "Moses, have you seen him?" The sea replied, "Since the day that he made Israel pass through me, I did not see him." He then went to the mountains and the hills and asked them, "Moses, have you seen him?" They replied, "Since the day that Israel received the Torah on Mount Sinai, we have not seen him." He thereupon went to Gehenna and asked it, "Moses, have you seen him?" She replied, "I have

---

[14] For a discussion of some of the literary and thematic elements of this episode, see Rella Kushelevsky, "The Crossing of Boundaries and Liminality in the Rabbinic Aggadot on the Death of Moses and on 'Those to Die in the Wilderness': Analogous Aspects," in *Exodus: Border Crossings in Jewish, Christian and Islamic Texts and Images*, ed. Annette Hoffmann, Judaism, Christianity, and Islam—Tension, Transmission, Transformation 11 (De Gruyter, 2020), 137–38.

heard his name, but I have not seen him." He then went to the ministering angels and asked them, "Moses, have you seen him?" They replied, "Go and ask human beings." He finally went to Israel and asked them, "Moses, have you seen him?" They said to him, "God has fathomed his way, and has secreted him for the life of the world to come, and no creature knows his whereabouts," as it is said, *And he was buried in the valley* (34:6).

In this imaginative account, Moses again becomes the successful rebuker, berating (גער) the angel of death and sending him away. When the angel tries again, he is unable to find Moses, questing across the celestial and terrestrial planes in a vain attempt to find him again. Moses is not to be found on land or at sea, in the netherworld below or in the heavens above. Yet, the midrash concludes by noting that Moses is buried in the valley. Moses is ostensibly deceased, but in death he is unlike others whose places of burial can be located. While this text seems to ultimately conclude with Moses' physical demise, some passages in the early *midrashim* suggest that Moses was actually successful at achieving immortality. *Pisqa* 357 in *Sifrei Devarim* records a tradition on Deut. 34:5 ("So Moses the servant of the Lord died there") that Moses never actually passed away: "Others say: Moses never died, and he stands and serves on high, as is shown by the use of the same adverb *there* in this verse and in the verse, *And he was there with the Lord* (Exod. 34:28)." The verse in Deuteronomy that describes Moses' death employs the word "there" (שָׁם) just as a verse about Moses on Mount Sinai during revelation uses the word "there." Moses' "death" is thus understood to be like Moses' ascent to speak with God rather than the normal mortal way of leaving this world.

Aside from a few midrashic passages which intimate that Moses was actually able to escape death, most sources assume that he died at the ripe old age of 120.[15] However, in contrast to the midrash from *Sifra* quoted above, in which only some of the Israelites were distraught at Moses' death, *Sifrei Devarim* suggests that a vocal contingent of the people tried to prevent Moses from dying. In this midrash, the Israelites sought to protest against God taking Moses in order to keep their precious leader. Commenting on Deut. 32:48 ("And the Lord spoke unto Moses that selfsame day"), which introduces God telling Moses that he will ascend Mount Nevo to die, *Pisqa* 337 relates:

---

[15] *Sifrei Devarim* includes Moses among a list of four people who died at 120 (*Pisqa* 357; Hammer, *Sifre*, 382).

> What was Scripture's purpose in saying *that selfsame day* here? The reason was that Israel said, "By our oath, if we see Moses (leaving us), we will not let the man who had brought us out of Egypt, had split the (Red) Sea for us, had brought down manna for us, had supplied us with the quail, had performed miracles and wonders for us—we will not let him go." Said the Holy One, blessed be He: "Behold, I will bring him into the cave at midday, and if anyone wishes to stop (Me), let him come and try." Hence Scripture says, *And the Lord spoke unto Moses that selfsame day.*

Whether due to devotion to Moses, fear of carrying on without him, or otherwise, the Israelites claim that they will do what is necessary to prevent Moses from dying. Perhaps riled by the people's combative tone, God decides to take Moses at midday[16] when everyone can see and protest—if they actually dare. God's exasperation grows a few passages later, in *Pisqa* 339, when Moses himself suggests that it would be better if he were not to die:

> Moses said to God, "Master of the universe, why must I die? Would it not be better for people to say 'Moses is good' out of personal knowledge rather than as mere rumor? Would it not be better for people to say, This here is Moses, who had brought us out of Egypt, had split the (Red) Sea for us, had brought down the manna for us, and had performed miracles and wonders for us,' rather than to say, 'Moses was like that, and did such-and-such?'" God replied, "Enough, Moses. Such is My decree, which applies equally to all men," as it is said, *This is the law: when a man dieth in a tent* (Num. 19:14).[17]

Striving for immortality, Moses suggests to God that it would be better if he could keep on living rather than die before the people enter the land. His argument is built upon the notion that firsthand knowledge is better than rumor and oral tradition. Judaism would simply not be the same without the presence of Moses to serve as a testament to the great things he did with God's help. But God rejects this attempt to evade death and shouts

---

[16] See Hammer's note that "'selfsame,' is understood as meaning at the very height of the day" (Hammer, *Sifre*, 504).

[17] As Hammer notes, "The emphasis is on *a man*, i.e., any man whatsoever" (Hammer, *Sifre*, 505).

"Enough!" (כלך).[18] Like all other humans, Moses must die.

While the early rabbis generally do not attempt to forestall death, they are also concerned about what it means for them to die and the impact of their death on the Jewish people. Unlike Moses, whose legacy will endure, the *tannaim* were not particularly influential figures in their day.[19] They thus evince a degree of anxiety that their passing will not be taken so seriously. This concern manifests itself at the conclusion of Mishnah and Tosefta Sotah in which the rabbis imagine all of the important things in the world that cease with the deaths of significant rabbis (mSot. 9:15): "When Rabbi Meir died, the tellers of parables ceased; when Ben Azzai died, the diligent ones ceased… when Rabbi Yehoshua died, goodness ceased from the world… when Rabbi Akiva died, the honor of Torah ceased.…" While this passage (and its parallel in Tosefta Sotah) may have been compiled sometime after the death of these figures by their ardent followers, the highly exaggerated depiction of loss not only denigrates the accomplishments of the surviving generation but also reflects a need to overemphasize the impact of the earlier rabbis.

Tosefta Sotah 14 paints an image of a population abounding with murderers, adulterers, and people who distort judgement.[20] While this derogatory depiction of a Jewish community that actively flouted Torah prohibitions may be an exaggeration, it suggests that the rabbis were cognizant of a general indifference on the part of the population to Jewish law. If the people ignored the basic tenets of the Pentateuch, then it is no surprise that they also disregarded the rabbis. I see these passages at the end of Mishnah and Tosefta Sotah, which highlight the values lost to the world with the deaths of various rabbis, as attempts to combat this disregard. In a world in which people went around killing one another, the lives of the early rabbis held little esteem in the eyes of the general populace. Although none of the

---

[18] On the use of the term כלך, particularly in the expression או כלך לדרך זו, see N. Berggrün, למילון התלמודי: כלך, או לכה לך, הולכה לך, *Leshonenu* 33:2-3 (1969): 129-34; N. Berggrün, (129 'עמ ,לג לשוננו) "למאמרי כלך", *Leshonenu* 34:3 (1970): 240; Yaakov Elman, "The Order of Arguments in כלך-Baraitot in Relation to the Conclusion," *JQR* 79 (1989): 295–304; Shamma Friedman, "או כלך לדרך זו - The Term and its Usage in the Tannaitic *Midrashim*," *Sidra: A Journal for the Study of Rabbinic Literature* 9 (1993): 61–74.

[19] Seth Schwartz, *Imperialism and Jewish Society 200 B.C.E. to 640 C.E.* (Princeton: Princeton University Press, 2001), 119–28.

[20] Saul Lieberman, *The Tosefta: According to Codex Vienna, with Variants from Codex Erfurt, MS. Schocken and Editio Princeps (Venice 1521) - The Order of Nashim*, vol. 3 (New York: The Jewish Theological Seminary of America, 2007), 235–38; Saul Lieberman, *Tosefta Ki-Fshutah: A Comprehensive Commentary on the Tosefta Part VIII Order of Nashim* (New York: The Jewish Theological Seminary of America, 2007), 750–56.

rabbis were immune to death itself, by portraying the early rabbis as tied to significant values such as goodness and Torah, these passages attempt to create an enduring legacy so that the *tannaim* would not be forgotten even after they were gone.

Conclusion

In tannaitic literature Moses becomes a rabbi—*Moshe rabbeinu*.[21] More than simply an illustrative example of what it means to be a rabbi, this label is used "injunctively" to single Moses out as distinctive and a model for others: Moses is *the* rabbi for the rabbis.[22] Moses serves as the exemplar for the activities and qualities to which the early rabbis aspired—religious authority, recognized judicial prowess, and an immortal legacy. But rather than construct the literary image of Moses as perfect, the ultimate ideal, tannaitic sources instead embrace Moses' humanity. The tannaitic *midrashim* from the school of Rabbi Akiva highlight Moses's faults and failings alongside his major successes. This presentation paints a portrait of a leader who mirrors the rabbis in both their successes and their deficiencies. The figure of Moses captures the limitations that the rabbis themselves experience and thus serves as an even more productive role model than an angel-like model of perfection. Moses is a remarkable leader who is nevertheless human and imitable—a projection of rabbinic aspirations and insecurities. In this way Moses serves as the ideal rabbinic role model.

---

[21] See *Sifrei Devarim* 305, 307, 343, 355 and 356 as well as many other places in the tannaitic midrashic corpus.

[22] Matthew Roller distinguishes between examples used "illustratively" and those employed "injunctively," where the former is "an utterly typical instance of a series of similar objects" and the latter is "singled out as distinctive." (Matthew B. Roller, "Exemplarity in Roman Culture: The Cases of Horatius Cocles and Cloelia," *Classicial Philology* 99, no. 1 [January 2004]: 52).

May Women Serve as Mohalot?

David Golinkin

האם מותר
לנשים לשמש כמוהלות?[1]

דוד גולינקין

לכבוד החוקרת והמחנכת
ד"ר אורה הורן פראוזר
בהגיעה לגיל "זקנה" (אבות ה':כ"א)
ו"אין זקן אלא מי שקנה חכמה" (קדושין ל"ב ע"ב)

שאלה: האם מותר לנשים לשמש כמוהלות?[2]

תשובה:

א. תקופת המקרא

משתמע מן המסופר על אברהם ויצחק (בראשית כ"א:ד') שאב חייב למול את בנו. מצד שני, אנו קוראים בספר שמות (ד', כ"ד-כ"ו) כיצד מלה ציפורה את בנה "במלון", בדרך ממדין למצרים:

ויהי בדרך במלון, ויפגשהו ה' ויבקש המיתו. **ותקח צפרה צר ותכרת את ערלת בנה** ותגע לרגליו, ותאמר: כי חתן דמים אתה לי. וירף ממנו, אז אמרה: חתן דמים למולת.[3]

חז"ל התייחסו למעשה ציפורה בחיוב. במדרש (שמות רבה ה':ח', מהד' שנאן, עמ' 157-158) אומרת ציפורה: "שהרי קיימתי המצווה". אפשר להסיק מהסיפור המקראי

---

[1] תשובה זאת מבוססת על תשובתי באנגלית שהופיעה בספרי: *Responsa in a Moment Vol. II*, Jerusalem, 2011, pp. 219-226 ושוב עם כמה עדכונים בספרי *The Status of Women in Jewish Law: Responsa*, Jerusalem, 2012, pp. 204-211.

[2] ההפניות הקצרות להלן מתייחסות לרשימת הספרות שבסוף התשובה.

[3] לאיור של מעשה צפורה מספרד מן המאה הארבע-עשרה ראו *The John Rylands Haggadah*, Tel Aviv, 1988, fol. 14a (תודתי נתונה לדוד אוברמן שהפנה את תשומת לבי לאיור זה.). לאיור מאשכנז בסביבות 1450-1500, ראו הגדת נירנברג השנייה, דף 13 ע"ב, אצל באומגרטן, עמ' 66.

שתמיד מותר לנשים למול את הבן **או** שמותר לאשה למול את הבן **בדיעבד**, בשעת הדחק, למשל, על מנת להציל את חייו של משה שלא קיים את המצווה.

ב. תקופת בית שני

ספרי המקבים מכילים כמה גירסאות של סיפור על נשים שנהרגו או שמתו מכיוון שמלו את בניהן. מסופר בספר מקבים ב' (ו':י', מהד' כהנא, עמ' קצ"ז; והשוו מהד' שוורץ, עמ' 155) על שתי נשים שנרצחו על ידי היוונים יחד עם בניהן "כי מלו את בניהן". בקטע המקביל בספר מקבים א' (א':ס'-ס"ג, מהד' כהנא, עמ' ק"ג; והשוו מהד' רפפורט, עמ' 121) מסופר: "ואת הנשים **אשר מלו את בניהן** המיתו על פי הפקודה. ויתלו את העוללים בצוואריהן ואת בני בתיהן **ואת המלים אותם** [המיתו]". מדובר ברישא בהמתת הנשים שמלו את בניהן, אבל בסיפא זה נשמע כאילו המיתו את בני המשפחה, הגברים אשר מלו את הבנים. לבסוף, מגילת אנטיוכוס נכתבה כנראה בארמית בארץ ישראל בין המאות ה-2-5. נאמר שם (פסוקים 35-36, במהדורת מ"צ קדרי, בר אילן א' [תשכ"ג], עמ' 94; ובתרגומו, עמ' 103): "ואף אשה אחת ילדה בן אחר מות בעלה **ומלה אותו לשמונה ימים**" ואז היא קפצה מחומת העיר יחד עם בנה ושניהם מתו.[4] אם כן, שניים מתוך שלושת המקורות הללו מספרים שנשים מלו את בניהן במהלך מרד המקבים נגד היוונים. סיפורים אלה עשויים ללמדנו **שתמיד** מותר לנשים למול את הבן **או** שמותר לאשה למול את הבן רק בשעת גזרה, כשאין ברירה.

ג. ספרות חז"ל

שנינו בתוספתא שבת ט'ו:ח' (מהד' ליברמן, עמ' 70 ומקבילות):[5]

היתה יולדת זכרים והן נמולין ומתין [=ומתים],
מלה ראשון ומת, שני ומת, שלישי תמול, רביעי לא תמול.
מעשה בארבע אחיות בציפרי [=בציפורי]
שמלה ראשנה ומת, שניה ומת, **שלישית** ומת, ובא מעשה לפני חכמים ואמרו **רביעית לא תמול.**
אמר ר' נתן: כשהייתי במזגת של קפוטקיא [=Mazaca בירת קפדוקיא, בטורקיה של היום] היתה שם אשה אחת שהיתה יולדת זכרים והן נמולין ומתין,
מלה ראשנה [=ראשון] ומת, שני ומת, שלישי הביאתו לפני, ראיתיו שהוא ירוק... המתינו לו **ומלוהו** וחיה, והיו קורין אותו נתן (הבבלי) על שמי.

בכל המקרים הללו נאמר שהאם מלה **עצמה** את בנה. יתר על כן, כל אלה הם מקרים של

---

[4] ראו זיו, עמ' 40 והערות 5-7. שוורץ בהערותיו למקבים ב' מנסה ללמוד ממקבים א' שהבנים נימולו אבל לאו דוקא על ידי האימהות. רפפורט בהערותיו למקבים א' מרחיק לכת עוד יותר וקובע ש"אין להניח שהאימהות מלו את בניהן בעצמן, שכן זה מנוגד להלכה היהודית". הוא לא מביא אף הוכחה לטענה זאת. כפי שאנו נראה, רוב רובם של הפוסקים החל מן התלמוד הבבלי סברו שמותר לאשה למול את בנה או לכתחילה או בדיעבד.

[5] השוו למקבילות בשבת קל"ד ע"א; חולין מ"ז ע"ב; ירושלמי יבמות פרק ו', ז' ע"ד; וכן שיר השירים רבה ז:ג' המצוטט אצל זיו, עמ' 41-42.

לכתחילה ולא בדיעבד, ובניגוד למקורות הנ"ל בספר שמות ובספרי המקבים שניתן לפרש בשני הכיוונים.

המקור התלמודי העיקרי על נשים כמוהלות נמצא בעבודה זרה כ"ז ע"א:

איתמר: מנין למילה בעובד כוכבים [בכתבי יד: בגוי] שהיא פסולה?
דרו בר פפא משמיה דרב אמר: "ואתה את בריתי תשמור" (בראשית י"ז:ט')
ורבי יוחנן [לומד מן המילים] "המול ימול" (שם, יג, כאילו כתוב: המל - ימול]. מאי בינייהו?...
אלא איכא בינייהו אשה. למ"ד [למאן דאמר, למי שאומר] "ואתה את בריתי תשמור" [=רב] ליכא, דאשה לאו בת מילה היא; ולמ"ד "המול ימול" [=רבי יוחנן] איכא, דאשה כמאן דמהילא דמיא [=כמי שמהולה דומה].
ומי איכא למאן דאמר אשה לא? והכתיב (שמות ד', כ"ה) "ותקח צפורה צר"?! קרי ביה "ותקח" [קרא אותו כאילו כתוב ותקח בפתח, בבניין פיעל].
והכתיב "ותכרות"? קרי ביה "ותכרת" [שוב, בבניין פיעל] דאמרה לאיניש אחרינא ועבד [שאמרה לגבר אחר ועשה].
ואיבעית אימא: אתיא איהי ואתחילה ואתא משה ואגמרה [ואם אתה רוצה אמור: באה היא והתחילה ובא משה וסיים].

כלומר, לפי התלמוד, האמורא רב (בבל, דור ראשון) היה אוסר על נשים למול את הבן, ואילו האמורא רבי יוחנן (ארץ ישראל, דור שני), היה מתיר לנשים למול את הבן. רוב המתירים לאישה למול מתבססים על העיקרון התלמודי הידוע (ביצה ד' ע"א) "רב ורבי יוחנן - הלכה כרבי יוחנן". ויש המסתמכים גם על התקדים המקראי של ציפורה. אחד המקורות הבודדים האוסרים על נשים למול (תוספות לעבודה זרה כ"ז ע"א, ד"ה אשה) אומר כי רב צדוק מכיוון שהתנא רבי יהודה הנשיא פסק על פי אותו פסוק מוקדם יותר בסוגיא כשהוא אוסר על גוים למול את הבן.

ד. גאונים וראשונים

יעקב שפיגל ויוסי זיו כבר בדקו פוסקים ומדרשים ופיוטים רבים שנכתבו בין המאות ה-8-16 וחילקו אותם לשלוש קבוצות.[6] והרי החלוקה שלהם בתוספת כמה פוסקים נוספים:

א. **שלוש-עשרה מקורות מתירים לנשים לשמש כמוהלות לכתחילה בלי שום הגבלות:**
רב אחאי גאון, שאלתות, בבל, שנת 750 לערך; ספר בשר על גבי גחלים, סוף תקופת הגאונים; ר' טוביה ב"ר אליעזר, מדרש לקח טוב, בסביבות 1100, אזור הבלקנים; ר' מנחם ב"ר שלמה, מדרש שכל טוב, בשנת 1139; ר' אברהם בן יצחק אב בית דין נרבונא, נפטר 1179, לפי הנוסח המובא בספר תמים דעים; ר' אלעזר ממיץ, ספר יראים, צרפת, נפטר 1198; ר' משה מקוצי, ספר מצווֹת גדול, צרפת, נפטר 1236; הרב יצחק בן משה מווינה, אור זרוע, וינה, נפטר 1250; הרב מרדכי בן הלל, המרדכי, אשכנז, נפטר 1298; הרב מאיר

---

[6] שפיגל, עמ' 150-154; זיו, עמ' 43-46. בשל ריבוי המקורות, לא חזרתי על ההפניות המדויקות הרשומות במאמריהם בהערות השוליים.

הכהן מרוטנבורג, הגהות מיימוניות, אשכנז, בסביבות 1300; ר' ישעיה די טראני הזקן, רי"ד, איטליה, המאה ה-13; הרב מנחם רקנטי, איטליה, סוף המאה ה-13(?); ר' זכריה בן שלמה הרופא, מדרש החפץ, תימן, 1428.

ב. עשרים ושישה מקורות מתירים לנשים לשמש כמוהלות בדיעבד, אם אין שם גבר שיודע למול את הבן: ר' שמעון קיארא, הלכות גדולות, בבל, בסביבות 825; רב עמרם גאון, בסביבות 858 (המצוטט בסידור רבנו שלמה ב"ר נתן, ירושלים, תשנ"ה, עמ' קמ"ב); הרב צמח גאון, בסביבות 872 (שפיגל, הערה 17); הרי"ף, רבינו יצחק אלפסי, מרוקו וספרד, 1013-1103; הרב אברהם בן יצחק אב בית דין נרבונא הנ"ל, כפי שהוא מצוטט בספר האשכול, פרובאנס, נפטר 1179; הרב יצחק בן אבא מארי, ספר העיטור, פרובנס, נפטר 1190; רמב"ם, מצרים, נפטר 1204; הרב אליעזר בן יואל הלוי, ספר ראבי"ה, אשכנז, נפטר 1225; הרב אברהם בר יצחק הכהן בפיוט "אות בריתות" (שפיגל, עמ' 152); ר' יעקב הגוזר ור' גרשום ב"ר יעקב הגוזר, שניהם באשכנז במחצית הראשונה של המאה ה-13; הרב צדקיהו בן אברהם ענו, שבלי הלקט, איטליה, המאה ה-13; הרב אהרן הכהן מלוניל, ארחות חיים, פרובנס, בסביבות 1300; כל בו, פרובנס, בסביבות 1300; הרב מנחם המאירי, בית הבחירה, פרובנס, נפטר 1315; הרב אשתורי הפרחי, כפתור ופרח, ארץ ישראל, בסביבות 1322; הרא"ש, רבינו אשר, טולדו, נפטר 1327; הריטב"א, ספרד, נפטר 1330 (שפיגל, הערה 11); הרב יעקב בן אשר, ארבעה טורים, טולדו, נפטר 1343; רבינו ירוחם, תולדות אדם וחוה, טולדו, נפטר 1350 (שפיגל, שם); הרב חיים בן שמואל, צרור החיים, ספרד, המאה ה-14; רבינו נסים גירונדי, ספרד, נפטר 1380 (שפיגל, שם); הרב מנחם אבן זרח, צידה לדרך, ספרד, נפטר 1385 (שפיגל, שם); הרב ישראל אלנקאווה, מנורת המאור, טולדו, נפטר 1391; הרב יוסף אבן חביבה, נמוקי יוסף, ספרד, תחילת המאה ה-15; הרב יוסף קארו, שלחן ערוך, צפת, נפטר 1575.

ג. שישה מקורות אוסרים על נשים למול את הבן: תוספות לעבודה זרה כ"ז ע"א הנ"ל; תוספות רבינו אלחנן, שם; תוספות שנץ, שם; רבינו יצחק מקורביי"ל, ספר מצוות קטן, צרפת, נפטר 1280; ר' ישעיה די טראני הצעיר, ריא"ז, איטליה, נפטר 1280 (שפיגל, הערה 9); והשו"ת הרמ"א, ר' משה איסרליש, בהגהותיו לשלחן ערוך, קרקוב, נפטר 1572.

ה. מדוע גברה הגישה המחמירה על הגישה המקלה?

אם נשים במקרא, בתקופת בית שני ובתקופת התנאים מלו את הבן; ואם רבי יוחנן התיר, וההלכה בדרך כלל נפסקת לפי רבי יוחנן מול רב; ואם כל כך הרבה פוסקים מימי הביניים התירו את הדבר לכתחילה או בדיעבד—למה אנו לא שומעים על נשים שאכן מלו את הבנים בימי הביניים?

יוסי זיו (עמ' 46-49) ניסה לפתור את התעלומה על ידי בדיקת מנהגי יהודי אתיופיה אותם אסף מ-38 ראיונות שנערכו בישראל בין השנים 1999-2003. לאחר שאישה אתיופית יהודייה יולדת, היא טמאה במשך 40 יום לבן ובמשך 80 יום לבת. היא עוזבת את ביתה עם התינוק וגרה מחוץ לכפר ב"בית היולדת". קרובות משפחה נלוות אליה על מנת לסייע לה בטיפול בתינוק. מכיוון שהיא והתינוק היונק עדיין טמאים ביום השמיני, היא או אחת מהנשים האחרות מלות את הבן. הדבר אף פעם לא נעשה על ידי גבר, מכיוון שהוא היה נטמא על ידי נגיעה בתינוק. ביום ה-40 לתינוק או ביום ה-80 לתינוקת, האם והתינוק טובלים בנהר ומיטהרים.

זיו משער כי האתיופים שמרו על המנהגים הארצישראליים המקוריים של טהרה, כפי שהם משתקפים בפסיקתו של רבי יוחנן, לפיהן מותר לנשים למול את הבן. בבבל, לעומת זאת, הלכות טומאה וטהרה כבר נעלמו ולכן רב קבע שאסור לאשה למול את הבן.

זו תיאוריה מעניינת, אך היא אינה עומדת בפני הביקורת:

1. אי אפשר לקבוע את מוצאם של יהודי אתיופיה, אך חוקרים רבים מסכימים שהם היו אתיופים ממוצא אגאו (Agau) שאימצו זהות ישראלית בשלב כלשהו. לרוב האמונות והמעשים שלהם יש מקבילות בכנסייה האתיופית-אורתודוקסית. הם בדרך כלל נוהגים על פי הספרות המקראית או הספרים החיצוניים, ובניגוד להלכה התלמודית או הימי-ביניימית.[7]

2. אין שום רמז בעבודה זרה כ"ז ע"א שיש קשר בין הלכות טומאה וטהרה לבין מילה על ידי נשים. אכן, רב ור' יוחנן דנו באמת בשאלה אם מותר לגוי למול את הבן; זהו "סתם התלמוד" שהעביר את המחלוקת ביניהם למילה על ידי נשים.

3. אם המנהג האתיופי היה קשור לרבי יוחנן, הוא היה מחייב נשים למול את הבן, ולא רק מתיר זאת.

4. ככל הנראה רוב הפוסקים רק התירו לנשים למול את הבנים בדיעבד או אסרו זאת לגמרי מכיוון שהנטייה הכללית של הראשונים היא למנוע מנשים לקיים מצוות שהתלמוד מתיר ואף מחייב אותן לעשות. דוגמאות טובות הן תפילין, ציצית, קידוש בליל שבת, ונשים בתור סנדק בטקס ברית המילה.[8]

ו. סיכום והלכה למעשה

אין ספק שמותר לנשים יהודיות למול את הבנים לכתחילה. פסק זה מבוסס על:

א. התקדימים של ציפורה, ספרי המקבים והתוספתא;

ב. הסוגיא התלמודית בעבודה זרה כ"ז ע"א - רב ורבי יוחנן, הלכה כר' יוחנן;

ג. שלושה-עשר גאונים וראשונים הפוסקים על פי הסוגיא בעבודה זרה לכתחילה;

ד. אין שום בסיס תלמודי להתיר לנשים למול את הבנים רק בדיעבד, והסמכות העליונה בהלכה היא התלמוד הבבלי.[9]

דוד גולינקין
ירושלים עיר הקודש
י"ג אייר תשפ"א

ספרות

---

[7] ראו סטיבן קפלן אצל מיכאל קורינאלדי, יהדות אתיופיה: זהות ומסורת, ירושלים, תשמ"ט, עמ' 6-10.

[8] לגבי נשים ותפילין ראו ספרי מעמד האשה בהלכה: שאלות ותשובות, ירושלים, תשס"א, עמ' 23-45. לגבי נשים וציצית ראו שו"ת מהרי"ל החדשות סימן ז'; הרב משה פיינשטיין, אגרות משה, אורח חיים, חלק ד', סימן מ"ט; Aviva Cayam, in: *Jewish Legal Writings by Women*, Jerusalem, 1998, pp. 119-142. לגבי נשים וקידוש ראו Rabbi Eliezer Berkovits, *Jewish Women in Time and Torah*, Hoboken, 1990, pp. 92-100; לגבי אשה כסנדק, ראו הרב דניאל שפרבר, מנהגי ישראל, חלק א', עמ' ס'-ס"ו וכן באומגרטן, עמ' 65-77.

[9] ראו מה שכתבתי בספרי הנ"ל (לעיל, הערה 8), עמ' 62-64. חלק מהראשונים אומרים שהרעיון של בדיעבד מבוסס על סיפור ציפורה – אך התלמוד אינו מעלה טענה כזו.

באומגרטן—Elisheva Baumgarten, *Mothers and Children: Jewish Family Life in Medieval Europe*, Princeton and Oxford, 2004, pp. 65-66

גרוסמן—אברהם גרוסמן, חסידות ומורדות, ירושלים, תשס"א, עמ' 331-332

זיו—יוסי זיו, "מילה בידי אישה בספרות חז"ל ובמנהג יהודי אתיופיה", נטועים יא-יב (אלול תשס"ד), עמ' 39–54

רובין—ניסן רובין, ראשית החיים, תל אביב, תשנ"ה, עמ' 91

שפיגל—יעקב שפיגל, "האשה כמוהלת – ההלכה וגלגוליה בסמ"ג", סידרא ה' (תשמ"ט), עמ' 149-157

שפרבר—הרב דניאל שפרבר, מנהגי ישראל, חלק א', ירושלים, תשמ"ט, עמ' ס"ו, הערה 18 וחלק ד', ירושלים, תשס"א, עמ' ח'-ט'.

The Story of the Story as the Focus of Engagement

Edward L. Greenstein

For a period of four years, I headed a large interdisciplinary graduate program in general hermeneutics and cultural studies at Bar-Ilan University. I would sometimes get a ride home to Jerusalem from one of the brilliant younger lecturers in the program, a secular Israeli who is an expert on contemporary critical theories as well as psychoanalysis and modern French literature and culture. I always enjoyed our rides for the intellectual stimulation they routinely provided. During one of our last such journeys together I asked my colleague about his recent work; but before he would respond, he chose to ask me about a project I've been working on. For a long time now, I have been seeking to reconstruct what we can of the pre-biblical Israelite literature in general and the early Hebrew epic in particular.[1] For over a century, scholars have found traces in the Hebrew Bible of Israelite epic—by which I mean relatively long narrative poems about a hero or heroes, divine and/or human.

What my colleague found perplexing was that a religious, theologically-oriented person like me would be interested in ancient literature that was pre-scriptural, unauthorized, non-canonical. He assumed correctly, I think, that all of us have some personal stake in the objects of our research and writing; but he could not figure out what my stake might be in studying and trying to reconstruct pre-canonical Hebrew literature. The pre-biblical literature, one could argue, was cast aside in forming what became the canonical biblical texts. The earlier sources' erstwhile integrity and status were consigned to oblivion as newer texts were produced that would supersede them as scripture, as literature that would be sacred to a community.

---

[1] See, for example, my overview "Signs of Poetry Past: Literariness in Pre-Biblical Hebrew Literature," in *Strength to Strength: Essays in Appreciation of Shaye J. D. Cohen*, ed. Michael L. Satlow (Providence, RI: Brown Judaica Studies, 2018), pp. 5-25. My work on reconstructing early Hebrew epic was supported by Israel Science Foundation grant no. 673/16. On the background of biblical prose narrative in earlier Canaanite epic, see my essay "Biblical Narrative and Canaanite Narrative," in *Some Wine and Honey for Simon: Biblical and Ugaritic Aperitifs in Memory of Simon B. Parker*, ed. A Joseph Ferrara and Herbert B. Huffmon (Eugene, OR: Pickwick, 2020), pp. 1-22. I am very pleased and proud to publish the present essay in honor of my former student, cherished colleague, and friend, Dr. Ora Horn Prouser. This essay derives from a lecture I gave at a conference on "Word and Wisdom," held at the University of Notre Dame, in April 2019.

My answer to the question of what's at stake for me in studying pre-canonical literature along with that literature which became a community's canon, my community's canon, is not straightforward. But it can be expressed by way of two broad perspectives. One is historical and the other is phenomenological. My colleague James Kugel in his widely read book, *How to Read the Bible*, effectively distinguishes the historical-critical study of the Bible as a rewarding intellectual activity from the religious interpretative endeavor of drawing meaning out of the Bible as it became scripture.[2] I do not make this distinction. For me, one can find, or make, meaning in the study of how biblical texts came to be—within the evolution or the story of the story—as well as one can in the phenomenological reading of the text in its received form—or in any other form. That is, one can find meaning—general as well as personal—in the process of text formation as well as one can in the text that has been formed.[3] I hasten to add, lest I be misunderstood, that the reading of a text is also a process, and one that keeps meaning fresh and new, as the great medieval Jewish northern French exegete of the twelfth century, Rabbi Samuel ben Meir, or Rashbam, put it: in the interpretations that are proposed as new every day.[4]

My own work on pre-biblical Israelite literature has taken a number of different, and sometimes overlapping, forms. I have been studying and writing on a widespread ancient Near Eastern narrative paradigm that I call the fugitive hero story pattern.[5] This rather particular narrative structure, numbering by my analysis as many as fourteen plot or motivic features, is attested in at least three literary compositions that antedate the earliest Hebrew literature by centuries. The pattern is adopted and adapted in virtually all the major narratives of the Hebrew Bible—those of Jacob, Joseph, Moses, David, and the early history of the people Israel—and it is also known in two compositions from Mesopotamia from the biblical period.

In order to appreciate what is special and interesting about any of the relevant biblical stories, one must know in what ways a particular narra-

---

[2] James L. Kugel, *How to Read the Bible: A Guide to Scripture, Then and Now* (New York: Free Press, 2007).

[3] For an example of this approach, from a somewhat different angle, see Benjamin D. Sommer, *Revelation and Authority: Sinai in Jewish Scripture and Tradition* (New Haven-London: Yale University Press, 2015).

[4] See his comment on Genesis 37:2; Martin I. Lockshin, *Rabbi Samuel ben Meir's Commentary on Genesis: An Annotated Translation* (Lewiston-Lampeter-Queenston: Edwin Mellen, 1989), pp. 240-42.

[5] See, for example, my study "The Fugitive Hero Narrative Pattern in Mesopotamia," in *Worship, Women, and War: A Festschrift for Susan Niditch*, ed. John J. Collins et al. (Atlanta: Society of Biblical Literature, 2015), pp. 17-35.

tive departs from or elaborates the fundamental story scheme. For example, knowing that the fugitive hero tends to plan his return home by mustering an army, one begins to discern the moves made by Jacob, during his return from Aram Naharaim to the land of Canaan, as the organization of his household as an army—a *machaneh*, a term that appears numerous times throughout that part of the narrative.[6] Or, knowing that the fugitive hero in exile tends to seek a divine oracle in order to learn whether the time for his comeback is propitious, one begins to realize that when Moses in Midian drives his herds into the wilderness toward the Mountain of God, he is not simply looking for a new pasture but rather homing in on the site of an established oracle. There he can discover whether it is safe for him to return to Egypt or whether his life is still being threatened. The present version of the book of Exodus almost completely suppresses the purpose of Moses' maneuver and overwhelms it with an episode in which it is the Deity who seeks out Moses in order to commission him to rescue the Israelites from Egyptian bondage.[7] One can find in this compositional or redactional dynamic a lesson on how one's personal interests should be subordinated to the community's welfare. But whatever one learns from such an analysis, there is clearly a history to this text, and to all other texts, and in that history there is meaning to be found or made.

I have also been studying the mythological and epic poems from Syria and Canaan in the centuries preceding the formation of the earliest biblical texts as well as the evidence for Israelite poems, epic and otherwise, preceding the composition of the literature known to us in the Hebrew Bible. Without going into exceeding detail, one can remark that for the better part of a century scholars have been discerning an unbroken stream of literary tradition beginning somewhere in the early Canaanite period and stretching through the entire biblical period and beyond.[8] The contours of this tradition may be hard to see, since only parts of it are familiar to us; but many of the details are evident.

One cannot be sure that the character of Job as a righteous sufferer harks back in any way to the figure of Kirta, in the Ugaritic (North Canaanite)

---

[6] I have delivered a paper on that aspect of Jacob's story at the conference "Migration and the Bible," held at Princeton University, March 2019. I plan to publish an article derived from that paper in the near future.

[7] See my article "Moses and the Fugitive Hero Pattern," *TheTorah.com* (on-line, 27 December 2018).

[8] See, for example, my article "The Canaanite Literary Heritage in Ancient Hebrew Writing," *Michmanim* 9 (1996), pp. 19-38 (in Hebrew). For a brief overview, see my "Tales from Ugarit Solve Biblical Puzzles," *Biblical Archaeology Review* 36/6 (November/December 2010), pp. 48-53, 70.

epic of that name, who is also portrayed as a pious sufferer.⁹ However, one can be certain that the prose framework of Job, in which one finds the widespread narrative formula, "they raised their voices and cried," similar to the widespread formula, "he raised his eyes and saw," belongs to the same literary stream as the centuries-earlier Ugaritic epic, where the specific formulas "he/she/they raised their voices and cried" and "he/she/they raised their eyes and saw" are first widely attested.[10]

Passages in Ugaritic epic have strikingly similar reflexes throughout biblical poetry. A well-known example is the following. In Ugaritic epic the god Baal's moral outlook is characterized thus:

> For two feasts Baal hates (šna), /
> three the Rider of the Clouds:
> A feast of shame and a feast of contention (dnt),
> And a feast of the lewdness of maids.[11]

It is hard not to see the influence of this or a similar passage in the following characterization of Israel's YHWH in Proverbs 6:16-19:

> These six things YHWH hates (שנא),
> And seven are abominations to him:
> Haughty eyes, a lying tongue, and hands that spill innocent blood;
> A heart that devises evil schemes,
> Feet that run quickly to (do) evil;
> A deceitful witness giving false testimony;
> And one who spreads contention (מדנים) among brothers.

The passage from Proverbs is more elaborate, but in its structure, its language, and its content it echoes its Canaanite predecessor. I am not adduc-

---

[9] For the Ugaritic narrative texts in transcription and English translation, see Simon B. Parker (ed.), *Ugaritic Narrative Poetry* (Atlanta: Society of Biblical Literature, 1997). For the Kirta Epic, see my edition and translation in *ibid.*, pp. 9-48, with bibliography at the end of the volume.

[10] For this phenomenon and selected bibliography, see Greenstein, "Signs of Poetry Past," pp. 21-22.

[11] For the text, see Mark S. Smith in *Ugaritic Narrative Poetry*, p. 124. For discussion and some bibliography, see my "Wisdom in Ugaritic," in *Language and Nature: Papers Presented to John Huehnergard on the Occasion of His Sixtieth Birthday*, ed. Rebecca Hasselbach and Na'ama Pat-El (Chicago: Oriental Institute of the University of Chicago, 2012), pp. 69-89, at 72-73.

ing this example in order to make a direct comparison for exegetical purposes. I simply want to share a bit of the evidence for the claim of cultural and literary continuity between early Canaanite sources and later biblical compositions. The author of Proverbs 6 surely did not inherit the model for his text directly from Ugaritic. But he far more likely than not found his inspiration in an earlier Israelite composition, whether oral or written, that formed an intermediary link on the chain between early Canaanite and later Hebrew literature.

In the following case, not knowing the Canaanite mythological background of a biblical verse prevents one from making sense of it. Psalm 48 describes the beauty of Jerusalem, whose aura owes greatly to the fact that God's temple is located within it. In verse 3 "Mount Zion" is referred to as "far reaches of the North (Hebrew *tsafon*)." Anyone who knows any geography will find this reference enigmatic at best. In the New American Bible, a note is appended, explaining that "in Palestine and Syria" it is "a traditional name for the earthly abode of God." In the Norton critical edition of the King James Version, Herbert Marks explains: "The north" "is also Mount Zaphon in northern Syria, seat of the Canaanite god Baal. Zion is in fact in the south, but the psalmist here suggests that its reach is universal, incorporating the mythical mountain of the gods."[12] I would second Marks's explanation but go further: this is one of many verses in the Bible in which features and powers that are ascribed in the neighboring Canaanite cultures to Baal and Baal worship are here attributed to the God of Israel and his cult. It is the battle between Elijah and the prophets of Baal on Mount Carmel (1 Kings 18) fought by means of literary parody, by adopting and reassigning a phrase from one reference to another.

My larger point, however, is that the Hebrew Bible develops out of and in dynamic tension with earlier Canaanite *and* Israelite materials. Of course, the most prominent example of a pre-biblical epic that is quoted, alluded to, adapted, and transformed in biblical literature—all the way through the Book of Revelation in the Christian Scriptures[13]—is the myth of combat between the Storm-god and the Sea or Sea-god and his associates.[14] The

---

[12] Herbert J. Marks (ed.), *The English Bible: King James Version: The Old Testament* (New York-London: Norton, 2012), p. 1003.

[13] See Hermann Gunkel, *Creation and Chaos in the Primeval Era and the Eschaton: A Religio-Historical Study of Genesis 1 and Revelation 12*, trans. K. William Whitney, Jr. (Grand Rapids, MI-Cambridge, UK: Eerdmans, 2006).

[14] See, e.g., John Day, *God's Conflict with the Dragon and the Sea: Echoes of a Canaanite Myth in the Old Testament* (Cambridge: Cambridge University Press, 1985). For a comprehensive analysis of all the pertinent source material, see Noga Ayali-Darshan, *The Storm-God and the Sea: The Origins, Versions, and Diffusion of a Myth throughout the*

fact that Israel's God in his storm-god persona is called "the Rider of the Clouds" in Psalm 68:5,[15] assimilating an epithet used of the Canaanite god Baal in Ugaritic epic, and that one of the guises of the Canaanite sea-god, "the Twisting Serpent," is used of an adversary of Israel's God in Isaiah 27:1, make the dependence of the Hebrew Bible on the Canaanite, and later Israelite, epic tradition virtually certain. In some instances of re-use or adaptation, the biblical version will simply substitute a theological claim by Canaanites made for the efficacy of Baal with a counter-claim for the primacy of Israel's YHWH. However, as numerous studies have shown, the transformations tend to go far deeper.

In biblical narrative there tends to be de-mythologization.[16] Accordingly, the priestly creation story of Genesis 1:1-2:4a removes the element of struggle from the relationship between the Creator-God Elohim and the ubiquitous and inchoate waters from the plot; and it reduces the water to an inanimate mass, de-personifying it in the process. As a result, Elohim, whose wind, a telltale vestige of the *Chaoskampf*, hovers over the dark waters, divides the water and sets a boundary between it and the land. He does not run it through as though it were a dragon (see Isaiah 51:9-11), and he does not need to vanquish it. And yet, it is essentially the same story, and it remains the same myth. Following Theodor Gaster, Ian Barbour, and others, I understand myth to refer to a narrative that functions like a metaphor.[17] It describes a paradigm—such as the world order, or the structure of the Israelites as a family of twelve sons—by telling a story about how that paradigm emerged *in illo tempore*, when it all began. And so, to this very day, whenever you stand at the seashore and watch the tide come in and then recede, stopping short of inundating the land, you are experiencing the defeat of the Sea-god by the Storm-god, or, in more mundane terms, the limits set on the wild water by an orderly God. Similarly, as Frank Moore Cross most famously suggested, when the sea is split for the Israelites to escape the Egyptians, and the Egyptians and their Pharaoh are submerged in

---

Ancient Near East, trans. Liat Keren (Tübingen: Mohr Siebeck, 2020).

[15] This interpretation of the Hebrew *rokeb ba'arabot* (compare Ugaritic *rkb 'rpt*) is widely accepted; see, for example, Artur Weiser, *The Psalms*, trans. Herbert Hartwell (Philadelphia: Westminster, 1962), p. 484 with n. 1.

[16] Compare my essay "The God of Israel and the Gods of Canaan: How Different Were They?" in *Proceedings of the Twelfth World Congress of Jewish Studies*, Division A: The Bible and Its World (Jerusalem: World Union of Jewish Studies, 1999), pp. 47*-58*.

[17] For references and some discussion, see my essay, "The Torah as She Is Read," *Essays on Biblical Method and Translation* (Atlanta: Society of Biblical Literature, 1989; reprint: Providence, RI: Brown Judaica Series, 2020), pp. 29-51, especially 40-44.

the sea, we have another transformation of the combat myth, in which the Deity vanquishes his human enemy at the de-mythologized sea, cleaving the sea in two, and then pulling the water back together so that it blankets and drowns the enemy.[18] Typically, in the Song at the Sea in Exodus 15, YHWH blows the sea apart by a blast of his breath, preserving in poetry the epic character of the myth. But in the preceding prose narrative in Exodus 14:21, the Deity causes a dry desert wind to blow, separating the water and drying up the seabed temporarily, as the Israelites cross.

As Michael Fishbane, for one, has seen, the paradigmatic function of the myth finds expression even post-exilically in the prophecy of the anonymous prophet in Babylonia we tend to refer to as Second Isaiah (51:9-11).[19] There the prophet presents a three-stage typology:

> Be aroused, be aroused, put on power, O arm of YHWH!
> Be aroused as in former days, primeval times!
> You are the one that cut through (the sea monster) Rahab,
> The one who pierced through the Serpent.
> You are the one who dried up Sea,
> The waters of the Great Deep.
> Who made the depths of Sea into
> A path for the redeemed to pass through.
> And so, the people ransomed by YHWH will return,
> They will re-enter Zion in jubilation,
> Eternal glee on their heads.
> Rejoicing and glee will overcome them;
> Grief and groaning will leave them.

In the first iteration of the paradigm, the Deity sets the scene for Creation by dividing the waters, here personified as the Sea-god. In the second, the Deity splits the sea and provides a path of dry land for the redeemed of the Exodus to escape. And in the third, the act of clearing a path of return from the Babylonian Exile to Jerusalem, or to the Persian province of Yehud, is conceived as yet another splitting of the sea by the Supreme God. The image is expressed elsewhere in Second Isaiah (40:4) this way: "Every valley will be elevated, and every mount and hill will be lowered; the crooked

---

[18] Frank Moore Cross, Jr., *Canaanite Myth and Hebrew Epic: Essays in the History of the Religion of Israel* (Cambridge, MA: Harvard University Press, 1973), pp. 111-44.

[19] Michael Fishbane, "The 'Exodus' Motif / The Paradigm of Historical Renewal," *Text and Texture: Close Readings of Selected Biblical Texts* (New York: Schocken, 1979), pp. 121-40.

will become straight; and the hilltops a plain." One may add, not altogether parenthetically, that herein lies an important difference between Jewish and Christian visions of messianism. In the Jewish paradigm, the messianic age is imaged, as in Isaiah 51, as a return from the Diaspora to the Homeland; whereas in Christianity the messianic age is figured as the advent of Jesus, the story of whose ministry is replete with allusions to the Exodus.[20]

By adducing the transformations of the myth of combat between the Deity in his storm-god persona and the Sea, I do not mean to suggest that the myth's pertinence is only in its adaptations—that meaning should be made only in the conversion of the more original form (and please note that I did not say "primitive" form) of the myth into a more prosaic or historical version. In his brilliant book, *Creation and the Persistence of Evil*, Jon Levenson finds significance in the fact that the more mythological, or mythopoeic, form of the combat myth continues to serve theologians of the Hebrew Bible, by which I mean theologians in the Hebrew Bible.[21] Even in the Ugaritic combat myth, the sea-god Yamm is not forever destroyed; he is placed in captivity (according to my interpretation) or temporarily eliminated (according to others).[22] In the diverse biblical versions of the myth, the power of the Sea, often represented by a mythological figure such as the Leviathan, the monster is defeated, imprisoned, suppressed, or merely controlled. It is not annihilated but left around to rear its head, or its many heads, and threaten our existence. As Levenson suggests, the survival of the Leviathan, as a plaything of the Deity (in Psalm 104) or as the pride of God's creation (in the second divine speech from the whirlwind in Job), symbolizes the fact that evil and chaos are often repressed and restricted, but they are not eliminated. The Deity, as the agent of Creation, must continually exert himself in order to prevent the disorderly from overwhelming the orderly.[23] And thus, the story of combat between the Creator God and his terrible creature retains its mythic character in the Bible, and, for those who adopt the bibli-

---

[20] For a historical survey, see Marinus de Jonge, "Messiah," *Anchor Bible Dictionary*, ed. David Noel Freedman (New York: Doubleday, 1992), vol. 4, pp. 777-88. The background of the Jesus narrative in the Exodus story is widely acknowledged; see, e.g., I. Howard Marshall, "An Assessment of Recent Developments," in *It is Written: Scripture Citing Scripture: Essays in Honor of Barnabas Lindars, SSF*, ed. D. A. Carlson and H. G. M. Williamson (Cambridge: Cambridge University Press, 1988), p. 16.

[21] Jon D. Levenson, *Creation and the Persistence of Evil: The Jewish Drama of Divine Omnipotence* (San Francisco: Harper & Row, 1988; reprint: Princeton: Princeton University Press, 1994).

[22] See my study "The Snaring of Sea in the Baal Epic," *Maarav* 3/2 (1983), pp. 195-216.

[23] Compare Robert D. Miller II, "Dragon Myths and Biblical Theology," *Theological Studies* 80 (2019), pp. 37-56.

cal imagery, in our world as well. Levenson himself draws the following poignant conclusion:

> The present is bereft of the signs of divine triumph. It is a formidable challenge to faith and a devastating refutation of optimism. On the other hand, the dialectic of this vision does not allow for an unqualified acceptance of the pessimism that attributes to innocent suffering the immovability of fate.[24]

The myth, I would say, describes an existential reality of life that parallels the more physical reality, in which the land on which we live is often threatened but rarely overrun by destructive forces.

The study of pre-biblical myth and epic is essential for tracing the development of biblical literature. However, I, as a scholar of the pre-biblical material, am not interested in it solely for its role in the evolution of the Hebrew Bible. I, like some others, seek and find meaning in the pre-biblical and extra-biblical material as well. It may sound strange to say it this way, but it is as much if not more the postmodern in me as the antiquarian in me that leads me to draw inspiration from what we may regard as pagan literature. For me, meaning is not inherent in texts; texts are not receptacles containing meaning. Rather, meaning is made by a reader in the act of reading, just as the sound of a tree falling in the forest is, to my way of understanding, the product of the hearer, not the tree making its fall. The falling of the tree makes waves in the air. An ear picks up the air waves as sound. I, as a reader of ancient texts, may choose to find meaning, and even inspiration, in the act of reading whatever sources I read.[25]

A biblical text is meaningful to me not because it needs to be, not because it is inherently so; but rather because as a member of a religious tradition and community, I make a commitment to read and seek meaning in biblical texts, as I do in texts that follow in the same tradition. I do not have the same commitment to draw inspiration from pre-biblical or extra-biblical texts from the ancient Near East. However, I may *choose* to read them for personal meaning. I may choose to be moved by them. That does not make me a pagan; it makes me a humanist as well as a religionist.

In recent decades more and more texts from the ancient Near East have been read as occasions for finding or making meaning. For example, the

---

[24] Levenson, *Creation and the Persistence of Evil*, p. 24.

[25] See, for example, my essay "Reading Strategies and the Story of Ruth," in *Women in the Hebrew Bible: A Reader*, ed. Alice Bach (New York: Routledge, 1998), pp. 211-31.

second earliest known fugitive hero narrative (see above) relates the personal story of King Idrimi of Alalakh, a town west of Aleppo in northern Syria.[26] Idrimi was born in Aleppo, but when his town was overrun, he fled with his brothers to Emar in east central Syria. With the support of the Storm-god he managed to muster an army, return to northern Syria, and, with political support from the dominant rulers, took the throne in Alalakh. Once established there, Idrimi says emphatically that he built himself and his allies houses; and that for all the homeless of his newly adopted town he provided homes. It is hard not to be impressed by the public works Idrimi performed. A man who lost his home and lived in temporary homes for many years came to appreciate the value of home. And so he made use of his resources to provide homes to all whom he governed.

To take another example. The old Canaanite epic of the Storm-god Baal is ordinarily understood as a drama of nature played out in the metaphysical realm. On the one hand, Baal must suppress the Sea in order to protect the land. On the other, he must overcome desiccation and the death of plant life that characterize the summer months in order to rise, triumph, and provide life-giving rain in the winter and spring. The plot, in such a reading, gives expression to the perennial human anxiety about the renewal of life and prosperity, which we know from experience is, in any given year, tenuous. But in more recent years, scholars such as Johannes C. de Moor in the Netherlands and Aaron Tugendhaft in the United States, have read the struggles of Baal for kingship over the gods and the machinations and intrigues that are entailed in those struggles as reflections of political cynicism concerning how real government operates.[27] De Moor sees in the conflicts among the gods a reflex of the breakdown of the international political order toward the end of the second millennium BCE. Tugendhaft interprets the conflicts of Baal and his opponents, Sea and Death, not so much as myth as sociopolitical critique. Watch the gods in their interactions and see what is wrong with the way people govern and interact. Whether one is convinced by such a reading or not, my point is that the Baal epic is here being read for its own meaning, and not for its significance as one of the sources of what will later become the biblical corpus.

---

[26] For a translation and literary commentary, see my article "Autobiographies in Ancient Western Asia," in *Civilizations of the Ancient Near East*, ed. Jack M. Sasson (New York: Scribner's, 1995), vol. 4, pp. 2421-32.

[27] Johannes C. de Moor, "The Crisis of Polytheism in Late Bronze Ugarit," in *Crises and Perspectives: Studies in Ancient Near Eastern Polytheism, Biblical Theology, Palestinian Archaeology, and Intertestimental Literature*, ed. A. S. van der Woude (Leiden: Brill, 1986), pp. 1-20; Aaron Tugendhaft, *Baal and the Politics of Poetry* (London-New York: Routledge, 2018).

The Ugaritic epic of Kirta has also been read for its theological and political themes. Gary Knoppers published a perceptive analysis of this ancient Canaanite text in which he delineated the pros and cons of divinely ordained kingship, as exemplified in multiple ways in the story.[28] In one of my own essays on Kirta,[29] I underscored the ironies of life the story illustrates, as a man who wished for nothing but a son to inherit his kingship saw that son grow up to threaten his throne, leading him to curse the son with whom he was blessed. Moreover, the king, by departing from the strict instructions of the high god El and making a superfluous vow in an act of emotion and piety, nearly lost his life to disease as a result. The lesson one may draw—that being overly pious or conscientious can lead to trouble, as Qohelet (7:16) had warned ("don't be overly righteous")—may not comport with one's preconceptions of a pious tale about a controlling yet caring god and his devoted human servant. But if one remains open to surprise and the unconventional, one may tease out such a meaning. When one is sensitive to people and their foibles, one can find meaning in any well-told tale.[30]

There is much more I could say about the transition from early Canaanite epic to biblical narrative.[31] For now, let me only add that the transition was certainly not direct. One must posit an intermediary stage of native Israelite epic, which emerged in the wake of Canaanite epic on the one hand, and which was drawn upon by the early Hebrew narrative writers, on the other. There are several reasons for positing a pre-biblical Israelite epic, as Umberto Cassuto, Sigmund Mowinckel, and others had suggested several decades ago.[32] First, this was the common method of relating stories in the ancient Near East in general and in Syria-Canaan in particular. Second, right in the middle of very prosaic prose in biblical narrative one may encounter a burst of archaic verse. The best known example is this couplet, appearing in one of the driest passages in the flood story (Genesis 7:11):

---

[28] Gary N. Knoppers, "Dissonance and Disaster in the Legend of Kirta," *Journal of the American Oriental Society* 114 (1994), pp. 572-82.

[29] Eliezer (Ed) Greenstein, "The Ugaritic Epic of Kirta in a Wisdom Perspective," *Te'uda* 16-17 (2001), pp. 1-13 (in Hebrew); see in brief Greenstein, "Wisdom in Ugaritic," pp. 77-80.

[30] Compare Ora Horn Prouser, *Esau's Blessing: How the Bible Embraces Those with Special Needs* (Teaneck, NJ: Ben Yehuda, 2012).

[31] See, e.g., my essay "Biblical Narrative and Canaanite Narrative," in *Some Wine and Honey for Simon: Biblical and Ugaritic Aperitifs in Memory of Simon B. Parker*, ed. A Joseph Ferrara and Herbert B. Huffmon (Eugene, OR: Pickwick, 2020), pp. 1-22 (first published in Hebrew in 2003 in a volume in honor of our teacher, Avraham Holtz).

[32] For references see my "Signs of Poetry Past" (n. 1 above).

> All the springs of the great watery deep split open,
> And the windows of the sky opened up.

Recent work by Guy Darshan shows that an epic poem of the flood was known at the ancient city of Ugarit, making the theory of an epic lying behind the biblical flood story highly plausible.[33] In any event, one can hardly explain the poetic couplet in the midst of biblical prose without positing an Israelite epic of the flood on which the prose author drew.

A third basis on which to maintain the existence of a pre-biblical Israelite epic is the presence of certain poetic, and often archaic, lines scattered throughout biblical literature, in prose but mainly in poetry. Thus, for example, in Proverbs 3:20 we find the line "the watery deeps were split open," which echoes the first line of the couplet I cited from the flood story; and in Isaiah 24:18 we find the line "For the windows from on high opened up," which echoes the second line of the couplet from the flood story. There are many additional examples of this phenomenon. The most likely explanation is that poets and prose writers alike in composing their own poems and narratives would excerpt lines from classic poems, like the epic of the flood. That is how traditional writing works. One draws on the classics, thereby lending authority and prestige to one's own compositions.

Yet a fourth piece of evidence for a pre-biblical Israelite epic was alluded to above. The epic formulas "he raised his eyes and saw," "she raised her voice and cried," are abundant in Ugaritic narrative verse and in biblical prose narrative as well. Since the biblical prose writers no longer had access to Ugaritic literature, from what source did they adopt these formulas? Not from biblical poetry, where the formulas are barely ever attested and then, never in the third person and never in a narrative context. The widespread use of such formulas in biblical prose narrative can only be explained if there was an Israelite epic literature from which to borrow and adapt them. There must have been epic poems in pre-biblical Hebrew literature. Reconstructing as much as possible of these poems is one of my own academic preoccupations. I want to restore as much of the missing link as possible.

But rather than speculate about what the Israelite epic of creation looked like or whether there was an epic of the plagues in Egypt (I think there may well have been),[34] I would like to devote the remainder of this essay to the

---

[33] Guy Darshan, "The Calendrical Framework of the Priestly Flood Story in Light of a New Akkadian Text from Ugarit" (RS 94.2953). *Journal of the American Oriental Society* 136 (2016), pp. 507-14.

[34] I presented a lecture on that topic at a conference on new directions in the study of

evolution of the biblical text I have been most extensively and intensively studying in recent decades—the book of Job.[35] There is no question that a legend of Job pre-existed the biblical version.[36] The prophet Ezekiel (14:14, 20) twice refers to a trio of righteous gentiles who, at the time of God's destruction of Jerusalem, would not by virtue of their own righteousness be able to save anyone but themselves. They would not, like Noah in the great flood, like Danel—a Canaanite judge who seems to have been able to restore his dead son to life at least part of every year[37]—and like Job, be able to save their children's lives from disaster by dint of their own piety and virtue. In Ezekiel's version of the Job story, Job apparently prays for the restoration of his dead children, and they are returned to him at the end of the tale. In the biblical account, after his test of devotion ends, Job is provided with a new set of ten children. In any event, in the background of the book of Job lies a traditional story, known perhaps to Canaanites as well, which served as the starting point for one of a series of biblical authors who contributed to the formation of the canonical book. It has even been proposed that the original Hebrew Job narrative was epic in form.[38]

What I would like to suggest is that the meaning of Job can be deepened and rendered more dynamic and dialectical by examining the probable historical process by which it became the text we know. The process begins with what was surely an oral tale of a good man who lost his wealth and his family and, perhaps through keeping his patience and his piety, regained them by the grace of his god. We cannot really know if Job was tested or needed to perform any particular acts in order to receive his restoration, but in the first written stage of the composition of which we are aware, in the prose narrative that frames the biblical book, his estate was decimated and his children stricken. It is not clear why the Deity restored the fortunes of Job, but it may

---

myth in the Hebrew Bible, held at Tel-Aviv University, January 2018. In a forthcoming article (in Hebrew) I argue that an early Hebrew epic stands behind the narrative of Balaam in Numbers 22-24.

[35] See my translation with introduction and annotations: Edward L. Greenstein, *Job: A New Translation* (New Haven-London: Yale University Press, 2019; lightly revised paper edition, 2020).

[36] See already Shalom Spiegel, "Noah, Daniel, and Job, Touching on Canaanite Relics in the Legends of the Jews," in *Louis Ginzberg Jubilee Volume* (New York: American Academy for Jewish Research, 1946), pp. 305-55.

[37] For the Ugaritic text and English translation see Simon B. Parker, "Aqhat," in *Ugaritic Narrative Poetry*.

[38] Nahum M. Sarna, "Epic Substratum in the Prose of Job," *Journal of Biblical Literature* 76 (1957), pp. 13-25.

be because throughout all his suffering, he did not complain.

The test of Job's devotion to the Deity appears for certain only in the second stage of the prose narrative's formation.[39] The test, which has no precise parallel anywhere in the ancient Near East, is prompted by the Deity and is administered by the Satan, the member of divine court whose job it is to trip people up and then to malign them for it. The Satan's secondary appearance in the prose tale is evident in the syntax. Briefly described, in Job 1:13 it is related that "On a (certain) day, his sons and his daughters were eating and drinking wine in the house of their brother, the firstborn, when a messenger came"—and told Job of an attack on his herds and servants. The possessive pronoun "his"—"his sons and his daughters"—refers clearly to Job. But Job was last spoken of in verse 5 above; he had not been mentioned for several verses. The nearest antecedent of the pronoun would be the Satan. One must conclude that the intervening section, in which the Deity speaks with the Satan, has been secondarily added. Otherwise, the text would read that "on a certain day, the Satan's sons and daughters were eating and drinking wine," etc. The secondary addition of the Satan to the story jibes with an increasing trend in Second Temple Jewish texts, to remove direct responsibility for doing evil or wreaking disaster from the Godhead itself to some lesser agent, in this case, the angel known as the Satan.[40] In the conclusion of the prose narrative, in the epilogue at the end of the book, the Satan is not mentioned at all; nor is the skin inflammation with which the Satan afflicts Job. These facts support the analysis holding that the Satan and his role in the story were added belatedly in an effort to remove any taint of meanness or unfairness from the Deity.

What this means, of course, is that in an earlier version of the biblical book, the Deity's behavior was understood to be unjust and, if not immoral, incomprehensible; and a literary effort was made to protect the Deity's righteous character by ascribing the shadier aspects of the story to another agency. One finds a similar tendency in the other stages by which the canonical book of Job came to be.

---

[39] See my Hebrew essay, "God's Test of Job," in *Shai le-Sara Japhet: Studies in the Bible, Its Exegesis and Its Language*, ed. M. Bar-Asher et al. (Jerusalem: Mossad Bialik, 2007), pp. 263-72; some of this study is summarized in my essay, "The Problem of Evil in the Book of Job," in *Mishneh Todah: Studies in Deuteronomy and Its Cultural Environment in Honor of Jeffrey H. Tigay*, ed. Nili S. Fox et al. (Winona Lake, IN: Eisenbrauns, 2009), pp. 333-62.

[40] For example, in 2 Samuel 24:1 it is YHWH who takes out his anger on Israel by inducing David to take a census of the people, an act that for some reason leads to a plague. When the same episode is retold in the Persian period revisionist history (1 Chronicles 21:1), it is the Satan who induces David to undertake the census.

In the prose tale, as S. R. Driver pointed out over a century ago,[41] the question at issue is: Can there be piety without reward? Do people require a material motivation in order to be devout? The major part of the biblical book of Job is the poem forming the large core of the work. Here the question is transformed into the linchpin of theodicy, and some would say of all theology: Is God just? Does the Deity govern the world in such a way that the good are rewarded and the bad are punished? However, while Job and his companions are debating that question, much else is going on in the poetic dialogues. I shall indicate only two of the concomitant issues that are being developed, as I read the book.

One issue is epistemological—on what basis does or should one base one's arguments?[42] Job's friends rely on the wisdom of the ages, on tradition, on what they claim to have learned from their ancestors. Truth is a content that is transmitted from generation to generation. Job himself relies on experience: on the realities of his own case—a good and pious man who finds himself mysteriously afflicted—and on a revelation he receives from a divine source. (I cannot elaborate here, but I am basing this claim on extensive work by others and by me that demonstrates that the hair-raising nocturnal appearance of the spirit in the second half of Job 4 has been misplaced and belongs to Job, not Eliphaz.)[43] Tradition versus revelation becomes a central theme in later religious thought as well.

A second issue is, to my mind, the most innovative and inspiring element in the book of Job.[44] So far as I know, it was Immanuel Kant who first put his finger on it. The question is: Is there any limit to speaking truth when talking about God? Truth in God-talk is, in my reading, the most consistent strain running through the book. At the outset Job expressed his concern that his children, in the midst of their partying, might, under the influence of wine and a festive atmosphere, blaspheme. The test of Job also revolves around speech: Will Job maintain his piety or curse the Deity after he loses his fortunes and family, and after he is physically afflicted? The

---

[41] S. R. Driver, *An Introduction to the Literature of the Old Testament* (Cleveland: Meridian, 1956; originally published 1906), pp. 409-10.

[42] See my study "'On My Skin and in My Flesh': Personal Experience as a Source of Knowledge in the Book of Job," in *Bringing the Hidden to Light: Studies in Honor of Stephen A. Geller*, ed. K. F. Kravitz and D. M. Sharon (New York: The Jewish Theological Seminary / Winona Lake, IN: Eisenbrauns; 2007), pp. 63-77.

[43] See now also Ken Brown, *The Vision in Job 4 and Its Role in the Book* (Tübingen: Mohr Siebeck, 2015).

[44] See my essay "Truth or Theodicy? Speaking Truth to Power in the Book of Job," *Princeton Seminary Bulletin* 27 (2006), pp. 238-58.

bulk of the book is dialogue—it is a drama of speeches. And at a number of junctures, Job makes the claims that he would never lie, never speak corruptly; and that he has never blasphemed. The most extraordinary moment comes near the end of the book, when the Deity addresses Job's companions, telling them that they did not speak "truthfully" or "in honesty" (*nekhona*) about him in the way his servant Job has (Job 42:7-8).

In an earlier form of the book, many scholars imagine, the Deity's compliment to Job was made in the reverse context. Job had resisted the urgings of his friends, who, like Job's wife, had urged him to curse God for his suffering. Job refused and was therefore praised. However, in the present form of the book, the author, who has given Job much more to say than he has any of the companions or the Deity himself—the author has God praising Job for speaking truthfully, sincerely, on the basis of what he knows, rather than parroting the pieties of the tradition. This is the book's most radical moment—when the Deity seems to favor complete truth in speaking of God over the rehearsal of time-honored doctrine.

This for me is the climax of the book. But it is not, I'm afraid, the last stage in the composition of the canonical text. I prefer the book at this stage in its formation, as I understand it. However, in my analysis, there are two passages, one very brief and one very long, that have been added to the more radical book of Job.[45] The first is a difficult passage I believe has been interpolated in chapter 24, in response to a challenge from Job. In his counter to Eliphaz in the third round of disputation, Job maintains that the Deity indulges the wicked, allowing them to prosper, calling into question the Deity's commitment to the just treatment of human beings. Job ends his discourse with a provocative challenge: "If it is not so, then who can prove me false? / Who can dismiss my words as nothing?" (24:25). The seven preceding verses, which are particularly difficult in language and form, seem to make the contrary claim: that the wicked cannot escape divine punishment. I maintain that these verses were inserted secondarily by an early reader of the book who rose to meet Job's challenge—"who can prove me false?" This reader sought to prove Job wrong about divine justice.

The extensive interpolation in the canonical book of Job is the four-part uninterrupted discourse of Elihu. Most modern scholars understand that these speeches were added to an earlier version of the book. Carol Newsom refers to them as the first reader's response to the book.[46] In the Deity's discourses to Job from the storm, he takes pride in the predatory and in-

---

[45] See pp. 110-12 in my translation for references and brief explanations.

[46] Carol A. Newsom, *The Book of Job: A Contest of Moral Imaginations* (Oxford-New York: Oxford University Press, 2003), pp. 200-33.

timidating creatures he has made and expresses very little concern for human beings. More disturbingly, he makes no claim to maintain a system of just retribution—he appears to be about power and not about justice.[47] This distressed an early reader of the book, who composed the Elihu chapters in order to anticipate and put a spin on the Deity's answer, or lack of an answer, to Job. Elihu introduces the theme of divine providential care for humans and portrays the Deity as just and moral as well as powerful and mysterious. It is thereby implied that whatever justice Job fails to perceive in the world is a result of its esoteric nature, not of its absence. For example, in contrast to the Deity, who proclaims that he makes it rain where no human can benefit from it (38:25-27), Elihu (36:27-28) insists that the Deity showers humanity with rain.

In summary, the book of Job deals in a number of dialectically presented positions within the dialogues between the protagonist and his companions, on the one hand, and between the human sufferer and the afflicting Deity, on the other. But dialectic and argument are found not only in the dialogues as presented in the book. They also characterize the process by which the book as we know it was composed, as themes and perspectives are shifted with each addition or alteration in an earlier version of the text. There is a distinct attempt to blunt the subversive thrust of the original book by championing the belief in a just God. The argument between Job and his companions is doubled in the process by which the book attained its canonical form. There is drama in the story of the story just as there is in the story itself.

---

[47] See my essay "In Job's Face/Facing Job," in *The Labour of Reading: Desire, Alienation, and Biblical Interpretation* (Festschrift for Robert C. Culley), ed. F. C. Black et al. (Atlanta: Scholars Press, 1999), pp. 301-17.

The Free Exercise Clause and the Challenge to a Civil Society

Debra E. Guston

There is a saying that goes: "Your right to swing your fist stops at the tip of my nose."

Its origin is unclear, but it appears to have originated in the 19th Century and is alternately attributed to Abraham Lincoln or Nathaniel Hawthorne. Even without such auspicious attribution, the saying is a clear representation of the compact required for the American aspiration of a truly diverse civil society—*e pluribus unum*—out of many, one. A variation on this theme comes from Rabbi Israel Salanter, founder of the Mussar Movement, which is focused on the continual refinement of personal character and scrupulous attention to moral norms. Rabbi Salanter is reputed to have said, "When, in your personal spiritual fervor, you wrap yourself in a Tallis, make sure you don't slap the person standing next to you with the tzitzis!"

The Constitution

The First Amendment to the United States Constitution states that "Congress shall make no law respecting an establishment of religion, or prohibiting the free exercise thereof...." This article focuses on the second clause, the "free exercise" clause and what happens when a person's sincerely held religious belief and expression collide with civil law and community engagement and access. In its simplest reading, the Free Exercise Clause clearly makes it unconstitutional for the government to prohibit an individual from worshiping as they wish. That concept is complicated by what happens when the government tries to enforce a law that appears to a citizen as infringing on their freedom to worship or manifest their sincerely held beliefs in their daily lives. Courts, academics and others have struggled mightily to weigh the competing interests of trying to maintain religious pluralism while championing individual religious rights.

There are dozens of cases that have come before the Supreme Court of the United States involving issues concerning the Free Exercise clause. This summary is just that, a summary of cases that will help focus in on the central theme of this article.

The Cases

To start this review, we need to look back to 1948 when the Supreme Court ruled in Prince vs. Massachusetts[1] that a mother who adhered to the Jehovah's Witness faith could not hide behind her faith to permit her minor child to sell newspapers on the street contrary to child labor laws. The Court opined that the Free Exercise Clause protects one's right to practice one's religion as one pleases, so long as that exercise does not run afoul of "public morals" or a "compelling" governmental interest. The Court ruled that the mother's parental autonomy and free exercise rights were not absolute and the state's interest in protecting the child outweighed the mother's interest in having her child engage in the proselytizing activity of selling the newspapers as was common and acceptable in her faith practice. The Court set upon the balancing of the Free Exercise clause with other interests of the state.

In 1960, Braunfeld vs. Brown[2] started a long line of "blue law" challenges. Mr. Braunfeld owned a retail clothing business in Philadelphia. As an Orthodox Jew, he closed his shop on Saturdays. The state blue laws only permitted certain types of businesses to open on Sunday and so Braunfeld challenged the constitutionality of the law, claiming it violated his religious liberty, forcing him to lose two weekend days of business as a result of his religious practice and the state's Sunday restrictions. In a 6-3 decision, the Court found that the blue laws had a secular basis and rationale and did not directly intend to hinder one religious observance over another. The blue law was upheld, despite its indirect burden on religious observance. The Court reasoned that unless the state can accomplish its secular goal of providing a uniform day of rest for all through other means, an indirect burden, such as economic sacrifice, may be a result of the statute, but that does not make the blue law unconstitutional.

In a companion case, Gallagher vs. Crown Kosher Super Market of Massachusetts, Inc.,[3] argued that same year but decided in 1961, the Court came to a similar conclusion as it had in Braunfeld: the blue law was upheld.

Next, we move to 1972 when the United States Supreme Court held in Yoder vs. Wisconsin[4] that the Amish plaintiffs could be exempt from state education law that made education compulsory through high school. The

---

[1] Prince vs. Massachusetts, 321 U.S. 158 (1948)

[2] Braunfeld vs. Brown, 366 U.S.599 (1960)

[3] Gallagher vs. Crown Kosher Super Market of Massachusetts, Inc., 366 U.S. 617 (1961)

[4] Yoder vs. Wisconsin, 406 US 205 (1972)

Amish argued that the compulsory education laws were antithetical to their religious and cultural lifestyle. Their children, they argued, should be allowed to complete their studies after the 8th grade so they could take their place in the community to train in farming, trades and crafts. The Supreme Court tried to differentiate between a lifestyle that was entwined with the religious belief (the Amish lifestyle) or simply a lifestyle choice, "admirable or virtuous" as it may be. Their example was of Thoreau's rejection of social norms and values—Thoreau's was not a practice of religion but a philosophical choice. Enforcing compulsory education on the Amish, the Court reasoned, might lead to an end of their religious-based lifestyle. Here the balancing of the religious lifestyle of the Amish weighed more heavily than the state's interest in compulsory secondary education for the children involved.

In 1978, the high court heard McDaniel vs. Paty.[5] This case challenged Tennessee's 18th Century law that prohibited members of the clergy from serving as state legislators. Clearly deriving from the founders' wariness of the intermingling of religion and government and meant to address the first clause of the First Amendment that the government should not "establish" religion, Tennessee's law had been in place since 1796. Ruling for a unanimous Court, Chief Justice Warren E. Burger found the law to be unconstitutional, as it required the surrender of one's religious practice as a condition to exercise a civil and civic right—to run for office in a representative democracy.

And now come the cases that led us to new federal laws and give rise to the central question of whether religious freedom and expression can, without restraint, co-exist in a diverse civil society.

In Goldman vs. Weinberger,[6] Goldman was a commissioned officer in the U.S. Air Force. He was also an ordained rabbi and under the military's uniform regulations, he was not permitted to wear his yarmulke while on duty and in his Air Force uniform. The regulation was neutral in content—no head coverings were to be worn indoors, except by armed police in the performance of their duties. No intent there to restrict a Jewish service member from wearing a yarmulke. By a 5-4 decision, the Court upheld the regulation, giving deference to the military and its needs for regulation, as the Court said, to "foster instinctive obedience, unity, commitment, and esprit de corps." A year later (1987), Congress passed a new law[7] to allow members of the armed services to wear religious garb in a "neat and conservative" manner.

---

[5] McDaniel vs. Paty, 435 U.S. 618 (1978)

[6] Goldman vs. Weinberger, 475 U.S. 503 (1986)

[7] 10 U.S. Code §774

The same year as Goldman, the Court heard Bowen vs. Roy.[8] A seemingly odd case, Bowen's holding is consistent with Free Expression jurisprudence in its period, a jurisprudence that will significantly change a few decades later. Plaintiffs were a Native American couple with a small child. The family was receiving federal support as a low income family and refused to provide their daughter's social security number in connection with the benefits. The government terminated the benefits for their failure to comply. The family argued that the use of the social security number would "rob the spirit" of their daughter and being forced to provide the number would violate their free exercise rights. An 8-1 Court held that the requirement of a social security number for federal benefits was a neutral, legitimate state requirement to prevent fraud. The important position is that the government was not required to provide aid to individuals to assist them in practicing their religion by either bypassing otherwise valid laws or creating new pathways for accommodation.

This same reasoning continued in O'lone vs. Estate of Shabazz[9], in which Muslim prisoners argued that work assignments outside the prison did not permit them to attend sabbath services on Fridays and violated their free exercise. The Court held that given the serious security concerns of prisons, there was no requirement to create alternatives to otherwise valid, neutral policies to promote the safety and security of the prison community.

O'lone was followed by Employment Division, State of Oregon vs. Smith[10] in which two employees at a drug rehabilitation center were fired for using peyote during a Native American religious service. The State denied them unemployment benefits as they were fired "for cause." At the state level, a court of appeals found that their rights of free exercise were violated and the state Supreme Court reversed. The United States Supreme Court remanded (returned) the case to the Oregon Supreme Court with instructions that the state court needed to determine whether the firing for the use of peyote was only an employer policy (presuming that would be unconstitutional) or whether the state had a policy to prohibit the use of peyote, which would be something the state could defend on that balancing test between the state interest and the interference with religious practice. The case came back to the U.S. Supreme Court in 1990.[11] The Oregon Supreme Court had found

---

[8] Bowen vs. Roy, 476 U.S. 693 (1986)

[9] O'lone vs. Estate of Shabazz, 482 U.S. 342 (1987)

[10] Employment Division, Department of Human Resources of the State of Oregon vs. Smith, 485 U.S. 660 (1988)

[11] Employment Division, Department of Human Resources of the State of Oregon vs. Smith, 494 U.S. 872 (1990)

that the state prohibited the use of illegal drugs even for sacramental purposes, but then found that such a prohibition was unconstitutional in that the state could not condition benefits upon a person's willingness to give up a religious practice. The U.S. Supreme Court, however, reversed and held that the state could deny the unemployment benefits for violating the law, even though the drug was used in religious ritual. While the U.S. Supreme Court agreed that a government cannot condition a benefit on giving up a religious practice, that was not the case when the religious practice was an otherwise illegal act. Oregon's law against carrying or use of peyote was a neutral law, applying to all people and not targeted at Native American religious practice.

With the "yarmulke case" of Goldman and the "peyote case" of Employment Division v. Smith, the Congress saw a growing restlessness with this line of Supreme Court cases and a consistent flow of disputes taking years to filter through the courts. The Congress passed the Religious Freedom Restoration Act of 1993.[12] The law, known by its acronym, RFRA, was passed by a unanimous House and had the votes of 97 senators and was signed into law by President Bill Clinton. The law reinstated prior Supreme Court standards of review for cases involving religious exercise—all such cases in federal court must withstand strict scrutiny—the highest and toughest level of review. The government must show a compelling interest in restricting a religious practice dealing with a core constitutional issue (other than the Free Exercise Clause) and RFRA mandates that the government, if it has a compelling reason to restrict religious exercise, must find the least restrictive manner in which to accomplish that interest.

Originally, RFRA applied to the states as well as the federal government, but that application was ruled unconstitutional in 1997 in City of Boerne vs. Flores.[13] In response, close to half the states have enacted their own "mini-RFRA's."

With RFRA, the tone and tenor of religious exercise cases seemed to change dramatically, which leads to the final spate of cases that illustrate the basic thesis of this article. Cases took a huge right turn—no longer were the major cases those of minority religious practitioners bringing cases when their rights to exercise were being curtailed, but majority Christian businesses and individuals began to bring cases where they felt the government was abridging their rights. The issues were being re-framed that in trying to promote minority interests, governments were hurting adherents to a majority religious culture. Free exercise should allow a person, or entity,

---

[12] 42 U.S.C. §2000bb et seq.

[13] 521 U.S. 507 (1997)

to exclude or to reject, that which the government sought to protect from discrimination or exclusion.

There is no more glaring example of the shift than Burwell vs. Hobby Lobby Stores, Inc.[14] The Hobby Lobby craft store chain is owned by a single family, a closely held corporation. When the Affordable Care Act was enacted, health insurance companies offering plans that were governed by the ACA were required to provide coverage for contraception for women. The ACA exempted religious organizations and non-profit religious organization employers from paying for such care by allowing them to opt out—in which case the insurer had to pick up the costs for the employee. The Green family, the owners of Hobby Lobby stores, are evangelical Christians who state that they have built their business model around their faith principles and that they did not believe in the use of contraceptives as a matter of religious principle and practice. They, as a for-profit organization, had no such exemption rights and if they did not provide the inclusive insurance, there would be tax penalties imposed under the law.

By a 5-4 majority, the Supreme Court held that under RFRA, Hobby Lobby and other for-profit corporations could not be compelled to provide contraceptive care to employees based on the religious principles of the company owners. In her vigorous dissent, Justice Ruth Bader Ginsburg heralded the concept that one's own rights end when exercising your rights hurts another. Justice Ginsburg, relying on years of the Supreme Court's case law, argued that the ability of an employee to gain access to contraceptive care through an employer sponsored plan was merely incidental to an otherwise neutral government mandate—provide insurance under the ACA or pay a tax penalty that will fund individuals to get their own insurance on the ACA marketplace. She further argued that the Green family beliefs must not burden or harm their employees who may not hold the same belief that contraceptive care was wrong.

The Supreme Court, having held in Hobby Lobby that closely held family businesses were comprised of individuals whose religious exercise should not be burdened by the government, opened the door for other noteworthy cases. The most publicized of those cases was Masterpiece Cakeshop, Ltd. vs. Colorado Civil Rights Commission.[15] Here, a Christian baker and shop owner refused to make a wedding cake for a same-sex couple. He had started to take the order when he learned for whom the cake was to be made and then refused. Colorado's civil rights laws make it illegal to discriminate in public accommodations on the basis of sexual orientation. The law is neutral

---

[14] Burwell vs. Hobby Lobby Stores, Inc., 573 U.S. 682 (2014)

[15] Masterpiece Cakeshop, Ltd. vs. Colorado Civil Rights Commission, 584 U.S. (2018)

on its face and appears to apply to businesses open to the general public. The baker, claiming that his cake-making was an artistic endeavor and an expression of his faith, defended a complaint made by the couple to the state's Civil Rights Commission. After a hearing, the Commission ruled in the couple's favor and fined the baker. The Supreme Court straddled the real issues in its decision—by a 7-2 vote, they overturned the fine, finding that the Commission had made so many derogatory remarks about the baker and his faith in the hearing, that the hearing itself had been tainted by religious animus. However, the Court went on to seemingly uphold, or at least ignore the two other central issues: was the Colorado law neutral on its face and in application and therefore constitutional to protect the rights of a minority community; and second, and perhaps the thorniest problems—is baking a cake for a wedding art and therefore expression or is it merely making and selling a commodity to the public? This combination of the Free Exercise Clause with the Freedom of Speech will likely dominate future litigation in this area.

A sigh of relief was heard from all "sides" in June 2021 when the Supreme Court ruled in Fulton vs. City of Philadelphia.[16] In a classic confrontation between a government and a religious non-profit, Philadelphia had a neutral non-discrimination law that bars it from contracting with organizations and businesses that discriminate against, among others, LGBTQ people. The City barred Catholic Charities from city contracts in the placement of children in foster care because it refused to place children with LGBTQ foster parents. Catholic Charities argued that it had to reject otherwise qualified LGBTQ people under its religious principles. In a narrowly tailored decision, the Supreme Court held that as the law allowed for a religious exemption that was not granted to Catholic Charities, the law was not one of "general applicability." An exemption was permitted and should have been granted. Fear that the conservative court would overrule years of jurisprudence allowing laws of general applicability to protect disfavored minorities did not come to pass.

What Next?

And so, with this legal history considered, the Free Exercise Clause and its protections may find supremacy over other civil rights in the future. The First Amendment appears on its face to be a statement of complete neutrality. But it is hard to envision that the Founders could have imagined fights over same-sex marriage and wedding cakes, contraception and health insurance,

---

[16] Fulton vs. City of Philadelphia, U.S. Supreme Court Docket No. 19-123

and whether a prison grooming policy violated a Muslim inmate's religious observance.[17] We are left to ask—will any person, selling wares or providing services, be permitted to harken back to times we thought we had moved beyond in America with signs of "NO [fill in the blank] SERVED?"

This level of "Main Street anarchy" has already begun. States like Arkansas have passed laws prohibiting the provision of medical services to transgender children and banning trans kids from sport participation. Representative Marjorie Taylor Green has posted a sign outside her Congressional Office extolling her belief that God made only man and woman as immutable beings. States have passed "religious conscience" laws allowing professionally licensed people—doctors, nurses, pharmacists—to refuse to treat or sell to persons to whom providing service would violate their sincerely held religious beliefs. Mandatory vaccination to protect the public health can be rejected claiming a sincerely held religious belief—an issue made all the more timely during the Covid pandemic. Two grocery store workers recently filed an EEOC complaint because the company's rainbow heart logo was viewed by the employees as supportive of the LGBTQ community (though the company did not intend the design to be a "pride" emblem). Religious employers have refused even to sign a waiver request to opt out of contraceptive care, claiming the mere act of signing a waiver form makes them complicit in the disfavored provision of goods or services.

The conclusion to this chain of legal cases and mostly conservative Christian individual action and political advocacy, can only be that there will be an equal and opposite reaction. The "what goes around—comes around" maxim is clearly in our future. One can foresee members of minority religions, racial and ethnic groups, LGBTQ communities and others turning the table on those currently engaged in seeking primacy of their sincerely held religious beliefs over a cooperative and unified civil society. This has happened in the recent past—during the years of intense focus on marriage equality—clergy of more "liberal" denominations that supported the rights of same-sex couples to marry urged politicians and courts to adopt the position that to deny them their ability to join same-sex couples in marriage was an abrogation of their sincerely held religious beliefs. So, too, did same-sex couples who wished to marry argue that their religious beliefs compelled them to want to marry in their faiths.

It is clear that our current politics and the movement toward creating an ideologically uniform judiciary makes it hard for us to see a time when American society will come back to a place of moderation, tolerance and acceptance. It is further difficult to predict whether our courts will continue on a

---

[17] Holt vs. Hobbs, 574 U.S. 352 (2015)

pathway of favoring governmental neutrality in protecting an open and inclusive civil society or whether there will be a tacit or even explicit sanctioning of discriminatory action taken under claims of a sincerely held religious belief.

We can only hope that the swinging of fists truly does end at the tips of others' noses.

The Wonder of Trees: Musings in Honor of Tu B'Shevat

Jill Hackell

When I entered rabbinical school, many of my acquaintances in the scientific world asked me how I could 'cross over' to the world of religion from the world of biology. Surely that chasm is too wide to allow for easy passage! In fact, for me it was never a chasm. On the contrary, science was the passageway that flowed directly into my interest in Judaism.

In college, this biology major discovered Heschel. As luck would have it, the Somerville Havurah was just down the road from my dorm at Tufts, and Art Green and others came to campus to teach. Here, I was introduced to Jewish mysticism by way of Gershom Scholem, and to Heschel's "radical amazement." I remember the quote that went up on the wall of my room: *The wonder of facts is that there are facts at all.*[1]

This sustained me throughout college as I studied the mysteries of DNA and protein synthesis, and in medical school throughout the study of human embryology and development and the complexity of human physiology. Behind all the facts that were unfolding were a deep sense of mystery and wonder at the perfection of it all. And it sustains me still.

Recently I have been reading about trees.

Sure, I've studied trees before. And I knew quite a bit about individual trees—how to identify them by their leaves or their bark, how nutrients and water move up to their leafy tops, how photosynthesis works. What I've learned recently is the way in which trees form a community, to share all kinds of information and resources with other trees around them.

For example, a tree grows in Africa—the thorn acacia—which is part of the diet of giraffes. Clearly, it is a danger to the tree to have all its energy-making leaves eaten. So, these trees have evolved a response: they manufacture a toxin and send it to its leaves, making them inedible for giraffes. But the tree doesn't only respond to its individual danger. It also sends out a warning gas (ethylene) that travels through the air, to warn neighboring acacia trees of danger. All the forewarned trees begin to pump toxins into

---

[1] Paraphrased from *"He knows that there are laws that regulate the course of natural processes; is aware of the regularity and pattern of things. However, such knowledge fails to mitigate his sense of perpetual surprise at the fact that there are facts at all."* Heschel, Abraham Joshua, *God in Search of Man.* 1983, Farrar, Straus and Giroux, NY, p. 45

their own leaves, and the whole group is able to protect itself from giraffes.[2]

There are even more profound relationships between trees. In natural forests, they are all connected underground through a vast network of fungi intricately bound up in their roots, through which they share water, nutrients, hormones, and information. This system has been dubbed "The Wood-Wide Web." Older and larger trees have the most connections and can provide resources to younger and smaller trees. Underground alarm signals can warn other trees of danger. A tree that is cut off from this underground network is much more likely to die than those that are connected. And a connected, dying tree can donate its carbon to its neighbors.[3] For trees, just as for other creatures—like ants, bees, and humans—it is not always survival of the fittest individual with every tree for itself; cooperation can help a species survive.

This underground cooperation occurs both within and between species. The trees with the most connections (called "hub trees" or "mother trees"), can recognize their own seedlings, and hook them more efficiently into the network. Injured or dying mother trees can send carbon and defense signals to their offspring which can increase their resistance to future stresses (like bug infestation), thus protecting future generations.[4] But interspecies support can be just as important.

In one experiment, Dr. Suzanne Simard studied carbon flow between Douglas fir and birch trees. In the summer, the firs were shaded by the larger birch trees and were less able to produce energy through photosynthesis; at that time carbon flowed from birch to fir. In the fall, when the birch was losing its energy-producing leaves so that the evergreen fir no longer was in its shade, the flow of carbon reversed. The two species depended on each other to get through the time of year that was more difficult for each of them.[5]

Dig deeply into nature and a world opens. Or, as Richard Powers put it in his novel about trees and the people who love them, *"A chorus of living wood sings to the woman: If your mind were only a slightly greener thing we'd drown you in meaning."*[6]

---

[2] Wohlleben, Peter, *The Hidden Life of Trees*. 2015 Greystone Books, Vancouver/Berkeley, p. 7

[3] Jahr, Ferris, "The Social Life of Forests". In: The New York Times Magazine Dec 6, 2020, p. 34

[4] Ted talk by Simard: https://www.ted.com/talks/suzanne_simard_how_trees_talk_to_each_other?language=en

[5] Jahr, p. 35

[6] Powers, Richard, *The Overstory* 2018. W.W. Norton and Co. NY/London

Now, meaning can go in two different directions. When I grapple with meaning with my left brain, I think in words, linearly, using facts and logic to lead to conclusions. When I grapple with meaning with my right brain, the process is more holistic, imaginative, and intuition based.[7]

Dr. Simard uses her research on interrelationships in the old-growth forest to try to change the lumber industry. Much of the great forests has been cut down to provide wood for human needs. To replace these losses, scientists have planted tree crops—forests made of single species that will continue to supply human needs. But there are problems. Insects destroy large sections of these forests. And the interruption of the complex underground communication network that has been developed over many hundreds of years in old-growth forests, makes all trees more vulnerable. In the "Mother Tree Project," Dr. Simard is studying how preserving hub trees and assuring species diversity can help make forestry sustainable.

With this in mind, I turn to Torah, still using connections arising in the logical side of the brain.

Deuteronomy 20:19 states:

> "When in your war against a city you have to besiege it a long time in order to capture it, you must not destroy its trees, wielding the ax against them. You may eat of them, but you must not cut them down. Are trees of the field human to withdraw before you into the besieged city? Only trees that you know do not yield food may be destroyed; you may cut them down for constructing siegeworks against the city that is waging war on you, until it has been reduced." (NJPS translation).

The text begins with a general caution to spare trees in time of siege. It is followed by a sentence with strange Hebrew syntax, which seems to be comparing trees to humans.

כִּי הָאָדָם עֵץ הַשָּׂדֶה לָבֹא מִפָּנֶיךָ בַּמָּצוֹר׃

Rashi explains it like this:

> "Is the tree of the field perhaps [ki] a human, to enter into the siege because of you, that it should be punished by the

---

[7] https://www.healthline.com/health/left-brain-vs-right-brain

suffering of hunger and thirst like the people of the city? Why should you destroy it?"

The answer to this question seems to be "no"; trees are not like humans. They are not part of this war between humans; they cannot take sides; they cannot run away. Josephus takes this further:

> "…if they could speak they would have a just plea against you, because though they are not occasions of the war, they are unjustly treated, and suffer in it; and would, if they were able, move themselves into another land." [8]

The text then moves from concern for the trees to concern for human needs. It tells us that it is specifically the *fruit* trees that we must not destroy, because these trees provide food. Trees that do not provide food may be cut down to meet the needs of men, i.e., building siegeworks to help ensure military success. Humans are to avoid wanton destruction and wastage—no scorched-earth policy—but when there is a good reason, trees may be cut down.

Indeed, from this verse comes the concept of *bal tashchit*, which warns against wasteful destruction.

> Whoever breaks vessels, or tears garments, or destroys a building, or clogs a well, or does away with food in a destructive manner violates the negative mitzvah of *bal tashchit*, do not waste or destroy. (Rambam, Mishneh Torah, Hilkhot Melakhim u-Milhamot 6:10)

Certainly, the spirit of the verse in Deuteronomy is that humans may use natural resources for our own needs, but we must take all precautions not to destroy more than we have to. Dr. Simard's research, with its insight into the natural connections within old-growth forests, can teach us how to do that wisely.

But that question in the verse—*Are the trees of the field human to withdraw before you into the besieged city?*—still gives me pause. Although the verse seems to provide the answer—'no, the trees are not human, they are without defense, they are not our enemy and we should spare them'—why raise up this comparison with humanity in the first place? And why use Hebrew syntax that is so unclear. It sets up an equation between trees and humans,

---

[8] Josephus, Antiquities 4:299, quoted in The Torah.com "Are Trees of the Field Human?" https://www.thetorah.com/article/are-trees-of-the-field-human

but its direction is ambiguous. Without a "to be" verb in Hebrew, this text can read: "perhaps the tree of the field [is] a human" (per Rashi); but it can also read: "perhaps the human [is] a tree of the field." And suddenly my right brain lights us and answers—Yes! That is exactly the message!

We are all connected and interdependent and, in that way, we humans and the trees are the same. When we exhale carbon dioxide, the forest breathes it in, exhaling oxygen which we breath in. All life forms are dependent on other life forms, both within the species and between species, and change in one will create change in the other. It all works as one, it is all one, it is all the One. *Sh'ma Yisrael, Adonai, Eloheinu, Adonai echad*. Pay attention, people of Israel, everything is one, everything is God[9]—and behold it is very good.[10]

Scientific observation is one way to slow down, to pay attention, and to hone one's sense of wonder in the world. There are, of course, other pathways in. The *b'rachot* are designed for this. My favorite is the *b'racha* of gratitude in the Amidah: "for the miracles that are with you daily, morning, noon, and night." Stop, it says, and look around you, and see the miraculous in the things you often take for granted.

Another way of augmenting the ability to notice is to draw. The artist and writer, Frederick Frank, echoes Heschel in the following series of quotes:

> "Drawing is an immunization against the addiction to 'looking at'—it restores the gift of seeing, of being full alive."

> "I learn that what I have not drawn I have never really seen, and that when I start drawing an ordinary thing, I realize how extraordinary it is. It is a sheer miracle—the branching of a tree, the structure of a dandelion seed puff."

> "While drawing grasses, I learn nothing 'about' grass—but wake up to the wonder that there is grass at all."[11]

Rabbi Nachman of Bratslov taught that the best place for *hitbodedut* is in the forests or fields. "*Know, when a person prays in the fields, all the grasses join in his prayer, helping him and strengthening his prayer.*" He goes on to connect the word for shrub (שִׂיח) of the field, with conversation (שִׂיחה) with God, relating it also to the verse "Isaac went out to stroll/meditate/converse (לשוח) in

---

[9] The writings of Rabbi Art Green have helped me understand the Sh'ma as an expression of this feeling.

[10] Genesis 1:31

[11] From Franck's writings as displayed in his museum in Warwick NY

the field..."[Gen 25:63]—*"His prayer was with the help and power of the field."*[12]

Sometimes, our encounter with nature can be so immediate that it brushes with the Divine and draws forth a response from us. I recall such a moment, standing in the redwood forest in California, overwhelmed by something I can't put into words, except to call it a prayer.

---

[12] Likutei Moharan ll, 11:1-2

The Witch of En-dor:
Tending the Spring of Generations

Jill Hammer

Author's Note:
When I was in rabbinical school, I took a Bible class on the stories of King David with the wonderfully insightful Dr. Ora Horn Prouser. As an assignment for the class, I wrote a paper on the Witch of En-dor. I remember Dr. Prouser liked that paper and took me aside to speak about it. This essay is based on what I wrote in that original paper. I hope Dr. Prouser, to whom I owe many debts of gratitude, still finds it to her liking.

At first glance, the events of I Samuel 28:3-25 seem meant to discredit the first king of Israel. King Saul, rejected by both God and the prophet Samuel, is reduced to hiring a sorceress to contact his deceased ex-mentor, contrary to God's law and his own. But when we examine the story deeply, we find that the witch of Endor—or to use the Hebrew term, the *ba'alat ov* or spirit-keeper—is not at all a villain. She is intelligent, competent at her work, and compassionate to Saul—indeed, she is the only person who is kind to King Saul in the last days of his life. The text, in fact, portrays her sympathetically, and this is startling given the Bible's condemnation of her profession. While the *ba'alat ov* is marginalized according to kings and priests, she is connected to the world of the ancestral dead in ways that suggest she has a power of her own. One might say she is a midwife at the portal between worlds. As we watch the *ba'alat ov* at work, we may form a picture of what the practices of an ancient Israelite medium or spirit channel might have been like—or at least, a picture of how the book of Samuel imagines women spirit workers.

Seeking Answers from She'ol

As the story opens, King Saul is a desperate man. He is facing a battle with the Philistines, and Samuel, the prophet who once declared him king over Israel, has informed him that God has rejected him as king, and that this decision cannot be changed.[1] This does not bode well for Saul's success in battle. Meanwhile, David's power is on the rise: Samuel has anointed

---

[1] I Samuel 15:23, 28-29

David, and Saul himself has acknowledged that David will soon be king.[2] Saul's son Jonathan has gone over to David; Saul's daughter Michal, David's wife, helped David escape Saul's plans to kill him.[3] Meanwhile, Samuel has died, so even the possibility of receiving the prophet's counsel seems lost. Under these circumstances, the prospect of leading troops against the Philistine army unnerves Saul.

Camped at Gilboa, the king trembles with fear. Saul, who has never been of resolute character, needs help, and he tries to contact God for support. The prophet Samuel has already told him God's mind won't change, but Saul seems to have hope, because he makes multiple attempts to get God's ear. He tries to contact God in three ways: by dreams, by *Urim* (the priestly divination tools), and by prophets (though we are not told which ones). All of these attempts, we learn in I Samuel 28:5, are unsuccessful. God does not answer. Saul has now exhausted the channels of prophecy considered legitimate by his own government—for in 28:3, we learn that Saul has "forbidden *ovot* and *yidonim* in the land."

What are *ovot* and *yidonim*? How do they relate to the forms of divination Saul has already tried? "*Ov*" is often understood to be related to "waterskin" or "skin-bottle"—i.e., a person who is a vessel for a spirit.[4] Yet the word bears more than a passing resemblance to *av*, father—indeed, without vowels, the words *ovot* (spirits) and *avot* (fathers/ancestors) look exactly the same. Thomas Podella believes *ov* is related to *av* and that an *ov* is a deceased ancestor.[5] (In a related theory, Manfred Hutter understands *ov* to be related to *api*, a Hittite word for one who is buried, or for a burial site.[6]) Given that the *ba'alat ov*'s role seems to be to summon shades of the dead, we might read *ovot* as "ancestor spirits." *Yidonim*, the "knowing ones," seem to be other types of spirits (sometimes translated "familiar spirits"). Leviticus 20:27 prescribes death for a man or woman who has an *ov* or a *yidoni* inside them. And Deuteronomy 18:11 includes "one who inquires of an *ov* or a *yidoni*" in a list of forbidden kinds of divination. Scholar Alexei

---

[2] I Samuel 16; I Samuel 24:22

[3] I Samuel 23:17; I Samuel 19:15-18

[4] Brown, Francis, Driver, S.R, and Briggs, C. A. *Hebrew and English Lexicon of the Old Testament* (Oxford: Clarendon Press, 1906), p. 15.

[5] Podella, Thomas. "Nekromantie," in *Theologische Quartalschrift*, vol. 177 (1997), p. 121-133.

[6] Hutter, Manfred. "Religionsgeschichte Erwagungen zu Elohim in I Sam. 28:13," in *Biblishche Notizen* (1983), p. 32-36.

Kondratiev sees the *ovot* and *yidonim* as inherently connected to the dead.[7] Presumably divination by these beings (rather than through the *urim* and *tummim*) is forbidden because they elicit help from the dead (or other spirit entities) rather than from God.

Yet the very name of the underworld—She'ol, which means something like "the asking place"—suggests that early Israelites understood the realm of the dead as a place of divination and supernatural assistance. In Deuteronomy 18:11, one who divines by an ancestor-spirit is called *sho'el ov*, one who asks of the dead. The realm of She'ol, described as under the ground or under the sea, contrasts with God's realm in the sky, and may have been seen as an alternative avenue for appeal—Isaiah in fact claims the ability to journey either to Heaven or to She'ol for answers.[8] Several biblical texts mention the practice of offering food to the dead (while also forbidding that practice). For example, in Deuteronomy 26:14, a worshipper is required to make a declaration that none of the annual tithe has been offered to the dead. It seems that the practice of asking ancestors for help was not that easy to stamp out.

The Bible, however, wishes to direct the Israelites' attention away from She'ol. In many biblical texts, She'ol is described as a dreary place where nothing happens, or sometimes as a place of torment.[9] The priestly rules against entry into the sanctum if one has been in contact with birth or death (i.e. if one menstruates, gives birth, touches a corpse, etc.), as well as the rules against consulting and/or feeding the dead, may have been specifically meant to disempower those practitioners whose primary work was with the ancestors and the portals of death and life. Women, who may have been particularly involved in death rites, might have been especially vulnerable to such delegitimation.[10]

King Saul, who in accordance with these biblical rules has made consulting with spirits illegal, nevertheless conceives the idea that a *ba'alat ov*, a channeler of ancestor spirits, could contact Samuel for him. This is no doubt meant to be ironic—Saul is not so committed to forbidding witchcraft once he needs a witch. He specifically asks his courtiers to find an *eishet ba'alat*

---

[7] Kondratiev, Alexei. "Thou Shalt Not Suffer a Witch to Live," in *Enchante*, vol. 18, p. 11-15. www.darknet.com/proteus/Suffer.htm

[8] See Psalms 139:8; Jonah 2:3; Job 38:17; Isaiah 7:11.

[9] Ecclesiastes 9:10; Psalms 6:6; Psalms 116:3; Isaiah 38:18

[10] Peritz, Ismar J. "Women in the Ancient Hebrew Cult," in *Journal of Biblical Literature*, vol. 17 (1898), p. 137-138.

ov, a woman who is a keeper of an ancestor spirit.[11] Saul's specifying of the practitioner's gender may be because it is generally women who do this work—and/or it could be that Saul thinks a woman would be the best one to consult. Possibly the text means to create a contrast between the (sanctioned) male prophet Samuel and the (unsanctioned) female witch of En-dor. Having alienated the first, Saul must now go to the second. "I will go to her and inquire through her (*edrshah bah*)," he says in I Sam. 28:7. With the same language Genesis used to tell how Rivkah once went "*lidrosh et YHWH*," to seek God, Saul now goes to seek (*edrshah*) a witch who can contact underworld spirits. His courtiers/servants tell him that there is such a woman, in a town called En-dor.

We should note that the way *ba'alat ov* is translated into English is influenced by the culture of the translator. The woman is often called "the witch of En-dor," using the British term "witch" for a practitioner of magic. However, in the Hebrew, the woman is never called a *mechashefah* (a witch or sorceress). Rather she is called a *ba'alat ov*, a term that implies she is a spirit channel. The name of the woman's town is connected to her profession—she comes from En-dor, a name that means "spring of generations."[12] In Psalms 139:15, the psalmist speaks of, before birth, being woven in the depths of the earth. This perhaps suggests that one Israelite understanding of the spirit is that it arises from the earth prior to birth, and returns there, to She'ol, after death. We might read the name of the town to suggest that the *ba'alat ov* is a keeper of the well of life and death. She knows how to access the portal from where souls come, and to where they return.

The Journey to En-Dor

Saul disguises himself before setting out to visit the *ba'alat ov*. He changes his clothes, putting on *begadim acherim*, other clothes.[13] This might remind the reader of the only Torah text where "other clothes" are mentioned—the priest who brings the ashes of the altar outside the shrine must change into

---

[11] However, David Toshio Tsumura understands *baalat ov* to mean "Lady of Dead Spirits" and to refer to the Ugaritic sun goddess, who sometimes accompanied the dead to the underworld. An *eishet ba'alat ov*, in that case, would be "woman of the Lady of Dead Spirits." (Tsumura, David Toshio, *The First Book of Samuel* (Grand Rapids, MI: Eerdmans, 2007), p. 630-631.

[12] Interestingly, Manfred Hutter thinks En-dor may be related to *enna durenna*, the Hittite term for the gods. (Hutter, Manfred. "Religionsgeschichte Erwagungen zu Elohim in I Sam. 28:13," in *Biblishche Notizen* [1983], p. 32-36.)

[13] I Samuel 28:8

"other clothes."[14] Ezekiel 42 and 44 also mention that the priest must change clothes before going among laypeople in the outer court. The putting on of "other clothes" may indicate moving outside conventional sacred spaces, outside the bounds of what priestly authorities consider holy.

Saul sets out with two men, and the three of them arrive at the home of the *ba'alat ov* at night. This is a kind of ironic reversal of the three angels who arrive at the home of Abraham and Sarah. Saul isn't here to give news about birth—rather, he needs news about death. His request to the woman is: "Please divine for me (*kasami na li*) by an ancestor spirit, and raise up for me the one I shall say to you."[15] Saul's polite request uses the language of *kesem*, magic, rather than *sho'el*, divining or asking. Perhaps this is because he intuits the awkward similarity between *sho'el* (asking/divining), his name Saul/Sha'ul (the asked-for), and She'ol, the realm of the dead.

But the *ba'alat ov* is not a fool. Like a streetwise entrepreneur who can sniff out an impostor, she senses that something is not right. Perhaps the well-made clothes tip her off, or the courtly language. She says to the king: "You know what Saul has done; how he has banned the ancestor spirits and the familiar spirits from the land. Why are you laying a trap for my life, to get me killed?" Presumably, if her reputation has reached the king's courtiers such that they can recommend her, she does this work for people all the time. Yet in this case, she smells a rat. She seems to suspect she is being entrapped. And she is willing to speak up sharply to the three no doubt armed men who have arrived at her home. Already, we can sense that the *ba'alat ov* of En-dor is a significant personality.

Saul swears to her by God that "no one will call you to account for this." She must now suspect that he indeed is someone in authority. Consenting to his request, she asks: *Mi a'aleh lach*? "Whom shall I bring up for you?" Saul replies: "Bring up Samuel for me." The language of "up" is of course significant—the shades of the ancestors are under the ground. One goes "down" to She'ol, just as Jacob says: "I will go down mourning to my son in She'ol."[16] And, in reverse, one comes "up" from She'ol when summoned by the living.

Then, without any description of a ritual to summon Samuel's spirit, Samuel appears to the *ba'alat ov*. When the woman sees Samuel, she cries out and says to Saul: "You are Saul!" (We might notice that she says "Saul" and not "King Saul"—which suggests she is not very subservient, or that she is surprised.) Perhaps the biblical text is omitting to tell us what kind

---

[14] Leviticus 6:4

[15] I Samuel 28:8

[16] Genesis 37:35

of ritual such a practitioner might use to call a spirit. Or perhaps the text conveys that the *ba'alat ov* simply sees Samuel, without any ceremony or cajoling on her part, and this somehow lets her know that the one who has asked is King Saul. The medieval commentator Rashi suggests that she sees something unusual in the appearance of this shade—Rashi suggests that most spirits ascend upside down in form but Samuel is right-side-up.[17] Other readers of the text suggest that the appearance of Samuel dispels all deceit and Saul's disguise falls away.[18] But it might also be that the speed of Samuel's arrival suggests to the *ba'alat ov* that only the king could have called such a great prophet so quickly. Again, we see that she thinks fast on her feet. And the stakes, for her, have just gotten very high.

The king stops trying to hide who he is. "Don't be afraid," he says, presumably meaning that he does not intend to arrest or harm her. "What do you see?" We should note that there is an assumption that the spirit will appear visually. We should also note that Saul does not appear to see anything. The *ba'alat ov* is the one who can see Samuel's shade before her. Her report of what she sees is: *Elohim ra'iti olim min ha'aretz*—"I see divine beings coming up from the earth."

The use of the word *Elohim*, gods, here is complex. Normally, *Elohim* means "God" and takes a singular verb. Sometimes *Elohim* means denizens of the heavenly court, angels, gods, or perhaps other supernatural beings (as in Psalms 82, where God pronounces judgment among the *Elohim*, or in Genesis 6:3 where the "sons of divinities" are mentioned). In that case, the plural noun *Elohim* takes a plural verb. The verb here is plural, which suggests the second usage: gods, angels, or spirits.

We might read the *ba'alat ov*'s statement to mean that she sees many spirits from the underworld, Samuel being among them—that is, many ancestral entities have come through the portal to She'ol that she has opened. We might then imagine Samuel coming forward from a crowd. Or perhaps we might understand the plural *Elohim* to be a respectful plural. If we read the text that way, the *ba'alat ov* sees one supernatural being—Samuel—arising from the earth, and refers to that being with the reverential term *Elohim* as well as a plural verb.[19] We might imagine that here we are seeing a glimpse of the *ba'alat ov*'s spiritual life. The beings she reveres dwell below her, in the ground. She seeks her prophetic power from the ancestors and the earth,

---

[17] Rashi to I Samuel 28:12

[18] Reis, Pamela Tamarkin. "Eating the Blood: Saul and the Witch of Endor, in *Journal for the Study of the Old Testament*, no. 73 (March 1, 1997), p. 3-23.

[19] Rashi notices the issue with the plural verb, and comments on this verse that Samuel brought Moses with him to plead his case in case God had summoned him to judgment!

not from the heavens. This, perhaps, is why she is Saul's last refuge: God has refused him, but the ancestors, perhaps, might answer.

"What does he look like?" Saul presses. "An old man comes up," she says, "and he is wrapped in a robe (*me'il*)."[20] The robe, presumably, is the tip-off that this is Samuel. This is touchingly reminiscent of Samuel's early life—Hannah would make her son a robe and bring it to him every year during the annual pilgrimage.[21] It is almost as if Samuel is still wearing the robe his mother made him.

Yet the robe is also ominously reminiscent of Saul's last moments with Samuel, when Samuel turned in disgust to leave and Saul grabbed at the corner of Samuel's robe. When the robe tore, Samuel promised that it was a sign: God had torn the kingship away from Saul and given it to someone worthier.[22] So the appearance of the robe, while it identifies Samuel, is not a good omen.

And indeed, Samuel is immediately angry and unkind. "Why have you disturbed me to bring me up?" the deceased prophet complains. (And this does indeed sound like the usually irascible Samuel.) One gets the sense that he was asleep in She'ol, or resting, and a summons back to the world of the living is entirely unwelcome. (One wonders whether the rest of the spirits the witch summons are equally annoyed, or if this is particular to Samuel.)

Saul pleads that the Philistines are attacking, and God has refused to answer Saul by prophets or dreams. "I have called you to tell me what I am to do," Saul concludes with pathos.[23] We might accuse the king of being craven and unkingly here—his pleading with the offended Samuel hardly conveys an imposing authority figure. Indeed, Saul is frequently insecure and unstable throughout his reign. Yet we might also see Saul's request as concern for his people—what will happen to his soldiers, to his family, to the Israelite tribes, after a massive defeat by the Philistines? Saul is still king and responsible for the people's defense: how can he win the battle without God's support?

But Samuel has no comfort for Saul. "Why do you ask me, since YHWH has turned away from you and become your enemy?" the angry shade chastises the king. Samuel repeats the original prophecy that David will supplant Saul: "YHWH has torn the kingship out of your hands and has given

---

[20] I Samuel 28:14

[21] I Samuel 2:19

[22] I Samuel 15:27

[23] I Samuel 28:15

it to your fellow, David."[24] ("Fellow," *re'echa*, can also mean "friend" and might well be in quotation marks.) And the language of tearing invites the reader to imagine that Samuel is still wearing the robe Saul tore when Samuel made the prophecy the first time. Nothing has changed, except that now the news has gotten even worse.

Samuel again blames Saul for not obeying God's command to wipe out every last Amalekite. (Saul spared the Amalekite king and the cattle, but killed everyone else, so Samuel's fury at Saul's "disobedience" might be judged a little out of proportion.[25]) And then Samuel delivers a new prophecy: "YHWH will give [the portion of] Israel who is with you into the hands of the Philistines. Tomorrow you and your sons will be with me, and the army of Israel YHWH will give into the hands of the Philistines."[26] Samuel announces that Saul will die the next day along with his sons and all the warriors who have supported him. The very next day, they will all be citizens of the underworld.

This is terrible, bitter news for Saul. Saul has brought to his family and people not glory, but death and defeat. It is the end of his hope for a dynasty, and practically amounts to the erasure of his kingship. It is the worst possible outcome for him, and the message is delivered without a shred of empathy.

We should note that throughout the scene, Samuel clearly retains his personality, his mission, and his human motivations. While many biblical texts seem to suggest that She'ol is a place of gloom and nothingness, even a place of silence and oblivion, in this passage Samuel seems vibrantly himself. And, he has access to new information about Saul's death, so it appears he is still a prophet, even in death. This makes one wonder if in fact She'ol was a more lively place than Psalms 115:17 suggests when it says: "the dead do not praise God, nor do any who go down into silence." That the Bible is incurious about She'ol doesn't mean that ordinary Israelites were. If the people indeed had a practice of leaving food for those who had died, this implies that they expected to be in a relationship with their dead in a personal way. This passage may well reflect those folk beliefs and practices.

After his cruel prophecy, Samuel seems to disappear. Saul falls prostrate onto the ground, terrified by what he has heard. "And also he had no strength in him, for he had eaten no bread all that day and all night."[27] It might be that Saul has fasted prior to asking for the *ba'alat ov* to do her

---

[24] I Samuel 28:17

[25] I Samuel 15:7-9

[26] I Samuel 28:19

[27] I Samuel 28:20

channeling work, as a ritual matter; we see fasting as a propitiatory act often in the Bible.[28] Or, maybe he has simply been too upset to eat. Now, he seems near death in his despair. And, he's contacted the world of the dead, which may leave him with one foot in She'ol and one foot out.

The Ba'alat Ov as Midwife of Death

With Saul paralyzed on the floor of the house, Saul's two courtiers do nothing. They may or may not have seen or heard anything, and they seem to have no notion of how to comfort their king. But the *ba'alat ov* acts. It is unclear whether she has heard what Samuel says: it is possible she sees but does not hear and Saul hears but does not see.[29] But it is also possible, even likely, that she knows exactly what Samuel has just said to Saul. She cannot do anything about the king's fate. But she can do something about his state of mind.

She says to Saul: "Your handmaid listened to you. I took my life in my hands and obeyed the words you had spoken to me. Now, you listen to the voice of your handmaid. I will put before you some bread. Eat, and then you will have strength to go on your way."[30] Again, we have the sense of the woman's strong personality: she is not afraid to address the king, though now her language is somewhat more deferential.[31] She invites him to eat the food she will prepare. And she indirectly suggests that just as she "took her life in her hands," she now offers the king life through the meal he will eat from her hands.[32]

Why does she do this? Maybe she intuits that he is famished and cannot go on any further without nourishment. Maybe she is afraid the king will die in her house and get her in further trouble, and she is trying to get him moving. Maybe she offers hospitality so that the king is less likely to blame her and act violently toward her because of the unfavorable prophecy he has received. Maybe she simply seeks to show him some kindness.

Or, maybe she is trying to bring him back into his body after contact

---

[28] Judges 20:26; II Samuel 12:16 and 21; I Kings 21:27

[29] Rashi draws this conclusion in his commentary on I Samuel 28:14.

[30] I Sam. 28:21-22

[31] However, we should note that unlike the wise woman of Tekoa (II Sam. 14:9) or Abigail (I Sam. 25), she never calls him "my lord" or "my lord the king."

[32] A similar point is made in Simon, Uriel. "A Balanced Story: The Stern Prophet and the Kind Witch," in *Prooftexts* vol. 8 no. 2 (May 1988), p. 165. Simon imagines the witch to be saying that she has a right to the king's life. Yet perhaps, she might be saying that as she took her life in her hands, she will now give the king life through her hands—or at least strength enough to face his own life.

with a spirit, by offering food to ground him. She may even be seeking to guide him toward the world of the dead, since Samuel has foretold how soon Saul will need to go there. This last possibility may be reflected in the words she says: *Yihyeh bach koach ki telech badarech*—"there will be strength in you as you go on your way."[33] The king does have a difficult road to walk in the next twenty-four hours. She suggests he eat before the journey—and maybe the journey she means is not his journey away from her home, but his journey to She'ol. She is, after all, the keeper of the *ein dor*, the spring of generations, and Saul is now perhaps closer to the dead than the living. Someone, she perhaps concludes, must help him to accept the passage to come. While no one else in Saul's orbit offers him any kindness or comforting ritual between this moment and his death, the *ba'alat ov* feeds him and speaks kindly to him, strengthening him for the journey.

Indeed, she slaughters a calf for him, and she likely is not wealthy enough to have many calves. This may indicate that she is making a sacrifice, an offering. It may be that the food is ritual food, food she prepares with magical properties to aid his journey between worlds. Spirit practitioners in a variety of traditions use meals and eating as a way to be in community with the spirits and also as a concluding "grounding" element to ritual. Some scholars understand the *ba'alat ov* to be conducting some kind of ritual to the ancestors to preserve her and Saul's safety, and/or concluding a covenant with the king via the meal in order to keep herself safe from his retribution.[34] These purposes may not be mutually exclusive.

The *ba'alat ov* of course is aware that Saul is the one who forbade her profession, and she aids him even despite this—perhaps because that is in her best interest, or perhaps because she sees that as her job. Scholar Uriel Simon notes that the witch is portrayed as kind; the text issues no moral judgment of her, and she exercises a motherly care for a person in a bad situation.[35] Simon also notes that she is the only one to be kind to Saul.

At first Saul will not eat, but then he gets up from the ground and sits on the bed, and eats the bread she has baked and the meat she has prepared. The *ba'alat ov* is, in a very real sense, feeding him his last meal. There is no one else to ease this news for him, no wife, child, or ally who offers him comfort. The *ba'alat ov* is, to use an anachronistic term, his death doula—a midwife to his dying process.

---

[33] I Samuel 28:22

[34] Reis, Pamela Tamarkin. "Eating the Blood: Saul and the Witch of Endor, in *Journal for the Study of the Old Testament*, no. 73 (March 1, 1997), p. 3-23.

[35] Simon, Uriel. "A Balanced Story: The Stern Prophet and the Kind Witch," in *Prooftexts* vol. 8 no. 2 (May 1988), p. 167.

We can, as scholar Diane Sharon has suggested, see this as the reverse of the story of Abraham and the three angels. In that story, three angels come, are fed a slaughtered animal and bread by their hosts, and bring a message that Sarah is about to get pregnant and give birth. Here, three men come, are fed a slaughtered animal and bread by their hosts, and receive a message that Saul is about to die.[36] Sharon understands this inversion as a condemnation of Saul—an anti-covenant that shows how far he is from God.

Yet the reverse pattern may also indicate something else. Both events—the annunciation to Abraham and the visit to En-dor—involve souls moving back and forth between realms: the soul of Isaac arrives, the soul of Saul leaves. Each event is accompanied by a feast with meat and bread. This parallel suggests that perhaps the portals of birth and of death are not so different. One has the sense that there is, indeed an *ein dor*, a well of generation, that opens at these moments. While the priests may keep far from birth and death, the *ba'alat ov* seems to represent forces that are inextricably entwined with these liminal transitions.

It could be regarded as a blessing that Saul encounters the *ba'alat ov* at this desperate moment. Saul's tragic character is that he tries hard to be a good king, and yet is judged a failure. He loses his family, friends, and supporters, and is supplanted by one of his court favorites. God and Samuel, after anointing Saul and raising him from an ordinary country life to be king, utterly abandon him. At the end, when the battle is lost and his sons are dead or about to die, even Saul's arms-bearer refuses to help Saul kill himself. According to I Samuel 31:4, he dies by falling on his own sword.[37] Were it not for the *ba'alat ov* of En-dor, Saul would have no one to show him any compassion in the last days of his life or help him on his journey to the ancestors. In a sense, the text allows mercy to Saul—not directly from heaven, but rather from the earth beneath, through the agency of the *ba'alat ov*. It is an unauthorized mercy, in the Bible's view, but mercy nevertheless.

---

[36] This parallel has been noted by Diane Sharon in her work on the pattern of doom in the story of the Witch of En-dor (Sharon, Diane, *Patterns of Destiny: Narrative Structures of Foundation and Doom in the Hebrew Bible* [Winona Lake, IN: Eisenbrauns, 2002], p. 182). Sharon suggests that the covenant between Saul and the *ba'alat ov* is patterned on the story of the angels' visit to Abraham and Sarah to create irony and show Saul's distance from God.

[37] In II Samuel 1, an Amalekite claims to have finished Saul off at Saul's request; it's unclear if he's telling the truth. If he is, it's a further irony that Saul spares the Amalekite king and an Amalekite kills Saul.

The Ba'alat Ov as Wise Woman and Bridge Between Worlds

The character of the *ba'alat ov* may in fact reflect the Israelite experience of wise women, mediums or witches who channeled spirits of the dead for ancient Israelites. Scholar Michael Moore points out that the Bible depicts Israelite wise women, including the wise woman of Avel, the wise woman of Tekoa, Abigail, and the witch of En-dor, as mediators of spiritual and political conflicts.[38] In consoling Saul and feeding him a covenantal meal that perhaps seeks to bring him some peace, the *ba'alat ov* of En-dor mediates between the spirit world and the human world. She is the bridge between the *Elohim* who come out of the earth, and the humans who seek knowledge from She'ol, the asking place.

I Samuel 31, in addition to showing us something about how the wise women of ancient Israel did their work, may also point out a truth about society: authorities condemn magic, witchcraft, etc., until they themselves need help. While we could read this story as a condemnation of Saul for his weakness in chasing after Samuel's approval even after the prophet is dead, it's not impossible we might see this story as a polemic against corrupt officials who ban certain practices but make use of those practices when they themselves are desperate. We can see this as similar to politicians today who get caught doing things in private that they have legislated against in public. The irony of the story in I Samuel is that it's the very person Saul has harmed with his legislation that shows him kindness in the end. If we focus on this aspect of the text, we could read the tale not only as a critique of Saul, but as a critique of priestly and kingly power—and perhaps even a subtle defense of the wise women, priestesses and mediums of ancient Israel.

The association of women with the underworld did not end with the Bible. In later Jewish life, women continue to be mediators of the realms of ancestral spirits. Women serve as professional mourners in the Bible, Talmud, and beyond.[39] A sixteenth century Yiddish manuscript describes mourning women who care for the dead and "stare out from their mourners' headdresses like owls…"[40] In early modern Jewish sources, it is predominantly women who become channels for the spirits of the dead.[41] Susan

---

[38] Moore, Michael S. "Wise Women or Wisdom Woman? A Biblical Study of Women's Roles," in *Restoration Quarterly*, vol. 35.3 (1993), p. 147-158.

[39] Jeremiah 9:16-18; Mishnah, Moed Katan 3:9.

[40] Fox, Harry and Lewis, Justin Jaron. *Many Pious Women: Edition and Translation.* (Berlin: Degruyter, 2011), p. 234.

[41] Chajes, J. H. *Between Worlds: Dybbuks, Exorcists, and Early Modern Judaism* (Philadelphia: University of Pennsylvania Press, 2003), p. 97-118.

Sered studied contemporary Yemenite and Kurdish Jewish women living in Jerusalem and wrote: "The women understand the concept of family in an extraordinarily broad sense, indicating descendants and ancestors, both biological and mythical. Seeing themselves as the link between the generations, old women are responsible for soliciting the help of ancestors whenever their descendants are faced with problems."[42] The role of the *ba'alat ov* has continued to find expression within Jewish life.

While the practices of the *ba'alat ov* of En-dor in I Samuel 28 can't be said to be biblically sanctioned, neither are they portrayed as grotesque. In fact, she is a sympathetic character. She intelligently sizes up the situation, does what she says she can do, and shows compassion to a desperate man even though he has done her harm. In the process, the *ba'alat ov* helps Saul to approach his death. Her role as midwife of She'ol, while portrayed as a forbidden practice, is also depicted as a needed kindness to an abandoned king.[43]

While Samuel speaks harshly with God's authority, the *ba'alat ov* speaks—with the authority of the earth? The ancestors? The narrative does not completely specify, but perhaps there is a hint in the name of her town: the well of generations. The *ba'alat ov*'s voice within the text, her sense of what is right, is different than Samuel's. She is not bound by the decree that Saul be rejected and friendless. Her tending of the portal of life and death comes with gentleness and without judgment. Hers is a separate spiritual realm, one that seems to exist in uneasy relationship with the divine realm on high.

---

[42] Sered, Susan. *Women as Ritual Experts: The Religious Lives of Elderly Jewish Women in Jerusalem* (Oxford, UK: Oxford University Press, 1992), p. 18.

[43] Simon, Uriel. "A Balanced Story: The Stern Prophet and the Kind Witch," in *Prooftexts* vol. 8 no. 2 (May 1988), p. 167.

A Rabbi Muses About "Entering the Zone" at Grateful Dead Concerts and at Synagogue Worship Services

Jeff Hoffman

At the end of May, 2017, I saw the Grateful Dead documentary "Long Strange Trip" on its debut night at the Capital Theater in Portchester, New York. It lasted four hours in addition to an intermission in the middle. (Since then, it has been available as a four-part series on Amazon video.) I wanted to see it there because The Capital Theater is kind of the East Coast headquarters of the Dead experience, so I'd be among friends. I'd be among the cognoscenti, so to speak. I went to see it there with my wife, Laurie, who first turned me on to the Dead in Jerusalem during our junior year of college, before we were married. We've been to many Dead concerts together since, and we've each seen a few apart from each other as well. But we're not Deadheads. Let me be clear about that. We've never gone to even as few as two concerts, two nights in a row, let alone a whole run at a venue. We've never abandoned our quotidian lives and followed the band around. But we have seen them a lot. You could say we're committed Grateful Dead fans, but we're really not Deadheads. For quite a few years, we'd see them each time they came to New York, which sometimes was three times a year, like the three pilgrimage festivals of the Torah. It was like a pilgrimage. It still is, in some ways.

At the end of the documentary, I felt that that the film maker, Amir Bar-Lev, a Californian with Israeli parents, and who spoke at the screening that night, achieved some great things. Authenticity, above all. And that's quite a feat for a musical experience that, for the dedicated, has a texture and feel as familiar as one's own family reunions. But I also felt that he didn't do what a review of the movie I read had claimed he did, namely, give the uninitiated a real sense of what a Grateful Dead concert was like. I don't blame the film maker for this; he never claimed that was his purpose. But as soon as the film concluded, I felt that I wanted to try and express my sense of what a Dead concert was like, for me at least. And in doing so, I got to musing about Jewish worship as well.

What was so great about Grateful Dead concerts? The magic didn't hit me at the first concert I attended, even though it was at the Dead's home arena, The Oakland Auditorium, in Oakland, California. It took place in

1979 or thereabouts, when we were in our mid-twenties. Laurie and I were married not long before and we were visiting her mother who lived in the Bay area at the time. What did hit me at that first concert was the surprising fact that there was no opening act. I had been used to lesser artists performing before the featured band at the rock concerts I had already attended. Probably the best concert I'd seen up to then was in the summer of 1972 before my senior year in high school, when the Rolling Stones played at Madison Square Garden in New York City, where I lived. The opening act was Stevie Wonder. In the middle of Stevie's act, a couple of fashion model types took his arms and escorted him from the keyboard to the drum set, and in the next song, he played a long drum solo, the likes of which I'd never heard before. I'm pretty sure that Richie, the drummer in our band at the time, was among the friends that accompanied me to the Stones concert, and we were both quite impressed by Stevie's drum chops. But it was the Stones I loved, and whose music I knew very well. By the end of that concert at the Garden, I had been brought so deeply into the zone that when I travelled home late that night on the Long Island Railroad, I rode outside, between the railroad cars with my shirt off, just enjoying the cool wind on a hot summer night. I developed a case of bronchitis as a result. But I had been in the zone! Sometimes you do crazy things when you're carried away like that. I was not the type—whether in High School or even in college—to take my shirt off in public or to ride between the cars of a train. I've always been more the type to go to sleep at a sensible time and do my homework diligently. The Stones got me to a place where I was willing to throw caution to the wind. A place where I felt altogether at home with myself and the world. That didn't happen very often. And it was a transcendent experience I wished to return to.

How the Dead got me to that place so consistently for years, and what that place, that "zone" feels like, is what I want to try and explain. I should add that I am a rabbi who was the spiritual leader of congregations for 23 years until 2004, and served as a professor of Jewish liturgy during more than half of that period. For the last 16 years, since I left the pulpit, I have continued to serve as a professor, and for the last 11 of those years I have served as an administrator at a Jewish seminary. And that a few years ago, I taught and participated in jam sessions at a weekend retreat meant to combine love of Judaism with love of the Grateful Dead. A reporter who wrote an article about that weekend for Tablet couldn't have painted a more negative picture of the retreat, but by her own admission, she came to the event with an unenthusiastic view of both Judaism and the Dead: http://www.tabletmag.com/jewish-arts-and-culture/music/126053/prayer-for-deadheads. I wasn't as down on the event as she was, and in fact, I will contribute, in the course of this essay, some thoughts about Jewish prayer that came to me as I reflected on the experience of Grateful Dead music.

"There is nothing like a Grateful Dead concert" the bumper stickers say. And a hand-made sign at an early concert turned into a commonly repeated idiom on the same theme: "They're not the best at what they do, they're the only ones who do what they do." I don't hold with these declarations. The Stones did it for me way back then. I know a rabbi, a mentor of mine in writing about Jewish prayer, for whom certain classical music concerts do it for him. I'm sure there are many paths to the sublime state I'm talking about, and not only through music. Of course, watching news programs with the crawl of the latest developments rolling at the bottom probably is not among them. But all sorts of activities can bring people there, activities from movement-centered endeavors like dance and sports to at-rest pursuits including prayer and meditation, and such seemingly passive events as watching an extraordinary film. When any of these experiences clicks for the participant, it deserves a bumper sticker. The Dead's music—anyone's music—is not the only path. But the Dead's music, and prayer, did it for me more often than anything, though each in its own way. And, I hasten to add, I am not a druggie. I never was. I've always been too chicken.

I do regularly enter a kind of blissful state through prayer and meditation. When it comes to worship services, while I've enjoyed communal singing, I have always been most drawn to the silent, meditative portions. There is a difference in the kind of zone that I often experience in prayer and the kind that I enter at Dead shows: the transcendence in prayer tends not to be quite as deep or produce as long-lasting an afterglow. That isn't necessarily a negative judgment on prayer, but rather a natural consequence of the fact that my prayer practice (into which I weave meditation) is a daily routine whereas my attending Dead shows is at most a three-time-a-year affair, and usually less often. There are many benefits to a daily spiritual practice. However, one of the detriments of a regular spiritual practice is that the zone one enters on any given day tends to be more low-key, yielding fewer epiphanies and lightning bolts (which themselves are one of the Dead's iconic symbols), and they don't usually clear the head to the same extent as less frequent spiritual experiences. Another major difference is that the worship services on the Sabbath in the large synagogue I attend, led by very talented clergy, do not offer an experience that comes close to the excitement of a rock concert in a large arena. Again, that's not a complaint. I would not want to attend a rock concert on a weekly basis. That would be sensory overload. At Dead shows, like most rock concerts, the music is LOUD, the drums are pounding, the vocals are audible to tens of thousands of people at once. You can sometimes feel the vibrations of the bass in your sternum. And I *like* all of that! It provides a kind of exhilaration and thrill that I welcome. But I wouldn't want that kind of thrill on a weekly basis. In any case, it would lose a good deal of its thrill on such a frequent basis. So, while my prayer practice is a wonderful regular spiritual routine, I do not expect, and I do not get, the deep, head-clearing, pleasure and delight that Dead concerts often yield. What I do get is a consistent, if brief, connection to God.

My friend, Alan, also a committed Dead fan, pointed out that part of the formula to achieve that transcendent state at Dead concerts—and really at many bands' concerts—is the shared familiarity many of us have with the band's music. The ability to sing along, to anticipate and appreciate both personal and communal favorite moments, as well as the pleasure in savoring how the variations, the harmonies, the solos, and the electronic effects add layers of richness and pleasure. A number of years ago, the fellow helping me pick out a new effects-pedal I wanted for my electric guitar told me how to emulate a certain sound that Jerry Garcia used. I paid attention to those sorts of things at Dead concerts just as a singer might pay more attention to the overtones of the harmony.

I remember attending a Grateful Dead show at the Garden before I really had become familiar with the collective highs and lows in the flow of their concerts, but I did know a lot of the songs. At that early stage in my Dead fandom, I had learned a few of the songs from FM radio but more from sitting outside on the terraces that connected the honeycomb configuration of the Resnick dorms at Hebrew University in Jerusalem during junior year of college, playing them on my acoustic guitar using Laurie's Grateful Dead songbook. At this particular concert, the band was playing "Lady With A Fan," a rambling take on the old theme from English ballads of two heroes vying for the love of a fair maiden: a staple of second set expansiveness. As the song approached its conclusion, I could feel a heightened sense in the more experienced crowd. I realized afterward that it was the anticipation of whether the band would segue, as they sometimes did, into the even lengthier and more spacey "Terrapin Station." And when the band did, in fact, follow through with "Terrapin"—signaled by the first word of that second song sung by Garcia, "Inspiration"—that word was accompanied by a roar of voices (mostly male voices; there always seemed to be more men than women), applause and fists pumping the air that signaled to me that this was a definite high in the rhythm of the evening. I caught on.

I've witnessed parallels to that sort of high in the rhythm of a rock concert at other bands' performances, including, for example, at Springsteen concerts. But I only ever attended two Springsteen concerts. I probably attended about 25 Dead concerts during Jerry's lifetime, and then perhaps another dozen or 15 of the various Dead configurations since his death in

1995. After a while, I got to know the Dead oeuvre so well that at concerts, Alan and I would occasionally indulge in the widespread competition to be the first to identify the song; within the first few seconds, if possible. Again, the men seemed to enjoy that kind of competition more than the women.

While it is true that joining the community of those who knew enough songs to feel really part of the fellowship and the rhythm of the evening enhanced the possibility of getting into the zone, it wasn't enough by itself. At least not for me. There was more to it.

When I entered the zone, the zone overtook me. It felt like it came from outside of myself. Though it is certainly not a prophetic state, this divine sensation reminds me of Ezekiel's frequent expression, "The hand of God was upon me." When it happened to me, it was usually during the second of the two sets the Dead would commonly play. By then, I had already had the whole first set under my belt—maybe an hour and a half of music. And in that first set, the thrill and excitement of loud rock 'n roll music that I love would usually have helped change my consciousness some and set me on the way to feeling pretty good. After the first set, a 25-30 minute intermission would ensue and then the second set would begin. By then, I had long since settled comfortably into the space. I'd gotten used to the hard, plastic seat, to the propensities of the various people in the seats around me, to the good looking, the weird looking, the loud, the quiet, the gyrating, the motionless, the stoned, the drunk, the sober. I had grown used to the view of the band from my location. I was used to the relative darkness of the arena and the super brightness of the spot-lit stage and the light show behind it. I had already abandoned my binoculars; they were for earlier in the show when my mindset was to focus on the movements of the band members.

There was something else, too: "Drums" (sometimes called "Rhythm Devils") followed by "Space." Toward the middle of every second set of music, the Dead inserted "Drums" and "Space." "Drums" was a long drum solo conducted by the Dead's two drummers, Billy Kreutzman and Mickey Hart (the one Jewish member of the band). This is not a token drum solo; we're talking 15-20 minutes. As the years went on, the instrumentation of the drum solos became more and more sophisticated, mainly as a result of Mickey's interest in world music and electronic music. The two whirling musicians would eventually be surrounded by dozens of percussion instruments of every kind, both acoustic and electronic. Some were set as usual on the floor, many were suspended from a huge, circular, metal frame. And they played them sitting, standing, crouched down, straight up, sideways, any which way. "Drums" would then morph into "Space." This happened as the rest of the band came back onto the stage, picked up their instruments and played another 15 minutes or so of atonal, spaced-out, eerie, electronic music. This music was usually slow of tempo, and while there could be occasional loud high or low notes, the tone was more subdued than the rest of the two sets of music.

I was never really into "Drums" and "Space." Laurie always enjoyed them, closed her eyes and meditated. Many fans seemed to share my reaction to these segments of Dead concerts because crowds of them could be seen streaming down the aisles to the bathrooms or to buy drinks and snacks or just to take a break into the well-lit walkways surrounding the concert space of the arena. Even though I wasn't into these parts of the concert, I didn't leave; I'd hang out and I would usually find myself in a kind of half awake, half asleep, dreamy state. During the years when I occasionally smoked a pipe—a tobacco pipe (which coincided with the years in which smoking indoors was permitted), I'd light up. Often enough, I'd be thinking through stresses of the past days or weeks. Somehow, by the end of "Space" I'd find that I'd actually transcended whatever sting remained of those stresses. It was kind of like what I'd undergo at the beginning of a vacation. Many of us can't just automatically go into vacation mode immediately on arriving at the hotel or the beach or the resort. My father, who was his own boss in a factory that made huge can-sealing machines, used to take only two weeks of vacation each year. My mother always said that it took my father the first week just to calm down. When I go on vacation, I, too, usually have to work through whatever tensions I still carried with me from the months of work since my last vacation. But at Dead concerts, after experiencing the evening up to and through "Drums" and "Space," I was able to speed up the de-stressing and processing that naturally occur at the beginning of a vacation. All of that would set me up for the magical moments to follow.

For me, the most enchanting and captivating moments began when the band gradually transitioned from the amorphous cacophony of "Space" into the beginnings of a slowly recognizable song from their repertoire. That's when I usually entered the zone.

It would start when I could just begin to make out what song was emerging from "Space." One time, it was "Eyes of the World." The lyrics are overtly spiritual; I've included study of this song one time or another in every Jewish institution in which I've taught to stimulate discussion of contemporary expressions of other-worldliness. But entry into the zone has been stimulated by other kinds of songs as well. "St. Stephen," for example. Well, that one, too, has overtly religious themes. OK, "Bird Song" has done it too. "Bird Song," I recently learned from the 2015 film "Janis: Little Girl Blue," was written by Jerry Garcia and his lyricist, Robert Hunter, in memory of Janis Joplin. Its imagery is ethereal and romantic, not overtly religious…

although that song contains the lyric "sleep in the stars." Truth is, I'm hard pressed to posit a clear distinction between the spiritual/religious and the poetic/romantic.

In any case, at this relatively late point in the concert, once the formlessness of "Space" gave way to a recognizable song, the hand of the music was upon me. I would begin connecting entirely with it. Everything else—which was most of my view since I rarely scored seats up front—faded away. It was still all there, that woman who danced up a storm, the guy yelling, and I mean shrieking, "JERRY!" as if Garcia could actually hear him (there was always at least one shrieker, and no other band member's name was invoked in this way, no matter where one sat, and it was always a guy; what's that about? The profound scholar of enigmatic sexual imagery in Jewish mysticism, Elliot Wolfson, could, no doubt, comment knowledgably). But all of that died away and it was just the music and me. Time slowed down. In fact, my usual neurotic concern with time, especially being on time, and worrying about how long it would take to drive home late at night after the concert, all of that disappeared. It didn't matter. In fact, when I entered this state—almost always sometime in the latter part of the evening in the second set—NOTHING MATTERED. EVERYTHING WAS ALRIGHT. This is what I mean by "the zone." It was a kind of bliss. When I'd be in that groove, my entire world consisted of the darkened, cavernous space of the arena, the several tens of thousands of fans, the band, and THE MUSIC, and all was aright in the world. At that point, there was nothing as delicious as "the sound of sweet guitars" (a lyric from a post-Jerry Dead song). When I'd nod my head up and down and side to side in rhythm to whatever song was then playing, the singer's words all rang true, and each musician's contribution, note after note, moment after moment, all blended so smoothly. It all added up to Beautiful Music.

But like many Dead fans, I was moved most by the long, improvised, rambling solos of Jerry Garcia's guitar. No two of his solos were the same. But there were patterns. Jerry loved playing at the very high end of the neck of the guitar producing dozens and dozens of staccato high notes, *very* high notes. In the hands of lesser guitarists, the effect could be too trebly, and painful to the ear. Not in Jerry's hands. He wasn't into treble. His high notes were *soft*. As he ascended the neck of the guitar, he brought me along with him to the heights. It's no accident that in many of the Dead's concert movies and videos (with Jerry often putting in the lion's share of post-concert editing), the images of the musicians morphed into images of outer space when they entered the musical jams that this venerable jam band pioneered. And the dominant instrument in the vast majority of those jams was Jerry's guitar. When I was in that state, I was "high." It wasn't drug induced; it was music induced. But it was also induced by everything else that contributed to that moment: familiarity with the band's songs—ultimately, extreme familiarity—the dark space, being removed from work, from the news, from the usual stresses of life, three hours or more of loud, live music from my favorite band that preceded that moment, including sitting through "Drums" and "Space."

If that kind of contentment could be brought on by alcohol or drugs, I'm not surprised that people return to that kind of inducement again and again. For me, the deep second set of Dead concerts brought me there.

Of course, this band consciously tried to create a communal experience of transcendence. The documentary about the Dead did bring out that point. One of the Dead's songs, "The Music Never Stopped," also makes that point:

> …The sun went down in honey
> And the moon came up in wine
> You know stars were spinnin' dizzy
> Lord the band kept us so busy
> We forgot about the time.
> They're a band beyond description
> Like Jehovah's favorite choir
> People joining hand in hand while
> The music played the band
> Lord they're setting us on fire…
> Keep on dancing through the daylight
> Greet the morning air with song
> No one's noticed, but the band's all packed and gone
> Was it ever there at all?

That is what the band always aims for: "Lord the band kept us so busy, we forgot about the time…The music played the band."

Of all the shows I went to over the years, I only encountered one at which there was a minyan for *Ma'ariv* (the brief evening service) during the intermission. It was at the New Jersey Performing Arts Center, and it was post-Jerry. It added a dimension of a community within a community. That minyan served the purpose of fulfilling the mitzvah of davening, but dare I say that for the purpose of providing a spiritual experience, at least for me, perhaps it wasn't necessary.

In the last few years, I haven't entered that blissful state as much at Dead shows. I'm not sure why. Of course, Jerry Garcia has been dead for over 20 years. I remember going to the first concert the band gave a year or so after Jerry died, wondering if the magic would still be there. I remember enjoying the concert, feeling that the band still put forth great music, as different as the experience had to be without Jerry. I cannot recall if I entered the zone at that concert or not. I have entered it at Dead shows in the post-Jerry era. But, as I say, not as often, and less and less over the last few years. While I will always miss Jerry, I have been enormously impressed by the musicianship of all of the guitarists that have taken the lead guitar role. Could it be that the much shortened "Drums" and "Space" has affected my ability to find the bliss? Or could it be that, like many fans of the Grateful Dead, I'm just getting older? Older or not, I still love rock 'n roll, and I still love playing it loud—both as an amateur rock musician and as a "player" of recorded music—though I have less and less tolerance for crowded venues, crowded parking lots and late nights out.

I have been thinking about how recently it's also been harder for me to derive the kind of spiritual joy I used to get regularly from attending synagogue services. I'm not sure that there's a connection to my diminished spiritual experience at Dead shows, but maybe there is. Too much familiarity with the material in both arenas? Perhaps.

The second century sage, Rabbi Eliezer, and the 21st century Jewish liturgy writer Marcia Falk (*The Book of Blessings*), both held that a worship service should not be the same thing every day. However, that did not become part of Jewish tradition; the opposite did. The traditional service emphasizes, well, tradition: saying the same things every day while de-emphasizing the need for immediate spiritual meaning. This was codified in Jewish legal compendiums: Deep devotion in prayer—truly connecting to the divine through the service—was barely required: out of the whole service, only the Shema (*Shulhan Arukh, Orah Hayyim* 61:1-2) and the first blessing of the prayer known as the *Amidah* require deep intention (*Shulhan Arukh, Orah Hayyim* 101:1). And even the requirement regarding the *Amidah* is disputed (see the gloss of the *Rema* on the previously cited source). What is required for the rest of the service is… saying the traditional words. Just saying them. Nevertheless, that worked for me consistently for many years. It still occasionally works for me, but not nearly as often. Furthermore, Jewish worship has accreted to itself more and more prayers over the centuries while few have been deleted. Therefore, there are more and more… words.

I wonder if the experience at Dead shows might have something to teach leaders of Jewish worship. While it is true that the Dead rarely played the same song over a short series of concerts, they certainly did repeat dozens, actually hundreds, of their songs over the long run. These were kept fresh not only because of the constantly changing set list, but also because when they did replay the same song, they never replayed it in exactly the same way. Now, I'm not suggesting that this pattern be cut and pasted to a synagogue service precisely the way it is followed by the Dead. Nor am I suggesting that the worship service should be cleared of all prayers that repeat. A certain kind of comfort may be attained by encountering the same prayers on a weekly, and even on a daily, basis. The main lesson I wish that worship leaders would take from the Dead experience is to consciously and deliberately design each prayer service with the goal of creating experiences of transcendence for the participants. I would submit that the vast majority of Jewish clergy do not aim for this even regarding the smallest portion of the services they conduct. And it is understandable why not: We have inherited a system in which even a typical service, whether traditional in style or not, on, say, a Shabbat morning, contains many, many prayers. It is quite difficult to sustain a sense of the transcendent over the course of many different prayers. We have also inherited a system in which, as I pointed out earlier, the codes of Jewish law have, for centuries, given up on promoting anything but the most minimal expectations of deep devotion in a prayer experience. That inheritance influences not only those sectors of the Jewish community that adhere to the medieval codes, but also the more liberal branches that do not. Let me add that while my words may be taken as harsh criticism of rabbis, cantors, and others who plan and run Jewish services, I, in fact, have enormous respect and empathy for those who conduct Jewish services. I've spent years on both sides of the pulpit and I know how easy it is to aim criticism at prayer leaders. My goal here is to share my musings in a spirit of collegiality and perhaps to stimulate some thought about the goals of Jewish worship.

I find that those places of worship that view spiritual transcendence as the main goal of prayer come closest to providing the kind of experience that I, at least, am after. This kind of goal is shared most consistently in Hasidic and Renewal circles (though there are other limitations to the style of worship in both of those circles). I frequently get the sense outside of those circles, and especially in non-Orthodox congregations, that prayer leaders try their best to reduce the amount of silent prayer to the absolute minimum. It feels to me as if they are afraid participants will get bored if more than a couple of minutes or so of silent prayer is offered. The common wisdom seems to be to increase communal singing to the absolute maximum, the more upbeat the better. I don't have a problem with communal singing, upbeat or downbeat. But what I'm after in a worship service is communing with God, cultivating the spirit, penetrating beyond my customary consciousness, connecting with the soul. If not the deep, lasting sense of transcendence available through the power of rock 'n roll at a Dead show, then the quieter, more peaceful and serene "normal mysticism" (Max Kadushin's venerable phrase) of prayerful meditation. Just as at a Dead show, music and singing can, indeed, bring people to that spiritual level. But unless the service is planned with the goal of reaching that level—and it seems to me that most services are not—the best that can be hoped for is the kind of mildly pleasant communal experience that may be achieved by singing the same words with mainly the same melodies week in and week out. More like what Israelis call *shirah betzibbur* ("communal singing") than *tefillah betzibbur* ("communal prayer").

As I say, I'm not at all sure that my difficulty in finding spiritual fulfillment in the type of synagogue services that had previously worked for me is connected to the same challenge I now have in attaining the zone at Dead shows. But the Grateful Dead documentary got me thinking about it and wanting to share my musings with others. And it is my hope that the decidedly unorthodox approach of thinking about Jewish worship through the prism of Grateful Dead music might lead those of us who play leadership roles in Jewish worship, and those of us who attend Jewish worship, to consider what our goals are in worship services, and what they might be.

"How Do You Sleep?"

A Sermon for Martin Luther King Day

Peter E. Hyman

It is no small task to speak with the community on this day when we celebrate the birth, life and legacy of Martin Luther King, Jr. For this is a day of conscience and memory. On this day history and hope converge, our painful past is measured against the promise of our progress, and we are answerable to Dr. King and to his dream. On this day we are judged against the undiminished challenge of his mission: a mission bequeathed to us in blood and tears. He continues to stir our souls and inform our actions.

The challenge and burden of this day increase because there are still people out there who stubbornly cling to perverse and ignorant notions, people who clutch desperately the prejudice of the past. Even they cannot ignore the power and efficacy of Dr. King's life and work. Ultimately, these folk and their descendants will surrender to the truth and capitulate to a society that fully rejects their bigotry and unequivocally condemns their racism. This day we celebrate the life of Dr. King, and thank God for the instructive and corrective power of his dream.

But today we also re-examine ourselves, for his challenge is our work. While this is, most certainly, a day of tribute and triumph, it is also a day of reckoning... for on this day we measure our progress against the promise of his dream. Especially on this day, the "dream" hovers above our heads and looms large on the horizon of our collective destiny. Who in this room does not hear his voice all the time? "I have a dream." Those words, spoken by that voice, propel us, inspire and motivate us, energize and strengthen us. The Prophet Amos asked: "How shall Jacob stand?" as he envisioned God holding a plumb line to measure Israel; using the plumb line to determine how faithful, how true and how committed to God's mission was Israel. Listen as Scripture speaks to the message of this day: "Said the Holy One: 'Amos, what do you see?' I said, 'A plumb line.' Said the Lord, 'I set this plumb line in the midst of my people; by it will I measure them.'" Today we are measured against that very same plumb line. How shall we stand?

You know, Dr. King begins eight paragraphs in that indelible speech with the phrase "I have a dream." We don't need a video clip. We don't have to Google YouTube. CNN need not show it every 10 minutes. Each and every one of us in this room can hear his voice, recall his intensity and remember un-mutedly both what he said and how he said it. And because this is so, on this day when we celebrate the dreamer and his dream, I am compelled to ask a question. The question derives from a story that you and I have read hundreds of times. The text, from the Book of Genesis, chapter 28, is the story of another dreamer, Patriarch Jacob and his famous dream. There Jacob sees angels climbing up and going down a ladder that connects Earth to Heaven…when he wakes up, he declares the spot holy and names it Beth-El, the House of God.

> "Now Jacob left Beersheba and headed toward Haran. The sun was setting so he stopped for the night. He took rocks from that place and using them for his pillow he lay down on the ground to sleep. And he dreamed…he saw a ladder set on the ground, its top reaching to heaven; and angels of God ascending and descending on it. And the Lord was standing beside him…When Jacob awoke from his sleep he exclaimed… 'How awesome is this place! This is no other but the house of God, and this is the gate of heaven.'"

This is as familiar a story as any in Scripture. Only in preparing these remarks for this day did the question present itself, and I believe the question is as profound as it is serious. How does one sleep on the ground using rocks for a pillow and dream about God's majesty, dream about the gateway into heaven and dream about the upright messengers of God? How do you sleep on a rock pillow and wake up shouting, "How awesome is this place?"

Some of you know that I am a Boy Scout. As a Boy Scout, I've slept on the ground more times than I care to remember. It is no exaggeration to say hundreds of nights, including two weeks last July on a mountain top in West Virginia! Let me assure you, that in all the times I've slept in the great outdoors, with Mother Nature for a mattress, not once…never…ever… did I wake up and shout: "This is awesome—God is in this place!!" There's always a stick jamming into my shoulder, a root poking my back, a pebble under my hip, a mosquito buzzing around my head! So, I don't know how you sleep on a rock pillow and exclaim: "How awesome is this place. This is no other but the house of God, and this is the gate of heaven."

Let me pose the question differently. How do you sleep in a filthy jail cell in Selma, Alabama, with images of bloodthirsty attack dogs in your eyes, the sting of water cannons still burning your body and the pernicious words of a despicable, racist governor and sadistic sheriff echoing in your ears… only to wake up and assert with unshakeable surety: "I have a dream that one day this nation will rise up and live out the true meaning of its creed: 'We hold these truths to be self-evident: that all men are created equal.'" How do you dream that? How did Dr. King stake his life on that, when it was not at all clear that any truth was self-evident?

How do you go to sleep in "a state sweltering with the heat of injustice" and wake up believing that someday our nation "will judge us not by the color of our skin but by the content of our character?"

How do you sleep in the most vile of circumstances and wake up convinced that soon "every valley shall be exalted, every hill and mountain shall be made low, the rough places will be made plain, and the crooked places will be made straight, and the glory of the Lord shall be revealed, and all flesh shall see it together?" How do you sleep on a rock and exclaim with unshakeable conviction: "How awesome is this place; God is here?"

The truth of the matter is this. The power of right and great dreams is never dependent on where you rest your head. Where you rest your head is never as important as where you place your heart.

The dreams that touch our hearts move our souls to action. The dreams that touch our hearts mobilize our spirit by the strength of their transcendent correctness and truth. The dreams that touch our hearts unite us, binding us together in common cause, compelling us to climb out on the shaky and dangerous ledge of uncertain consequence, moving us to heights thought unreachable and unattainable. That's the power of the dream that inspires our celebration this morning.

One last thought. It is sobering to acknowledge that all too often it falls on others to make real what we have dreamt. Sometimes all we get to do is provide inspiration and motivation.

Think about Moses. Can you imagine his disappointment in not being allowed to enter Canaan? Surely, Moses must have said to God: "Are You kidding me—I schlepped them out of Egypt, but I don't get to go into Canaan?" But, as we know, fulfillment of the dream fell to Joshua and the Israelite leaders of the next generation.

Here lies the essential insight. Moses not entering the Promised Land in no way diminished the magnitude, the immediacy or the imperative of his dream: getting the Children of Israel to the Promised Land. Sometimes others nurture the dreams we birth. In no way does that lessen the vitality of our dream.

On April 3, 1968 at the Bishop Charles Mason Temple in Memphis, Tennessee, Dr. King delivered yet another of his memorable messages. The title of that sermon was: "I've Been to the Mountaintop." The words of his concluding paragraph are familiar.

"I don't know what will happen now; we've got some difficult days ahead. But it really doesn't matter…because I've been to the mountain top. And I don't mind. Like anybody, I would like to live a long life—longevity has its place. But I'm not concerned about that now. I just want to do God's will. And He's allowed me to go up to the mountain. And I've looked over, and I've seen the Promised Land. I may not get there with you. But I want you to know tonight, that we, as a people, will get to the Promised Land. And so I'm happy tonight; I'm not worried about anything; I'm not fearing any man. Mine eyes have seen the glory of the coming of the Lord."

When Rev. Billy Kyles spoke at Union Baptist Church here in Easton, I asked him if Dr. King knew that he would not live to see the dream fulfilled. Rev. Kyles responded: "He knew something was going to happen. He was reconciled to that. But he knew others were ready to push forward, to march ahead and keep the dream alive."

We are those "others." Like it or not, the course has been charted, tasks assigned, and expectations articulated. "How shall Jacob stand?" How will we measure up?

History is filled with examples of dreamers who birthed a dream yet were denied the privilege of realizing their vision. This is not failure. I submit that this is the consummate act of genius and generosity. With righteous and upright dreams, it matters less who fulfills them and more that they ultimately be realized.

The Rabbis teach: "You are not obligated to complete the work, but neither are you free to desist from it."

The Gospel of Matthew instructs: "Where your treasure is, there lies your heart." Please note, Matthew did not say, "where your treasure is, there lies your head!"

Sleeping on the ground with a rock for a pillow is not a cerebral decision, an intellectual option. You sleep on the ground with your head on a rock when you believe with all your heart and with all your soul and with all your strength that your mission is sacred, your purpose righteous, and the stakes far too valuable to compromise. That's how you sleep on a rock pillow, see God, and exclaim, "How awesome is this place. Surely God is here."

"I may not get there with you. But I want you to know tonight, that we, as a people, will get to the Promised Land."

And so we dream.

Amen.

Light and Peace in Our Daily Liturgical Declarations

Michael Kasper

Dedicated to Dr. Ora Horn Prouser on the occasion of the renewal of her day of birth. As her name suggests, she helps to turn on the light.

In the history of the world,[1] humankind has not found a consistent way to settle arguments, disagreements, or scores of almost any magnitude better than to kill one another. Evolution has done little to temper our most base emotional state and it has not made much of a dent in our ability to resolve conflict in ways not leading to death for the loser. A sorry state of affairs to be sure, but especially so given how much time and energy many of us devote to talking about world peace and loving our neighbors.

Our sacred texts offer inspiration and reflect reality in a way human beings can sometimes understand and sometimes cannot: living and breathing people are loved and cherished by God but also severely punished when judged to be outside the pale of God's law.[2] Holy retribution can be swift and merciless.

The idea that Divine authority need make sense, in human terms, is quite beyond the scope of this brief paper. Nevertheless, the notion that mortals should accept the reality of God-induced horror is, in some way, like an unpleasant fragrance that hangs in the air; it is hard to take and harder yet to make sense of. Apparently, it was hard for our ancient rabbis as well. One need only to look at the *shelosh esreh midot* (thirteen attributes),[3] recited as part

---

[1] For the purpose of this paper it will make no difference if you calculate the beginning of humanity from a Jewish perspective (five thousand seven hundred eighty two years) or a secular/scientific perspective (between five and seven million years ago for our human ancestors). Either way—it is a very long while.

[2] For example: read Genesis 6:9 (Noaḥ), Genesis 19:23 (Sodom and Gomorrah), and Exodus 7-12 (Plagues). Also, Bruce Wells. "Punishments in the Torah and Their Rationale." *Zeitschrift Fur Altorientalische Und Biblische Rechtsgeschichte / Journal for Ancient Near Eastern and Biblical Law*, vol. 22, 2016, pp. 245-267. JSTOR, www.jstor.org/stable/10.13173/zeitaltobiblrech.22.2016.0245. Accessed 2 Feb. 2021.

[3] Compare the rabbinic version (Artscroll translation) "Hashem, Hashem, God, Compassionate and Gracious, Slow to anger, and Abundant in Kindness and Truth, Preserver of kindness for thousands of generations, Forgiver of iniquity, willful sin, and error, and who cleanses" with the Torah (Exodus 34:6-7 JPS translation) upon which the rabbinic language is based. "The Lord! The Lord! a God compassionate and

of the Torah Service during the *chagim* (festivals), to see how troubling texts have been reworked for more modern sensibilities.

Another text we might look at comes from the liturgy and comprises the first of two blessings which precede the recitation of *Shema*[4] in the morning. It includes three companion benedictions and is known as the *Yotser* (creation/formation) section[5]. It begins here with:

ברוך אתה ה׳ א-להינו מלך העולם יוצר אור ובורא חושך עושה שלום ובורא את הכל.

> Blessed are you, God, King of the Universe, Former of light, Creator of darkness, Maker of peace, Creator of all.[6]

This text, originally found in Isaiah 45:7, concludes with the words, ובורא רע—"and creates woe."[7] The Rabbis wanted a softer landing, a more uplifting message, a way to emphasize the idea that God is responsible for the creation of the extremes and all that lies between them: Peace and not-peace, light and its counterpart, darkness.[8] Furthermore, the blessing is clear about the thinking and order of priorities with respect to God's creative energy. God

---

gracious, slow to anger, abounding in kindness and faithfulness, extending kindness to the thousandth generation, forgiving iniquity, transgression, and sin; yet He does not remit all punishment, but visits the iniquity of parents upon children and children's children, upon the third and fourth generations."

[4] Recitation of *Shema* (from Deuteronomy 6:4) is a central part of the morning service. "Hear/Listen O Israel: The Lord is our God, the Lord is One."

[5] The three companion benedictions making up the first complete blessing which precedes the recitation of Shema are all on the theme of God's creation of light—the sun and moon. They are known by the common name *yotser*. Yotser means, literally, 'who creates…creation.' For a more fully fleshed out exposition of The Shema and its Blessings see: Rabbi Lawrence Hoffman, ed. *My People's Prayer Book: Traditional Prayers and Modern Commentaries: Vol 1*, Jewish Lights Publishing, Woodstock, VT, 1997, pp. 15-65.

[6] From Siddur HaGra (Elijah ben Solomon Zalman, The Vilna *Gaon*) as cited in the Complete Metsudah Siddur, Zion Talis Book Division, New York City, 1990, p. 96. Forming, *yotser*, is the act of refining or modifying an original substance whereas creating, *borei*, refers to the Divine creation of an original substance.

[7] יוצר אור ובורא חשך עשה שלום ובורא רע From the JPS translation: "I form light and create darkness, I make weal and create woe—" Other translations use "trouble" or "evil" instead of "woe."

[8] See also: Marc Brettler in Lawrence Hoffman, *My People's Prayerbook*, p. 45.

formed light, created its opposite, makes peace, and fashions all that is.

Genesis instructs us that on the first day God said, "Let there be light." All that comes after it is borne in the context of this first creation. Light is the prime mover, the energy that sets in motion all of the natural world's future creations.[9] Nevertheless, it is peace, that gorgeous and completely elusive state of being that the *mishnah* tells us is the one vessel that contains them (blessings) all.[10]

אמר רבי שמעון בן חלפתא, לא מצא הקדוש ברוך הוא כלי מחזיק ברכה
לישראל אלא השלום, שנאמר, ה׳ עוז לעמו יתן, ה׳ יברך את-עמו בשלום.

> Rabbi Simon ben Halafta said, The Holy One, blessed be He, found no vessel that could hold [the] blessing for Israel save peace, as it is said, The Eternal will give strength to His people; the Eternal will bless His people with peace.
> *Uktsin, 3:12*

In other words, although not first in the order of creation, it falls to peace as the ultimate sense of completion to hold the entirety of blessing. Peace and only peace is that container. As we review the order of God's handiwork we have light, darkness, peace, and everything else. Peace is gifted to us in a crucible of life-sustaining light. They, peace and light, are tied to each other for all time and although "for all time" does not necessarily include a place for humanity in a future world as we know the world now, nevertheless there seems to be an intuitive sense of peace and light as being connected to the future of humankind's place on planet Earth.

So why is it our lot to be on such poor speaking terms with peace? If we look to the natural world, we see an expression of Divine peace making itself known in so many ways. We can look to the trees and forests for inspiration and confirmation. In a recent *New York Times Magazine* piece Ferris Jabr wrote a stunning article called "The Social Life of Forests."[11] In it he chronicles time spent with Dr. Suzanne Simard, a professor of forest ecology at the University of British Columbia. Simard was a key inspiration for a

---

[9] See Rabbi Elie Munk, *The World of Prayer*, vol. 1, p. 92, Feldheim Publishers, Jerusalem/New York, 1961, 1963. In R, Munk's beautiful phrase, "light is…the element which awakens all other forces to life."

[10] The Mishnah ends the entirety of its writings with the quoted passage about peace as the only vessel that can hold the blessing for Israel.

[11] *The New York Times Magazine*, "The Social Life of Forests," by Ferris Jabr, 12/6/20, pp. 32-41.

central character in Richard Powers's 2018 Pulitzer Prize-winning novel, *The Overstory*.[12] Both the article and the novel instruct us in the incredible science of tree life where root systems, fungal conveyor belts called mycorrhizas, and the language of nature offer us God-like, inspirational, amazing, peaceful, generous, sophisticated, and life-affirming lessons laid at our feet by species and genera never before considered in this way. The humanity of these giants (Is it ridiculous to refer to their humanity?) begs each and every one of us to step back and consider our abject failure at getting along.

Simard's research has shown that trees, even those of varying species, meaning, they do not share kinship (i.e., they are altruistic), share resources to maintain health. A dying tree will sometimes offer a substantial share of its carbon to a neighbor. And resources seem to flow from older trees to younger ones. Consider Darwin's contribution to our understanding of evolution: it is an individual-centric system in which survival of the fittest supersedes all other growth schema. Contrast that to more recent forestry research which suggests an ongoing socialism as the norm. Jabr writes, "An old-growth forest is neither an assemblage of stoic organisms tolerating one another's presence nor a merciless battle royale: It's a vast, ancient and intricate society."[13] Jabr leaves us with the following realization: that tolerance might not be the highest form of a sanguine communal temperament. Perhaps there ought to be more. He also leaves us to anticipate the following question: "Is cooperation as central to evolution as competition?"[14]

What is it we need in order to emulate the lessons of trees? What is the missing connection in our own DNA that would push us to get along rather than to come out on top? Why is "kill or be killed" so injudiciously used to settle scores?

The Academy for Jewish Religion (AJR) has, in the last several years, pioneered a course of studies that moves its cantorial and rabbinical students toward this goal. AJR's cantorial students are required to complete a track of courses in Peace Studies.[15] These courses are designed to help the Academy's students understand the impulses leading to conflict and to offer resources toward resolving conflict, not only in large ways but in small ones as well. AJR's students are looking at Peace Studies from the point of view of Jewish texts, communal relationships, internal dialogues, and their own voices as

---

[12] *The Overstory*, Richard Powers, W.W. Norton & Co., New York, 2018.

[13] Jabr, "The Social Life of Forests," p. 34.

[14] ibid. p. 37.

[15] It is anticipated that the Academy's future rabbinical students will be required to take this track as well. Presently, rabbinic students can register for these classes as electives. To date, rabbinical student enrollment is at least half of each Peace Studies class offered.

instruments of peace.

Every member of the clergy is called on to deal with conflict, oftentimes on a daily basis. Sometimes it comes crashing in on the world stage (war, anti-Semitism, terror), sometimes it becomes manifest at the congregational level (board meetings, committee disagreements), and sometimes it makes its way into pastoral conversations (grieving families, divorcing couples, upset individuals). No matter the context, peace, or the lack of it, is part and parcel of the daily experience of professional clergy. Which begs the question: where is peace? What more is needed?

Light is what's needed. Light illuminates possibilities; light helps our vision. It focuses our eyes, illuminates paths, arouses our darkened hearts, and guides our journeys. Light awakens our senses. It is the atmosphere which enables creation, moves us to see the majesty of God's vision for Earth.

The morning liturgy equates the daily rising of the sun—that magnificent fire star—with the renewal of all that was, is, and ever will be created. But how does that renewal of the creative spark impact on our ability to make peace? Is there a relationship between daily renewal and peace? Is hope a necessary component of this process? Is faith? Is there a place for hope and faith in the daily creative rebirth? Is either a byproduct of daily renewal?

המאיר לארץ ולדרים עליה ברחמים,
ובטובו מחדש בכל יום תמיד מעשה בראשית.

You illumine the earth and its creatures with mercy;
in Your goodness, day after day You renew creation.[16]

Does God renew creation simply because God is good and therefore God is doing the sort of work we might expect a good God to do? Well, we don't really know, do we? Religion is, after all, a vehicle that affirms faith in things which must be described as unknowable. But if one were drawn to the idea that God does, in fact, renew creation each morning with the emergent light of the recurring sun, it might help lead us toward an understanding that a repeatable creation, coming from a singular creative moment in which God breathed life into a world for which all of existence is kept possible in a constant cycle of light and peace, darkness and war, could allow for the possibility that at any point in the daily cycle something new could happen. The cycle could yield a new result. The balance might tip and the trajectory of that arc

---

[16] This text is effectively the second sentence in the first benediction of the יוצר אור. The English translation comes from *Siddur Sim Shalom for Weekdays*, The Rabbinical Assembly, The United Synagogue of Conservative Judaism, New York City, 2002, p. 30.

might tip toward greater peace. How this never-ending cyclical repetition, forever and ever, has left us in the current state of affairs we find ourselves in is a great and solemn mystery. Evolution has not led us toward the completion of our rabbis' understanding that peace is the container that holds them all. And history has not shown humankind to have learned the lessons of the past, not nearly fast enough and not nearly well enough.

Nevertheless, we find a correlate expression of this idea, the renewal of creation, in the Passover Seder when we read the *Haggadah* as if we ourselves were slaves in Egypt. The two ideas share a similarity: the work of creation is renewed daily by God and we are told to treat the Exodus story as if it were our own. Each year at the appointed time the Jewish people renew our relationship to the struggle for freedom. The work of creation and the work of an experienced remembrance are renewed with perpetual regularity.

If God's creations and humankind's actions can be routinely created and remembered so that we not only give thanks but endeavor to act with more reverence for life and more awe for the majesty of our world, doesn't it follow that this mindfulness about the sanctity of God's creation would lead to a more perfect union, a life blessed with more peace?

Jewish wisdom has it that *shalom bayit*, peace in the home, is an idea so important that it deserves to be used as a Rorschach for how to live together in community. The *Otzar haMidrashim—Midrash haGadol 42*—helps to explicate rabbinic thinking about the relationship between peace and light.[17]

> גדול השלום שלא התחיל הקב"ה לברוא דבר בעולמו אלא בדבר שהוא שלום
> ואיזה זה האור שנאמר ויאמר א-להים יהי אור. ומנין שהוא שלום שנאמר יוצר
> אור ובורא חושך עושה שלום (ישעיה מ"ה ז'). מכאן אמרו חז"ל נר ביתו וקידוש
> היום נר ביתו עדיף משום שלום ביתו. פירוש האור נקרא שלום לפיכך מקדימין
> הנר שהוא אור ושלום ליין.

> Great is peace that the Holy Blessed One did not begin to create anything in God's world other than something that is peace—and what is this? The light, as it says, "And God said 'let there be light.'" And from where do we know that [light] is peace? As it says, "forms light and creates darkness, makes peace" (Isaiah 45:7). From here our sages of blessed memory said, "[When one has a choice between] a lamp for their

---

[17] *Otzar haMidrashim, Midrash haGadol 42*. Based on a sugya in Bavli Shabbat 23b. In discussing the merits of purchasing oil to light the Shabbat lamp vs. purchasing oil to light a Ḥanukkah lamp, a poor person should choose oil for the Shabbat lamp because without the light from a Shabbat lamp the family would be sitting and eating their meal in the dark. Having light in the home makes for peace.

home and [wine for] sanctification of the day, the lamp for one's home is preferable because of peace in their household."

Our understanding is that light equals peace and, therefore, candles are more important than Kiddush wine. Our sages understood that the value of peace was so great, so primary to all that followed, that if one had to decide whether to buy candles to illumine the room or wine to sanctify the meal, the choice was decidedly in favor of light, for light which is shared brings peace to the home.

Other cultures understand the relationship between light and creation in similarly essential ways. In Spanish, to give birth is called *dar a luz*, to give to [the] light. The phrase is the same in Portuguese and only slightly different in Italian: *dare all luce*. All mean the same, to birth a child. All point us toward the inescapable idea that the fact of existence, the fact of humans roaming the planet, the fact of community, all these are shown to us by the magic of the sun. By the magic of light. By the magic of peace.

None other than Rashi,[18] writing in the latter half of the eleventh century, makes a similar point about the goodness of light. Commenting on Exodus 2:2 he sees a connection between the words Jokhebed uses upon seeing her son, Moses, (*ki tov hu*—how goodly he is) and the Torah's own commentary in Genesis 1:4 (*ki tov*—God saw that the light was good).

וַיַּרְא אֱ-לֹהִים אֶת־הָאוֹר כִּי־טוֹב וַיַּבְדֵּל אֱ-לֹהִים בֵּין הָאוֹר וּבֵין הַחֹשֶׁךְ:

God saw that the light was good, and God separated the light from the darkness.
Genesis 1:4

וַתַּהַר הָאִשָּׁה וַתֵּלֶד בֵּן וַתֵּרֶא אֹתוֹ כִּי־טוֹב הוּא וַתִּצְפְּנֵהוּ שְׁלֹשָׁה יְרָחִים:

The woman conceived and bore a son; and when she saw how goodly he was, she hid him for three months.
Exodus 2:2

In fleshing out this connection, Rashi cites Sotah 12a:

וחכמים אומרים בשעה שנולד משה נתמלא הבית כולו אורה. כתיב הכא ותרא אותו כי טוב הוא וכתיב התם (בראשית א, ד) וירא א-להים את האור כי טוב

---

[18] Rabbi Shlomo Yitzḥaki (1040-1105 C.E.) was a medieval French commentator of both the Tanakh and Talmud.

The verse states, with regard to the birth of Moses, "And the woman conceived, and bore a son; and when she saw him that he was a goodly [*ki tov*] child, she hid him three months" (Exodus 2:2). And the Rabbis say: **At the time when Moses was born, the entire house was filled with light (*ora*)**, as it is written here: "And when she saw him that he was a goodly [*ki tov*] child," and it is written there: "And God saw the light, that it was good [*ki tov*]" (Genesis 1:4).
Sotah 12a

Reading Rashi, we get a glimpse of the power this creation of light enjoys. God saw the light and called it good, Moses' mother invokes the language of light to describe her son, and the rabbis posit an entire house, full of light, at the moment of Moses' birth. Light, Or/Ora, is good!

Is light all that's needed? What about hope? Hope may not be a prerequisite to this three-fold blessing of sun, light, and peace, but it is certainly a sort of amniotic membrane that allows us all to grow our desire for a better world. Humankind may not have sufficiently evolved past settling our scores with violence, but that doesn't mean we aren't capable. The *siddur* instructs us: day after day God renews creation. Each morning the sun rises; each evening it sets and when it is again time for its rays to poke upward, toward the heavens, birthing a new day, we have an opportunity to fulfill the rabbis' understanding of God's promise by putting the desire for peace in the center of our mind's eye. "The Eternal will give strength to His people; the Eternal will bless His people with peace."[19]

Are we willing to wait for evolution to do its work, to bring us to the place where our aggression, in the service of protection, is no longer as valuable to our survival as it once was? The historic record tells us that the evidence for waiting is suspect at best. A better choice would be to exercise our will and try harder. Education is always a key. Hope is, too.

Light and peace must be renewed daily, as we are taught, to move us out of the darkness and toward a new-old goal, toward a better world, toward a world where resolution of conflict is accomplished with a softer touch. A world where getting along is more important than winning a battle. We are born to give the light. May it be our blessing to use the light with wisdom and unending care.

---

[19] See footnote 10.

Large Issues in Small Spaces

What Jews Can Learn from Christians about "Public Theology"

Nancy Fuchs Kreimer

As protestors gathered outside meetings of the World Trade Organization in Seattle in 1999, a chant emerged that proved enduring. "Show us what democracy looks like!" someone shouted. And the crowd responded, "This is what democracy looks like!" In 2014, in Ferguson, Missouri, a young person of color with a vest that said "Clergy" shouted, "Show us what theology looks like!" And the crowd responded, "This is what theology looks like!"

For Christians who work in the field of public theology, there could be no more apt hashtag. In this essay, I will lift up some of the themes of public theology that resonate. I will suggest that these themes provide Jews with language to articulate what we already know and do well. At the same time, they inspire us to look toward our growing edges. In my experience, interfaith encounter at its best helps us recognize and appreciate our own tradition's strengths, even as it pushes us toward ever better versions of ourselves.

What is Public Theology?

Public theology is an emerging subfield within the larger field of Christian theology. There are Christian seminaries with chairs in public theology and some few where you can major in the area. Public theology is not the same as political theology. The latter is the study of how religion has thought about state and society through the ages. Michael Walzer's work on the history of Jewish thought in relationship to the public sphere is an example of political theology. Public theology, on the other hand, is about taking great abstract concepts about God out of the academy—and even out of the pews—and bringing them into the places where people are living their lives, what they call "micro-sites of engagement." As William Storrar of Princeton describes it, public theology is theology in the process of being constructed and reconstructed by "raising large issues in small spaces."

I first heard about the field of public theology from my colleague Reverend Katie Day who taught for four decades at the Lutheran Theological Seminary of Philadelphia (LTSP), now called United Lutheran Seminary

(ULS). Professor Day and I had the good fortune of co-teaching courses preparing Jewish and Christian seminarians to become religious leaders in a multifaith world. Our courses were part of a process Reverend Jenny Peace has taught us to call "co-formation."

Katie Day is a leading figure in the public theology world. She co-authored *The Brill Companion of Public Theology* (2017) and *Routledge Handbook of Religion and Cities* (2020). She wrote a position paper on gun violence prevention for the Presbyterian Church USA, and founded and chaired Heeding God's Call, a grass roots response to gun violence in Philadelphia. Upon her retirement, rather than a party with speeches about her, Professor Day requested a symposium on Public Theology. The symposium was held on April 9, the anniversary of her ordination. The date was intentional. April 9, 1945 is the day Reverend Dietrich Bonhoeffer, Lutheran pastor, theologian and anti-Nazi dissident, was executed at the age of 39. Katie Day chose that day to be ordained as a reminder of her mission.

The organizers of the symposium, asked me to speak about public theology from a Jewish perspective. My first thought: We Jews have *this* covered! I can tell. We certainly have the hashtags. Heschel's "my legs were praying," "Tikkun Olam." "Resisting Tyrants since Pharaoh." And going deeper, isn't that what Judaism is all about? The divide between theology and life that Christian public theology seeks to address does not appear to be a Jewish problem. Isn't our whole tradition focused on doing, not just believing?

Yes, and…

I will share four themes of public theology that feel important for Jews. They are place, empathy, disruption and embodiment. For each of these themes, I will offer examples from Jewish life. In each case, I will ask *What do we Jews do well that reflects this theme? What might we want to do better?*

Place

I attended the Reconstructionist Rabbinical College (RRC) when it was located in a rowhouse in North Philadelphia, where class could be delayed because we found a sleeping homeless man on the steps of the school. In 1982, just weeks after I graduated, the moving vans pulled up and RRC moved to leafy Elkins Park, not far from Old York Rd., a street lined with large synagogue buildings that had preceded us in that move, along with their Jewish congregations, in the 1950s.

When I returned to RRC in its new, suburban location to teach, I thought a lot about place because of what I learned from Katie Day. She passionately taught her "Torah" of place. She would remind her students that they were not becoming clergy just anywhere, they were becoming clergy here, in this place, on Germantown Avenue in Philadelphia, across the street from the Wawa. In fact, she wrote an entire book about that avenue, *Faith on the Avenue: Religion on a City Street* (2014), based on years of urban ethnography that she conducted with her students, very much an expression of her commitment to public theology.

Like many Americans, including American Jews, September 11, 2001 found me woefully under-educated in Islam. My first impulse was to begin to learn about the reality of this faith tradition that spanned the globe. I soon realized that what I was most ignorant of was my own location. It would be good to learn about Muslims, even better about Muslims in America, better still about Muslims in Philadelphia, people who were, quite literally, my neighbors.

Masjidullah, four miles down the road from RRC, became my go-to place to take rabbinical students to learn about the history of African American Islam through the eyes of elders who lived it.

When a Jewish woman, Pamela Geller, began a campaign to bring Islamophobic ads to public subways and busses in New York City, San Francisco and Washington, DC, it became a national issue that many of us addressed through Op Eds, petitions and social media. When SEPTA busses began carrying these ads in Philadelphia, it was showing up at Masjidullah for their press conference that mattered.

We Jews are often highly cosmopolitan people, with far flung family and friends and professional relationships. Many of us read several newspapers every morning, including the New York Times and an Israeli paper. We feel deeply connected to Jews around the world, and follow issues across the globe with passionate interest. This is a good thing. But it is also good to remember that we are accountable to the place in which we dwell and to the people among whom we live.

Disruption

Reverend Linda Noonan provided me with language to articulate something I knew, but did not know that I knew. We tend to think of public ritual as essentially conservative, as something we do to reinforce who we are and what we believe. But Noonan reminds us that communal ritual can become a site of disruption, a way to shake people up, to challenge what is, to actually break with tradition, even as it is reinforcing it.

In the Reconstructionist movement, we are familiar with this move and honor it each Shabbat in our synagogues. Mordecai Kaplan wrote about a theological move, rejecting the idea of the Jewish people being the chosen people of God. But then he did something even more provocative. He disrupted a key ritual moment with his idea. The moment is a public one, when individual Jews are called up to the Torah to recite a blessing. The words of the blessing include "who has chosen us from among all the nations." In his 1948 prayerbook, Kaplan proposed different words. By doing so, he was asking people to draw attention to an idea through a ritual disruption.

Today we see that happening in some communities through various liturgical moves to address gender issues. Depending on the community, these changes can be more or less radical. In many places, the Hebrew liturgy that is recited aloud remains conserving of tradition. Let it be said that Mordecai Kaplan himself ran into trouble when he announced that the words of the Kol Nidre prayer would be replaced with something more inspiring—Psalm 130. His congregation would not hear of it.

That said, public theology asks us to consider using ritual to bring important ideas into view, when people are not quite ready for them. Sometimes it involves taking a sacred event about which people have certain expectations and surprising them. The first time someone suggested I engage in that kind of disruption, I chose to demur.

The year was 1979. As I helped to plan the first wedding ceremony I ever performed, the young man and woman made what seemed an unusual request. They asked me to pause at the part where I say "by the power vested in me by the Commonwealth of Pennsylvania…" and to acknowledge the lack of rights of gay people to legally marry. At that time, there were very few people in my life whom I knew to be gay, and none who I knew wanted to be married. It seemed wrong to take a personal holy moment and interject a political message from the margins. I told the couple that it was just too weird.

Fast forward to the 2000s when I rarely performed a wedding without such a mention. In the Jewish circles in which I operated, it actually became a normative part of the wedding service until it was no longer needed. That happened in Pennsylvania in May 2014, and nationally in June 2015. Looking back, I am abashed at my response to that couple 35 years earlier, but glad that I ultimately became part of that effort in public theology. I know it was the courage of growing numbers of gay people to come out to their families and communities that shifted our culture and ultimately our laws. But I now see disruption of public ritual as part of that movement.

Obviously, this needs to be done with thoughtfulness. A funeral is likely not the place to try out radical new liturgy or introduce a message people may not be ready to hear. And public theology can also use ritual in ways that are not disruptive of what is. Two examples come to mind.

Several decades ago, Rabbi Arthur Waskow noticed that Abraham Joshua Heschel's yahrzeit and Martin Luther King's birthday often would fall very close to each other in January. He realized this was an ideal moment for ritual innovation, the institution of an entirely new observance, the Heschel-King weekend. Having created the first Freedom Seder in a church in Washington, D.C. in 1969, Waskow was familiar with how powerful it can be to bring people together across faith traditions to take big ideas like those of Heschel, King and the Passover ritual and find new ways for people to hear them.

Empathy

Jonathan Sacks wrote that the greatest challenge we have as human beings is seeing the image of God in people who are not in our own image. Turns out, empathy is tricky. It is not really about doing to others what we would have them do to us. Often, that is something we do not actually know. It's about listening hard and learning to see the world through others' eyes.

In the 1950s, I grew up singing "Let My People Go" at our family's seders. It was in our Haggadah, published in 1941 by the Reconstructionist Movement. By the 1960s, thanks to the popularity of Paul Robeson's rendition of the song which we knew as a "Negro spiritual," "Let My People Go" had become a staple of many American Jewish families' Pesach traditions.

Our traditional songs for the holiday were in Hebrew, but we were not Hebrew speakers anymore. American Jews needed a song in English, one that was powerful and singable. "Let My People Go" fit the bill. We were proud that our ancestors' story inspired people fighting for freedom thousands of years later. As I recall, we thought: this blending of cultures is America at its most beautiful! Needless to say, we were, with some exceptions, White Jews gathered at those tables.

In recent years, that has changed. Black Jews—who were there all along but at different tables—have been joined by Black people who are Jews through conversion, intermarriage, adoption and more. When some of these folks began to speak up, it was hard for us to understand. Evidently, what seemed so lovely from one perspective could look different through a different lens.

When Jews first hear that helping oneself to someone else's cultural product is not necessarily a compliment, we don't always get it. Jews have suffered persecution, no doubt, but being victims of economic exploitation is not part of the American Jewish story. The specific history of Black musicians and White Jews in the music business was news, at least to me. White Jews belting out, unattributed, a song first published by a Black man in 1851, is not neutral. As for the blending of cultures, that does not feel as benign to the marginalized as it does to those in the center, as we are learning from our indigenous tribal colleagues.

Rabbi Jacob Best Adler, a white colleague wrote:

> "While skimming through a Haggadah, my six-year-old son asked me about 'Go Down Moses,' a song which has not been part of our family's Pesach tradition. As I began to sing it for him in the style of Paul Robeson's iconic performance, the words felt uncomfortable in my mouth, like minstrelsy—a racist caricature—not intentionally, but still problematic. Even in our mixed-race African-American and white Jewish family, I would not feel comfortable including it in our Seder, and as a rabbi, I would not feel comfortable including it in majority white spaces. "

Another white colleague, Cantor Shira Stanford-Asiyo, offered her experience:

> "The issue is about being in relationship with those who have been impacted by this harm in a way that is responsive and accountable.... At our community seder we invited members of a progressive UCC Church to join us, and their gospel choir director explained the history of a spiritual/civil rights freedom song and then sang it in all its gospel glory... In our context that worked. But it was based on some long standing relationships."

This is how public theology evolves.

A recent example comes from my own growing edge. In some circles in which I travel, at the beginning of an event, people are asked to state the pronouns they use. (This past year, they were asked to put them with their name on their Zoom ID.) Since the pronouns I use correspond with the way I look, I thought it was unnecessary to have to state them. Only after people who are gender non-conforming explained this (more than once), did I understand how important it was to normalize this practice in order for everyone to feel included. Empathy is hard work, and we don't always get it right. But, public theology depends on the rigorous practice of listening.

Embodiment

In Christian discourse, this is where the word "incarnational" comes up. When Christians say public theology is incarnational, they mean it is not only about words. Bodies are involved. An example that comes to mind is the relatively new practice of the "mitzvah project" to supplement that traditional preparation for the Bar/Bat Mitzvah. As a puberty rite, our culture's emphasis on learning is on full display in how we welcome youth into the community. About twenty-five years ago, a custom began in some synagogues for the young person to undertake a project of gemilut *hesed/tikkun olam* in addition to their learning of Torah and liturgy.

It turns out that it is not always so easy to find a truly meaningful, hands-on project for a twelve-year-old to do in the busy months before their big day. It may require time and energy that a parent does not have to make a connection with a soup kitchen or a tutoring project or a nursing home. Many wonderful projects, including some truly creative ones, have indeed happened over these years in synagogues. At the same time, the project many young people now choose is to raise money for a cause they care about. This is a good thing, and arguably an excellent preparation for Jewish adulthood, in which fundraising is an important role in community life. That said, it is often worth the effort to find embodied ways for youth to engage with their world as part of their Jewish initiation.

In thinking about public theology, I realized how much we can learn from Israeli Jews who model all the themes I have mentioned. I think of Tag Meir, a group of Orthodox Jews who visit the homes of Palestinian citizens who have been harmed by Israelis. These individuals, working in their own locale, build relationships of empathy, disrupt business as usual, and bring their own bodies into places that may be challenging for them.

There are many organizations working alongside Tag Meir that reveal "what theology looks like" in the context of the Israeli-Palestinian conflict. But, if I had to focus on one public theologian, I would choose Rabbi Arik Ascherman, specifically because of his decades-long commitment to doing the work in the most embodied of ways. And here's the tricky thing about embodiment. It is not without personal risk.

Rabbi Arik Ascherman grew up in Erie, Pennsylvania. After college, he joined Interns for Peace, a coexistence project which sent him to the Israeli Arab city of Tamra and the Israeli Jewish city of Kiryat Ata to work from 1981 to 1983. After completing rabbinical school in the United States, he chose to make Aliyah and became an Israeli citizen in 1994.

Since then, under the auspices of various organizations that he has worked with, founded and led, Arik's goal has been clear: to hold Israel to its own highest vision of itself as a country dedicated to a prophetic understanding of justice. And he has done this not mostly through petitions and speeches, but by showing up. This means that times when Palestinians need defending from settlers, Arik is the rabbi who is willing to cross the border and to put his body on the line, not without risk of being beaten up by fellow Jews.[1]

What makes this "theology?"

By now you may be wondering why this is called theology at all. It sounds like social justice work on the local level, building relationships, cultivating empathy, using disruption to gain attention, and being willing to put one's whole self on the line. Where does theology come into that? For some Christians, the life and death of Jesus was not so much a project of salvation as a project of connection—God becoming human and able to understand our condition.

Shane Claiborne, an "urban monastic" who founded the Simple Way in the poorest section of Philadelphia, said, "Christianity is about God who decided to move into the neighborhood."

We Jews have various ways of explaining how God enters our lives. In Reconstructionist language, God as the process that makes for both communal and individual salvation. This connects these activities with faith, faith in our obligation to do the work and faith in our hope that the goals will be realized. When we work to bring about change on big issues in small places we are doing what is godly.

That language, however, is abstract, while public theology is a move from abstraction to the granular. Some of us find the poetry of midrash more evocative. We love to quote the Babylonian Talmud (Sotah 14a) that we "walk" in God's path by imitating God: providing clothes for the naked, as God made garments for the first humans; visiting the sick, as God visited Abraham after his circumcision; …burying the dead, as God laid Moses to rest.

In the end, I am encouraged by my encounters with Christian public theology to lift up and honor the way Jews have shown up to raise big issues in small places with sensitivity and with courage. I am also moved to think more about Heschel's famous "praying with my legs." I think many of us assume that the work we do in the world is a form of prayer. But the prayer part often takes a back seat to the work itself. I want to challenge myself to think more about how this aspect of my life is a response to God and a connection with God.

---

[1] See https://www.timesofisrael.com/rights-activist-rabbi-beaten-in-settler-attack-near-illegal-west-bank-outpost

Why Did He Die at Half His Days?

The Torah Student Who Wouldn't Touch His Wife

Dov Linzer

The Torah dictates that a man may not have intercourse with a woman who is experiencing her menstrual flow (is "in niddah") and if he does so, he and she have committed a weighty sin and are liable to *karet*, Divine excision (Lev. 18:19 and 20:18). The Torah also states that a woman who is in niddah does not become ritually pure until the seventh day from the beginning of menstruation (Lev. 15:19). While not clear in the text, the Talmudic rabbis state both that the woman leaves her ritual state of impurity only when the seven days are followed by immersion in a mikveh. They also state that the prohibition against intercourse is not limited to the time when the woman is actively bleeding, but applies throughout the period of ritual impurity, i.e., for a full seven days [see Bavli Shabbat 13b and Rav David Zvi Hoffman, Commentary of Leviticus, 18:19].

As stated, the Torah only proscribes intercourse when a woman is in niddah. The Rabbis, however, add to the Torah's prohibition and forbid a number of acts that are of a particularly intimate nature. The assumption is that they forbade such acts out of a concern that they could lead to intercourse. It is, however, possible that they were seen not as much as a slippery slope to sex, but as something inherently problematic. If intercourse is forbidden, the argument goes, then other forms of sex and sexual activity should be forbidden as well. These are acts that exist in the penumbra of the act of intercourse, and this alone makes them worthy of being forbidden (see Rashi, Ketubot 61a, *s.v. Aval* and *s.v. Hutz*).

Talmudic Forms of Distancing

Whatever the underlying reason, the activities that the Rabbis forbade are referred to in the later literature as *harchakot*, acts of distancing. What is surprising, however, is that when one looks discerningly at the Talmudic texts themselves, it becomes clear that the Talmud only proscribed five activities: three in one passage of the Talmud, regarding intimate but not overtly sexual acts, one in regard to gazing at her genitalia, and one regarding sharing a bed.

The three that are cited in Ketubot (61a) are as follows. A wife who is in niddah may not, says the Talmud:
- Lay her husband's bedspread
- Mix her husband's drinks
- Wash her husband's hands, face and feet

These acts, which appear relatively innocuous, are seen as particularly intimate ones, perhaps even acts that can be seen as an invitation to sex (see Rashi, *ad. loc., s.v. Hutz*). In fact, the Talmudic section immediately preceding states that even in a rich family that has many servants, the wife should still do these three acts for her husband because they are seen not as a chore that needs to get done, but rather as an expression of intimacy.

It goes without saying that if these acts are seen as too sexual or intimate, then unambiguous sexual activity and blatant sexual touch would be forbidden as well. At the same time, there is no reason to assume that touch that is not sexual would be a problem, and indeed, one commentator—Ra'avyah (no. 173) says so explicitly. His argument is simple: if the only thing a woman cannot do is wash her husband's hands, face and feet, then presumably she can touch him in a neutral way.

A Man Gazing on His Wife

The second Talmudic passage appears in Nedarim (20a) where it states that a man who gazes at his wife when she is in niddah will have unseemly children. This is followed by a statement of Rabbi Shimon ben Lakish who clarifies that the gazing that is prohibited refers to a man looking at his wife's genitalia. It is highly doubtful whether this should be seen as a distancing practice. The Talmud never says that it is forbidden, only that it is improper and has negative consequences. Even if it is a form of distancing, it is understandable why gazing at the genitalia should be forbidden, as it can easily lead to intercourse. Rambam (*Issurei Biah*, 21:4) does not cite this passage at all, indicating that he did not consider even the gazing of a man at his wife's genitalia to be a form of distancing. Ra'avad (*ad. loc.*) and Shulkhan Arukh (Yoreh Deah, 195:7) adopt the opposite conclusion. For them, all ways in which a man might gaze on the generally covered parts of his wife's body are forbidden, and considered to be a type of rabbinic distancing.

In sum, it is debatable whether a man gazing on his wife is considered a form of distancing. Shulkhan Arukh rules that it is so. This might reflect his reading of the Talmudic passage, but it might also reflect—and encourage—a more expansive approach to the scope of the *harchakot*. More on this below.

Sharing a Bed

The final Talmudic discussion regarding these acts of distancing occurs in the Talmud Shabbat (13a-b) which addresses the sharing of a bed. The Talmud raises the question whether a husband and wife may sleep in the same bed if they are both in their pajamas. The norm was that when the wife was not in niddah, they would sleep together naked. The wearing of pajamas is thus unusual, and might be able to serve as a sufficient reminder that the wife is in niddah to prevent sex from taking place.

In answering this question, the Gemara makes what would seem on the face of it a bizarre comparison. Let us argue—it states—that this case should be parallel to the case of two people sharing a table, one eating cheese and the other eating meat. Here is an excerpt of that passage, with loose translation:

> Beit Hillel says: Fowl may not be placed on the same table alongside cheese [*so we see that putting things next to one another may lead to sin*].
> There it is different as only one person is involved [*whereas here, with husband and wife, if one forgets that the wife is in niddah, the other will remember*]…
> As evidence that with two people it should be permitted is that fact that we permit two people eating at the same table, one fowl and one cheese.
> No—that is only because they are not familiar with each other [*so we are not afraid of one person accidentally eating from his neighbor's food*]; however, if they are familiar with each other it is prohibited to eat at the same table. And these, too—husband and wife—are familiar with each other, so they may not sleep in the same bed.

The analogy of husband and wife sharing a bed while sleeping in their pajamas to having meat and milk on the same table seems quite stretched. In fact, though, an important point is being made. Namely, concerns around the prohibition of sex when the wife is in niddah are no different than concerns around any other area of forbidden activity. This prohibition is just a prohibition—there is no special taboo associated with it. Based on the safeguards we put around other prohibitions we can deduce what safeguards are appropriate here as well.

We should note that the conclusion of the discussion, as the decisors see it, is that sharing a bed is forbidden even if both parties are clothed. The reason for this is not fully spelled out in the Talmud, and the commentators offer two reasons: (1) the sexual drive is more powerful than, say, the desire to eat, and thus requires additional safeguards (Tosafot, *ad. loc.*, s.v. *Mah Eishet Reyeihu*); or (2) the act of sleeping together is one of intimacy, which is forbidden here regardless of whether sex will ensue (Ramban, Glosses on Rambam's Book of Mitzvot, Negative Mitzvah 353). It needs to be underscored that neither of these reasons for extra stringency is unique to niddah. For example, the Talmud also prohibits a man and a woman who is not his wife being in seclusion, lest they have sex, even if the woman is not in niddah; it is the sexual urge that is the problem, not the prohibition of niddah *per se*.

The fact that the Talmud does not treat niddah differently from any other transgressions might be taken as something completely unnoteworthy. But it actually is quite remarkable that it does so. In the broader Jewish (and general) society, a woman in niddah was often seen as a source of dangerous, not just ritual, impurity. To eat food that she had touched, to be in the same space as she, to touch her, and certainly to have intercourse with her, would be to expose oneself to serious harm.

Societal Taboos and Braitta Di'mesekhet Niddah

The evidence for this pattern of belief can be found in many sources and is the topic of a good number of scholarly articles. One core text in this regard is *Braitta Di'mesekhet Niddah*, which reflects and reinforces societal attitudes that saw a woman in niddah as a source of danger, and demands many forms of distancing, such as avoiding the food that she touches, where she sits, and so on. Although these taboos and associated practices are not found in the Gemara, the text is believed by a number of Rishonim, including Ramban (Gen. 31:35), to be a Tannaitic work and to carry weight in dictating practices relating to a woman in niddah.

While these taboos existed in the surrounding society, the Talmud, significantly, never relates to these taboos but only to normal halakhic categories, as we have seen in the case of sharing a bed. In the entire tractate of Niddah, you will not find one explicit reference to this taboo-worldview. [The Talmud does have terms that reflect a certain disgust with the woman's genitalia, but this is unrelated to her niddah state.] After learning the tractate, a person would not be faulted for remaining ignorant of the fact that such attitudes existed, and this is indeed often the case for those learning the Talmud outside of an academic context.

In this, the Talmud made a wise move. As soon as you engage ideas you wish to reject you are giving a hearing and partial credence to what they are saying, and it becomes hard to free oneself of them. If the Talmud were to engage these taboos, even to refute them, they would become part of the Talmudic corpus, and could end up being interpreted as having some legitimacy.

However, in two instances the Talmud did not keep to this rule, and the result was that the position being rejected actually found its way into the canon, with implications for halakhic practice even until today.

Shabbat 64b—The Early Sages and Rabbi Akiva

The first exception is from Shabbat (64b) and reads as follows:

> It was taught: "And of her in her niddah impurity" (Lev. 15:33). The early Sages said that this means that she may not paint her eyes blue, and she may not rouge her face, and she may not adorn herself with colorful clothing.
> Until Rabbi Akiva came and taught: If you do so, you are making her unappealing to her husband, and her husband will divorce her. Rather, what is the meaning of that which the verse states: "And of her in her niddah impurity"? She shall remain in her menstrual status until she immerses in the water of a ritual bath.

There are some curious features of this passage. First, it is not clear how the early Sages derive from the verse that a woman in niddah must make herself unattractive. And Rabbi Akiva, who argues for pragmatic reasons, also seems to be promoting a different read of the verse. What exactly is the debate here?

Some have suggested that the early Sages read the word "niddah" as connected to the same word as *menudah*, or a woman who is distanced (see Avot d'Rebbe Natan A, ch. 2). To which R. Akiva responds that the word niddah does not have that association and the verse means nothing other than she is in her menstrual status. I believe that there is something even deeper at play.

The Sages are *early* Sages. They are reflecting a popular approach to niddah that had an influence on their understanding of halakha. Thus, a *niddah* is a woman cast out, perhaps because of the *menudah* association, but primarily, I believe, because of the word "impurity." A "woman in her niddah impurity" means that she must embrace and demonstrate her impure—read, taboo and dangerous—status, to give outward expression to it, and so that people will know to distance themselves from her.

To this Rabbi Akiva appears on the scene introducing a wholly new approach—"All of this was what was being said, until R. Akiva arrived." You have made a mistake, he says to them, both because the consequences of your approach are severe, but also because you read too much into the word. "Impurity" here means nothing different than it does in the rest of the Torah. When the Torah says she is in "her niddah impurity," it does not mean she must give expression to her taboo nature. All it means is that she is impure just like any other impurity. The significance of this is merely that this state will be removed by going to the mikveh, nothing more, nothing less.

My proposed reading of this passage has the taboo issues of niddah as a backdrop to the debate between Rabbi Akiva and the early Sages. However, these taboos are never mentioned explicitly, and it is possible to read their debate in absence of this context. And because the position of the Sages is rejected, there should be no lasting impact of their statement on later halakhic thought.

But this is not the case. First, the same position of the early Sages is found in Avot d'Rebbe Natan, without the opposing voice of R. Akiva. And the passage there concludes: "From here they said, whoever makes herself repulsive during her period of niddah, finds favor in the eyes of the Sages. And whoever adorns herself during her period of niddah does not find favor in the eyes of the Sages (Avot D'Rebbe Natan A, ch. 2 and B, ch. 3). So this position, which was originally cited only to be dismissed, has now been embraced and promoted.

This throughout the halakhic literature. In Shulkhan Arukh (Yoreh Deah, 195:9) we read:

> Only with difficulty did they permit a wife to adorn herself during the days when she is in niddah, lest her husband come to find her repulsive.

When this taboo-oriented approach is given voice—even if what follows is an emphatic rejection and a defanging of the idea of "niddah"—it is now part of the Talmudic corpus. And once that is the case, it can be endorsed and given staying power. It can be, and has been, concluded that the early Sages are right in principle, and that Rabbi Akiva's position should be attended to, at most, due to pragmatic reasons. Those aside, a woman who is in *niddah* should make herself look repulsive.

Shabbat 13a-b—The Student who Died Young

The second exception to the Talmudic silence around the taboos is from the Talmud Shabbat (13a-b). The passage reads as follows:

The School of Eliyahu taught: There was a case involving one student who studied much Mishnah and read much Bible, and served Torah scholars and died at half his days. His wife would take his phylacteries and go around with them to synagogues and study halls, and she said: It is written in the Torah: "For it is your life and the length of your days" (Deut. 30:20). My husband who studied much, and read Bible much, [13b] and served Torah scholars extensively, why did he die at half his days? No one would respond to her at all.

Eliyahu said: One time I was a guest in her house, and she was relating that entire event and I said to her: My daughter, during the period of your niddah, how did he act toward you? She said to me: Heaven forbid! He did not touch me even with his little finger.

And I asked her: In your white days, how did he act toward you? She said: He ate with me, and drank with me, and slept with me with bodily contact (naked). However, it did not enter his mind to do anything else (i.e., have sex). And I said to her: Blessed is the Omnipresent who killed him, as he did not show respect to the Torah. The Torah said: "And to a woman in the separation of her impurity you shall not approach" (Lev. 18:19).

There are two key points to focus on in this passage. The first is the woman's comment that during the niddah period, her husband did not "touch me even with his little finger." It is this statement that leads almost all medieval commentators and halakhists to rule that it is forbidden for a man to touch his wife even in the most casual, non-sexual way during the niddah period. This is how Rambam (*Issurei Biah* 11:13) and Shulkhan Arukh (Yoreh Deah 195:2) rule.

However, there is one outlier position. It will be remembered that Ra'avyah argued that casual touch is permissible as the "distancing acts" in the Talmud are limited to only the three intimate acts and sharing a bed. That this is permitted can, moreover, be inferred from the fact that the Talmud prohibits the wife to wash her husband's face, suggesting that simply touching it is permissible. This position runs up against this passage in Shabbat where the wife said that her husband did not even touch her with his small finger. We will return to this problem momentarily.

The second issue to focus on here is the distinction that Eliyahu made in his questioning between the "niddah days" and the "white days." To what do the "white days" refer and why did he suspect—correctly, as we see—that their practice might have differed between these two periods? The reading that most suggests itself is that the "white days" refer to the seven days after menstruation has ended, during which a woman does vaginal checks to make sure that she is not bleeding (hence, "white"—the checking cloth is white and blood-free). It is after these seven days that she may go to the mikveh. The problem with this reading is obvious—the practice of checking seven days is only mandated for a *zavah*, a woman who bleeds other than during her menstrual period. In the late Talmudic period this practice of seven blood-free days was added to the niddah practice as well (Niddah 66a, and see Rosh, Niddah, 36). That cannot be what this text is referring to, since this text is hundreds of years earlier.

The other way of reading this text can be found in Tosafot (Shabbat 13b, s.v. *Biymei Libunayikh*). Tosafot states that Eliyahu was querying her about different practices that she might be observing between the days that she was actively bleeding, and the remainder of the seven niddah days when she was not actively bleeding. There is no halakhic basis to distinguish between these two sets of days, as they are all equally—from a halakhic perspective—the seven days of niddah, and Tosafot states this explicitly. Yet, Eliyahu knew that they *did* practice differently based on whether she was actively bleeding or not and thus asked her about it.

This explanation is the best read of the Talmudic passage offered by the commentators. It only requires a little context to fully appreciate it. It is evident from many texts that present a woman's niddah impurity as a source of danger, that this danger is only or primarily present when the woman is actively bleeding. When she is not bleeding but has yet to go to the mikveh, she is halakhically impure, but no longer the source of danger.

Given that the danger is present only during the bleeding days, it stands to reason that there will be more stringencies during this time, and more leniencies during the "white period." Eliyahu knew that this was the practice of this woman. And when it turned out that they were overly lenient during the white period—sharing a bed, naked—he declared that God had killed the husband because he violated these halakhic strictures.

The story is making a stronger point about the outcomes of adopting these taboos. One could say: Why not adopt these taboos, it's just being stricter (we will bracket the impact on the lived experience of the couple)? This story teaches otherwise. If you adopt a taboo-approach it will lead you away from a halakhic one. Not only will you be stricter than halakha demands, there are times that you will also be more lenient. Sure, during the bleeding days you were very strict—based on the taboos. But during the non-bleeding, you were overly lenient, because you weren't thinking halakhically! You were thinking about taboos, and from that perspective you concluded that during the non-bleeding days there are no restricted acts of distancing—all that is forbidden is intercourse itself.

The Talmud is making the point—which is necessary to be heard by those who practice a more taboo-oriented approach—that this type of practice does not just result in additional stringencies. To the contrary: these stringencies will ultimately lead to leniencies. More than that. Stringencies and leniencies aside, acting this way is simply not following halakha.

This is what Eliyahu meant when he said: "Blessed be God who killed him, as he did not show respect for the Torah." He was killed not because of his transgressing the "distancing" prohibitions, but because he fundamentally abandoned halakha. He might have read a lot of Bible and learned a lot of Mishnah, but he did not show true respect for the Torah (perhaps because he did not also learn the Talmud—the more complex rabbinic discourse around these texts, which would have anchored him in a more halakhic, non-taboo approach). With all his learning, he failed to respect the verse that treats the entire period of niddah as one and makes no distinctions between the bleeding and non-bleeding period. He rejected a Torah approach for a taboo one.

This, then, is how Ra'avyah can argue that neutral touch between husband and wife is permitted. When the wife said that during the bleeding period "he did not touch me with his little finger," she was referring to their taboo-based practice and not the practices demanded by halakha.

Here we return to the principle of the importance of ignoring rather than debating these ideas. For in this story, the Talmud is attempting to fully reject and close down a taboo approach. "Do you see what happens when you follow the popular taboos? It will lead to unwarranted leniencies. Not to mention that God might strike you dead." And yet, although the goal was to refute this position, once it is in the Talmud it becomes part of the canon. And as such, it can easily move from a rejected position to an endorsed and even required one. For all decisors other than Ra'avyah, casual touch—even a pinkie!—is forbidden between husband and wife (Rambam, *Issurei Biah*, 11:18; Shulkhan Arukh, Yoreh Deah, 195:2).

As stated in the beginning, the Talmud ignores the world of taboos around niddah, leaving it as a mundane prohibition. But in two places it chose to take the time to reject the taboo approach without mentioning it explicitly. And yet, once this idea was engaged, it wouldn't go away. We are left with halakhic rulings that would never have been made had the Talmud ignored their existence to begin with.

One can speculate that the expansion of the distancing restrictions went further than the two or three cases we have been looking at. When the Talmud's explicit four or five restrictions expanded to include endorsing the position of the early Sages, the non-sexual touching of a pinkie, and possibly also forbidding a man to gaze upon his wife—weight was given to a taboo-based approach. This opened the door to restricting other practices that were similarly rooted in this approach, practices that were never forbidden by Talmud, certainly not explicitly so.

The lesson from all of this is clear. If you want something ignored, don't fight against it, just ignore it. No matter how tempting it is, don't argue. Just walk away.

"These Words"—A Letter to Ora

Barbara Horkoff Mutch

Dear Ora,

You asked me if it might be alright to think of us as friends once the accreditation process was complete. You couldn't have known how highly I hold friendship. I was honored by your question as I am now by your husband's invitation to contribute to this volume. I count it a privilege to offer a small reflection in the precious spirit of friendship and out of a little of the learning you have brought my way.

On my first visit to the Academy for Jewish Religion in 2017, an inscription in the library was brought to my attention and translated for me as, "These words and these words…both are the words of the Living God." Located in the physical heart of the AJR study and learning space, this provocative phrase introduced me to the "living laboratory of pluralism" that AJR has been for the last 65 years.

What is this pluralism you choose to write large on the walls of the school and for which you stand? The Merriam Webster dictionary tells me that pluralism is "a system in which two or more groups or sources of authority coexist." From you, Ora, I have learned it is so much more than mere coexistence. You have written, instead, that, "AJR's approach to pluralism expects members of our community to cherish one another."[1]

I am caught off guard by your choice of the word "cherish," Ora, by your courage to use in an academic context a word that speaks of loving care. What kind of a place is this, I wondered, that chooses such a "feminine" word to describe its way of being a community or that discerns in a "soft" image the capacity on which to build a rock-solid foundation? Indeed, what kind of woman is this who knows that the softest words are actually the strongest?

I am learning that you are the kind of woman who believes that pluralism, this cherishing of the other, is necessary because it enriches life. "Cherishing means finding value in ideas other than your own and truly believing that you can learn from them… Cherishing means not only that you respect others, but that you know that your perspective, your

---

[1] Ora Horn Prouser, "Living Pluralism at AJR" in *Studies in Judaism and Pluralism* (Teaneck, NJ: Ben Yehuda Press, 2016), 1.

life, and your approach to Jewish life are richer and deeper because of your interaction with other views and approaches."[2] Pluralism matters because it makes life more.

From what may be a like-minded teacher, I read that pluralism is necessary because "difference is the source of value... Because each of us has something someone else lacks, and we each lack something someone else has, we gain by interaction."[3] Jonathan Sacks draws a lesson from the market economy that seems to resonate with your own view—that value is located in variance rather than in sameness. He argues that if "our commonalities are all that ultimately matter, then our differences are distractions to be overcome."[4] To imagine difference as desirable, rather than distraction, transforms the way I engage the other. It changes my posture toward the unfamiliar and opens me to the possibility of something greater.

Sacks believes that what is most needed is a theology of difference, not a theology of commonality, claiming that:

> the proposition at the heart of monotheism is not what it has often been taken to be: one God, therefore one path to salvation. To the contrary, it is that *unity is worshiped in diversity*. The glory of the created world is its astonishing multiplicity: the thousands of different languages spoken by mankind, the proliferation of cultures, the sheer variety of the imaginative expressions of the human spirit, in most of which, if we listen carefully, we will hear the voice of wisdom telling us something we need to know. That is what I mean by *the dignity of difference*.[5]

From my own Christian tradition, I draw on the teaching that the "voice of God comes often from where we would least expect it, like a burning bush or a stranger or a dream ... And we must be listening for it... because truth is a mosaic of the face of God."[6] Perhaps, then, pluralism is necessary, not only because it enriches life, but because it is most like the Divine and so is closest to the created order.

---

[2] Ibid., 2.

[3] Jonathan Sacks, *The Dignity of Difference* (London: Continuum, 2003), 14-15.

[4] Ibid., 47.

[5] Ibid., 20-21.

[6] Joan Chittister, *Wisdom Distilled from the Daily* (HarperOne, 2009), 24.

If this is true, then, how might pluralism be lived out?

Turning toward and not away from difference is hard and demanding work. You acknowledge that, Ora, which encourages me. "True pluralism is very difficult... The key is strong communication within communal connection... [a] nurturing and sensitive communal atmosphere... provides the perfect backdrop for complicated conversations."[7] This sounds to me like differentiation from the world of Bowenian family systems theory, much like the ability to hold different opinions or values while staying emotionally connected to others. It's necessary for healthy human functioning, isn't it? You could have been talking about differentiation when you wrote that, "the goal is not to make every person comfortable with each decision. Rather, the goal is to make the discomfort a generative discomfort; one that leads us to think, struggle, push ourselves, and ask important questions."[8] Beyond this you wisely add, "The greatest single antidote to violence is conversation, speaking our fears, listening to the fears of others, and in that sharing of vulnerabilities discovering a genesis of hope."[9]

Could it be that pluralism is achieved primarily through listening and talking? Or at least that listening and talking are indispensable to the effort? If so, then how urgently we "must learn the art of conversation, from which truth emerges not, as in Socratic dialogues, by the refutation of falsehood, but from the quite different process of letting our world be enlarged by the presence of others who think, act, and interpret reality in ways radically different from our own... so that we can hear the voice of God in a language, a sensibility, a culture not our own... recognize God's image in one who is not in my image... feel not diminished but enlarged."[10]

It is not only linguistic and listening skills that are needed, though. It seems that imagination is needed, too, specifically, imagination that is compassionate. To cherish is an act of compassion, or at least it requires compassion to enact. In another of your writings, Ora, this time on the subject of how the Bible embraces those with special needs, you state, "...there is much to be gained from a compassionate reading of the text: It encourages seeing each character as having been created in the image of God."[11] You describe Esau as distractible, Jonah as living with

---

[7] Horn Prouser, "Living Pluralism," 2-3.

[8] Ibid., 5.

[9] Ibid., 2.

[10] Sacks, *Dignity,* 17-18.

[11] Ora Horn Prouser, *Esau's Blessing* (Teaneck, NJ: Ben Yehuda Press, 2011), xi.

depression, Joseph as having a gap between intellectual and emotional maturity. Through your treatment of the biblical texts and the selection of such a topic, you model how "the generosity of our moral and spiritual imagination"[12] must grow.

Wise teachers from many spiritual traditions seem to see the necessity in our interconnected world of learning to be enlarged rather than threatened by difference. Benedictine Joan Chittister writes that "Benedictine spirituality is, then, the spirituality of the open heart. A willingness to be touched. A sense of otherness. There is no room here for isolated splendor or self-sufficiency. Here all of life becomes a teacher and we its students… The listener can always learn and turn and begin again. The real disciple can always be surprised by God… listening has something to do with being willing to change ourselves and change our world."[13]

From another Roman Catholic tradition, Franciscan Richard Rohr views this as a generational wisdom, observing that, "In the second half of life, we do not have strong and final opinions about everything, every event, or most people, as much as we allow things and people to delight us, sadden us, and truly influence us."[14]

And you, Ora, write, "The biblical text itself includes conflicting approaches…we can agree or disagree about our reading of text, but… there is not only one legitimate reading. The fact that someone else has a different approach does not negate either view or person. It is the text itself that unites us as well as our shared commitment to that text and to one another as a community of learners."[15] We are united by the text, committed to turning toward difference, convinced that value lies in variance. Moreover, we become something more, something new, when we learn to cherish the other.

A number of years ago, I spent a few days with Avivah Zornberg and a living room of women. As introductions were being made, I was struck by the many references to Avivah as "my teacher." The connections being made by these women were not simply, "I took a class with her," or "her book influenced me" as they might have been in settings more familiar to me. Instead, I heard repeatedly the sure claim of relationship spoken in the present tense. "She is my teacher." In a quiet moment later that weekend, I asked Avivah what this meant. She responded, "You are miss-

---

[12] Sacks, *Dignity*, viii.

[13] Chittister, *Wisdom*, 19, 24.

[14] Richard Rohr, *Falling Upward* (Jossey-Bass, 2011), 122.

[15] Horn Prouser, "Living Pluralism," 8.

ing something if what you learn is not refracted through a person's life. We are taught[16] to 'Find a teacher. Find a friend.'"

I guess that makes you my teacher, Ora. And also, a friend.

Thank you.

Sincerely,

Barbara

---

[16] See Pirkei Avot 1:6.

The "Day of the Lord" and the Book of Esther

Joseph H. Prouser

The Prophet

The prophecy of Obadiah holds the distinction of being the shortest book in the Hebrew Bible: a single chapter totaling twenty-one verses. Obadiah delivers a concise oracle of doom against Edom, just recompense[1] for that nation's historic hostility, its record of violence and betrayal toward Israel,[2] and, in particular, "its perfidy against Judah during the siege and destruction of the First Temple."[3] In stark contrast to Edom's demise, Obadiah offers a promise of Israel's restoration, a reversal of political fortunes to be effected on the approaching "Day of the Lord."[4]

The Book of Obadiah is read as the haftarah for Parshat Vayishlach, providing a fitting prophetic counterpoint to the Torah's narrative describing the reunion of the estranged Jacob and Esau, progenitors of Israel and Edom, respectively.[5] Obadiah thus claims the further distinction—together with the Five Megillot and Jonah alone among the Books of the Hebrew Bible—of being read in its entirety on a single liturgical occasion. A careful analysis will demonstrate, however, that the Book of Obadiah and the Book of Esther have a great deal more in common than merely the manner of their public reading. An intertextual reading of these two Biblical Books, carefully tracing their shared themes and common vocabulary, suggests that the Book of Esther may be understood as a carefully crafted commentary, a fantastical depiction of the Prophecy of Obadiah fulfilled. No single linguistic parallel could justify such a claim; it is in the sustained pattern of

---

[1] W. G. Plaut comments: "God's motivation is not vengeance, but the need to keep evil in its bounds and to fulfill the terms of the divine covenant with Israel." *The Haftarah Commentary* (UAHC Press/New York, 1996), p. 89.

[2] See Bradford A. Anderson, "Poetic Justice in Obadiah." *Journal for the Study of the Old Testament* 35.2 (2010): 247-255. See also Elie Assis, "Why Edom? On the hostility towards Jacob's brother in prophetic sources," *Vetus Testamentum* 56.1 (2006): 1-20.

[3] Michael Fishbane, *JPS Bible Commentary: Haftarot* (Philadelphia 2002), p. 55.

[4] Obadiah 15. The "Day of the Lord" is also the subject, *mutatis mutandis*, of Isaiah 13:6, 9; Ezekiel 30:3. Joel 1:15, 2:1, 4:14; Amos 5:18, 20; and Zephaniah 2:2. See Rolf Rendtorff, "Alas for the Day! The 'Day of the LORD' in the Book of the Twelve" (1998).

[5] See Genesis 32:4ff.

their shared language and geo-politics that the critical relationship between the two Biblical works comes into focus.

Haman

As a descendant of Esau (by way of Eliphaz, Amalek, and Agag), Haman embodies much of the dark character and outright evil attributed to his nation of origin by Obadiah. "Your arrogant heart has seduced you (*hishi'ekha*), you who dwell in the clefts of the rock, in your lofty abode."[6] This indictment of Edomite delusions of grandeur (alleging a temperamental expression of its mountainous habitation) finds an instructive if distant echo in Esther's description of Haman's rise to power. "King Ahasuerus promoted Haman son of Hammedatha the Agagite; he advanced him (*vayinas'ehu*) and seated him higher than any of his fellow officials."[7] In his commentary on the Book of Esther, *Mechir Yayin*,[8] Rabbi Moshe Isserles (1530-1572) identifies the description of Haman's royal promotion (*ns'*) as word play echoing the description of Eden's serpent: "the one which deceived (*n-sh'*) Eve,"[9] signaling that Haman's rise is but temporary and illusory, as well as unsavory.[10]

Similarly, the verb (*ns'*) used to describe the political rise of Megillat Esther's most notorious descendant of Edom, thus resonates with Edomite pretensions *(n-sh')* to national superiority. The verb *ns'* conveys both meanings: deception and political ascent (so, too, physical elevation). A further literary connection to Esther 3:1 employing the same pun is found in Obadiah 7: "Your own allies have deceived you (*hishi'ukha*) and prevailed over you (*yakhlu lekha*)."[11] This verse provides a dual link to the Book of Esther, paralleling the admonition of Zeresh: "If Mordecai, before whom you have

---

[6] Obadiah 3.

[7] Esther 3:1.

[8] Poland, 1556.

[9] Esther 3:1, Rabbi Moshe Isserles, *Mechir Yayin*, ad loc. See Genesis 3:13, "The serpent deceived me, and I ate"—*hanachash hishi'ani (n-sh') va-okhel*.

[10] The same pun, linking deception/delusion with physical ascent or elevation to a prominent but perilous position, is to be found in the English expression "to set up." Merriam-Webster thus includes among its definitions of "set up" both "to raise to and place in a high position… to place in power or office" as well as "to put in a compromising or dangerous position usually by trickery or deceit."

[11] See P. Kyle McCarter, "Obadiah 7 and the fall of Edom," *Bulletin of the American Schools of Oriental Research* No. 221, Memorial Issue: Essays in Honor of George Ernest Wright (February, 1976), pp. 87-91

begun to fall, is of Jewish stock, you will not prevail over him (*lo tukhal lo*); you will fall before him to your ruin."[12] His wife's prescient prediction of Haman's downfall also reprises the imagery of Obadiah: "You say to yourself,[13] 'Who can pull me down to Earth?' If you rise as high as an eagle, should you nest among the very stars, even from there I will pull you down—declares the Lord."[14] The prodigious dimensions of the gallows/stake intended for Mordecai, which becomes the instrument of Haman's demise, aptly reinforce Obadiah's imagery of a dramatic Edomite fall.[15]

Furthermore, the phrase "You say to yourself" (*omer b'libo*) itself reprises imagery of the Book of Esther. When asked obliquely by Ahasuerus regarding a fitting reward for Mordecai ("What should be done for a man whom the king desires to honor?"[16]), Haman assumes that he is the intended honoree: "Haman said to himself (*vayomer Haman b'libo*): 'Whom would the king desire to honor more than me?'"[17] The same phrase, here linking the nation of Edom in Obadiah to the most infamous descendant of Edom, Haman, is originally used to describe the eponymic founder of Edom's vengeful designs against Jacob: *Vayomer Esav b'libo*: "Esau thought to himself, 'Let but the mourning period for my father come to an end, and I will kill my brother Jacob.'"[18] While this phrase (*omer b'libo*) is neither unusual nor exclusively associated with Edom and his progeny, it contributes to a sustained pattern of parallels linking Obadiah and Esther. The inner life and dark ideation of Obadiah's Edomites and Esther's Haman, significantly revealed with the same rhetorical formula, are critical to their respective narratives.

The Book of Esther describes the reversal by which Haman is quite literally hoisted on the lethal instrument of his own devise in no uncertain terms. "But when Esther came before the king, he commanded: '…Let the evil plot, which he devised against the Jews, be visited on his own head! (*yashuv… al rosho*)' So they impaled him and his sons on the stake."[19] This formulation

---

[12] Esther 6:13.

[13] Or, "You think in your heart…."

[14] Obadiah 3-4.

[15] See her chapter on "Haman's Fall" in Elaine Rose Glickman, *Haman and the Jews: A Portrait from Rabbinic Literature* (Jason Aronson 1999), pp. 79-113.

[16] Esther 6:6.

[17] Ibid.

[18] See Genesis 27:41. Unlike his ignoble progeny, Esau does not act on this malevolent fantasy.

[19] Esther 9:25.

is taken directly from Obadiah's prophesied punishment of Edom: "As you did, so shall it be done to you; your conduct will be visited on your own head (*g'mulkha yashuv b'roshekha*)."[20]

Esther

The reversal of roles and fortunes which is the essence of the Book of Esther is not limited to Haman's ignominious execution. His property, too, is transferred to those he conspired to murder: "That very day, King Ahasuerus gave the property of Haman, the enemy of the Jews, to Queen Esther,"[21] fulfilling the assurance of Obadiah: "The House of Jacob will dispossess those who dispossessed them."[22] Obadiah's execration of Edom, who "laid hands on its wealth," is similarly revisited in Ahasuerus' order that his Jewish subjects be massacred and their possessions plundered.[23] Significantly, this acquisitive evil is eschewed by Persia's Jewish population in their ascendancy.[24]

Perhaps the most compelling connective tissue linking Esther to Obadiah is found in the Jewish heroine's own words: "How can I bear to stand by and watch (*ra'iti*) the misfortune (*b'ra'ah*) which will befall my people!? And how can I bear to stand by and watch (*ra'iti*) the destruction (*b'ovdan*) of my kindred?!"[25] Esther's mournful expression of her motivation to action is drawn directly from Obadiah: "Do not stand by and watch (*tere'*) your brother on that day... the day of his destruction (*'ovdam*)... Don't you stand by and watch his misfortune (*b'ra'ato*) on the day of his calamity."[26] It should be noted that the New Jewish Publication Society translation of these verses renders them as interrogatives, even more closely aligned with Esther's plaintive words: "How could you gaze with glee on your brother that day, on the day of his calamity... How could you... gaze with glee... on its misfortune on its day of disaster."[27] Esther's doleful refrain is customarily

---

[20] Obadiah 15.

[21] Esther 8:1.

[22] Obadiah 17.

[23] Esther 3:13.

[24] Esther 9:10.

[25] Esther 8:6.

[26] Obadiah 12-13.

[27] Obadiah 12-13. This change to the interrogative appears unique among contemporary translations. See the 1917 JPS version: "But thou shouldest not have gazed on the day of thy brother in the day of his disaster...."

chanted using the musical mode reserved for the Book of Lamentations,[28] further reinforcing the connection to the downfall of Jerusalem which occasioned Obadiah's dire oracle.

Sacred Intoxicants

Excessive drinking of intoxicants is a familiar and conspicuous narrative element of the Book of Esther.[29] The miraculous reversals and Jewish national vindication depicted in the Book of Esther are famously celebrated on the holiday of Purim, which the Biblical Book establishes,[30] by recourse to sacred intoxicants as well. The "feasting" or "banqueting" (*mishteh*: from the root *sh-t-h*: to drink)[31] prescribed in Esther 9:18, significantly, provides the Biblical basis of this process. In reference to the drinking customary on Purim, Rabbi Shlomo Yosef Zevin (1888-1978) dryly comments: "Facts are facts: the halachic duties of this day have never been neglected."[32]

The Book of Esther's penchant for drinking may further reflect its literary relationship to the prophecy of Obadiah. Immediately following the Prophet's reference to "the Day of the Lord,"[33] Obadiah continues to recall Edom's cruel and triumphal celebration of Israel's downfall, promising just recompense for that heartless gloating: "That same cup that you drank on My Holy Mount shall all nations drink evermore, drink until their speech grows thick...."[34] The Book of Esther and the popular holiday it created give substance and dramatic expression to this element of Obadiah's prophecy. Jews drink in celebration of the defeat of an Edomite/Agagite despot, just as, Obadiah records, his Edomite ancestors drank to the fall of Jerusalem. Purim drinking thus finds its sacred origins in two Biblical Books.

---

[28] A. Weil, *A Practical Manual on the Scroll of Esther* (London, 1961), p. 23.

[29] See Trisha M. Gambaiana Wheelock, *Drunk and Disorderly: A Bakhtinian Reading of the Banquet Scenes in the Book of Esther*, ProQuest, 2008.

[30] Esther 9:28.

[31] Esther 8:17, 9:17-19, 22. Compare Esther 1:3, 5, etc. See also Joshua Joel Spoelstra, "The Function of the *mishteh yayin* in the Book of Esther," *Old Testament Essays* 27.1 (2014): 285-301.

[32] *The Festivals in Halachah*, Vol. II (Mesorah/New York, 1981), p. 176.

[33] Obadiah 15.

[34] Obadiah 16. The New JPS translation offers an emendation: "...shall all nations drink at My hand."

Further Literary Resonances

In the context of this complex relationship between Esther and Obadiah, a number of additional parallels and shared linguistic terms may be identified. Haman's recourse to "lots" (*pur, hu ha-goral*)[35] to determine a propitious date for the destruction of the Jewish People calls to mind the Edomites said by Obadiah to have "cast lots (*goral*) for Jerusalem"[36] in their despoiling of the Holy City. The attentive reader of Esther, aware of the Book's basis in Obadiah, recognizes immediately the ill-fated end of Haman's use of "lots."

Similarly, Esther's statement of self-sacrificing determination, "And if I perish, I perish" (*v'cha-asher avadeti avadeti*),[37] echoes the verse in Obadiah: "I will cause the wise to perish (*v'ha-avadeti*) from Edom."[38] Again, the reader attuned to the influence of Obadiah understands: it is not Esther but her Edomite antagonist who is to meet his doom.

The physical and political salvation of Persian Jewry recorded in the Book of Esther is effected through a protracted process of palace intrigue. The malleable character of Ahasuerus and his manifest moral turpitude are critical to the narrative. They also reinforce Esther's responsiveness to the Book of Obadiah, which concludes by asserting that God is uniquely worthy of Kingship: *v'haytah l'YHVH ha-meluchah*: "And Kingship shall be the Lord's."[39]

Finally, the mass conversion to Judaism[40] of the indigenous peoples of Ahasuerus' empire constitutes an homage of sorts to the Prophet Obadiah himself, widely asserted to have been an Edomite convert to Judaism.[41]

The Day of the Lord

While any explicit reference to the Divine is famously and conspicuously

---

[35] Esther 3:7, 9:24.

[36] Obadiah 11.

[37] Esther 4:16.

[38] Obadiah 8.

[39] Obadiah 21. Compare King James Version: "And the kingdom shall be the Lord's." So, too, New International Version and English Standard Version. The New Living Translation: "And the Lord Himself will be king."

[40] Esther 8:17.

[41] Sanhedrin 39B; Rashi and Radak on Esther 8:17; Vayikra Rabbah 18:2, Tanchuma (Buber) Tazria 10.

absent throughout the ten chapters of the Book of Esther,[42] God's name is invoked seven times in Obadiah's scant twenty-one verses. It is a grave injustice to Esther, however, to read that Biblical Book as lacking a central role for the Divine. Esther dramatically details the doom prophesied by Obadiah: "The House of Jacob shall be fire, and the House of Joseph flame, and the House of Esau shall be straw; they shall burn it and devour it, and no survivor shall be left of the House of Esau."[43] Indeed, in direct fulfillment of Obadiah's prophecy, the destructive force of the Jewish People in Esther devastates its enemies, the entire household of the leading Edomite among them: "The Jews struck at their enemies with the sword, slaying and destroying; they wreaked their will upon their enemies… In the fortress of Shushan alone the Jews have killed a total of five hundred men, as well as the ten sons of Haman. What then must they have done in the provinces of the realm?!"[44]

By repeated recourse to its literary origins in the Prophecy of Obadiah, and, specifically, by referencing that prophecy in articulating Esther's duty to act in the national defense, the work that bears her name provides an extended narrative sequel to the Hebrew Bible's shortest Book. The Book of Esther, far from Godless or even strictly anthropocentric, depicts the "Day of the Lord"—replete with its promised political reversals and national recompense—fulfilling the prophecy at the very heart of Obadiah's theologically explicit oracle of doom. Thus understood, Esther is to be counted among the most God-oriented Books of the Hebrew Bible… and Purim may be the closest we come to "the Day of the Lord" until that eschatological event itself arrives.

---

[42] For a thorough exploration of this issue, see David R. Blumenthal, "Where God is not: the Book of Esther and Song of Songs." *Judaism* 44.1 (1995): 80.

[43] Obadiah 18.

[44] Esther 9:5, 12.

The Politics of Kashrut: Preliminary Observations

Jonathan Rosenbaum

Rabbi Mordechai Eliyahu (1929-2010) served as *Rishon LeZion* (Sephardic Chief Rabbi of Israel) from 1983-1993. A renowned scholar and decisor of Jewish law (*posek*), he is regarded as a *machmir* (one who rules stringently), particularly in decisions relating to Shabbat and holidays. Among many halakhic roles, Rabbi Eliyahu stood out as an acknowledged expert in the kashrut of *etrogim* and participated in debates about the halakhic validity of *etrogim* grown in various parts of the Mideast.[1]

The longstanding practice, particularly for *etrogim*, is to purchase one that is *mehuddar*, literally, "beautiful," but more precisely, one that exceeds the requirements for simply being kosher for ritual use.[2] In the 19th century, European Jewish communities often sent delegations abroad to secure *etrogim*. When costs were especially high, it was not uncommon for one *etrog* to be utilized by an entire community. However, the modern cultivation of *etrogim* for ritual purposes has made the cost of a basic, kosher *etrog* reasonable for almost everyone (typically $30 to $50).[3] Nevertheless, many observant Jews spend hundreds of dollars on an *etrog* that is *mehuddar*. Each year, in preparation for Sukkot, purchasers of *etrogim*, *mehuddarim* or just kosher, would come to Rabbi Eliyahu for his inspection. Many were meticulous in their observance; others, as Rabbi Eliyahu would subtly observe, seemed motivated more by the status conferred by his designation of their etrog as *mehuddar*.[4]

---

[1] "מרדכי אליהו," in ויקיפדיה, April 4, 2021, https://he.wikipedia.org/w/index.php?title=%D7%9E%D7%A8%D7%93%D7%9B%D7%99_%D7%90%D7%9C%D7%99%D7%94%D7%95&oldid=31071183.

[2] "*Shulchan Arukh, Orach Chayim*," 656, accessed April 13, 2021, https://www.sefaria.org/Shulchan_Arukh,_Orach_Chayim.

[3] Adele Berlin and Maxine Grossman, "ETROG," in *The Oxford Dictionary of the Jewish Religion*, ed. Adele Berlin (Oxford, UK: Oxford University Press, 2011); Jehuda Feliks, "Etrog," in *Encyclopaedia Judaica, Edited by Michael Berenbaum and Fred Skolnik*, (Macmillan Reference USA, 2007).

[4] "Etrog or Wife—On Which Should a Jew Spend More? - Israel National News," accessed April 13, 2021, https://www.israelnationalnews.com/Articles/Article.aspx/12279.

One middle-age man's recollection of Rabbi Eliyahu's view of *etrogim*, posted years after Rabbi Eliyahu's death, stands out:

> "When I was a boy of eight, my father, of blessed memory, was killed in traffic accident. The burden of financial support fell on my mother's shoulders. The situation was not simple at all, but somehow, we survived.
>
> "I reached the age of 13, but what I remember from the celebration of my bar mitzvah was a sad experience without my father…As the holidays of Tishrei grew near, I told my mother that I had learned in Talmud Torah that after reaching the age of mitzvot, one is required to shake the Four Species according to their halakhic requirements. My mother responded to me with pain, 'My dear son, it seems that I cannot give you money for buying an *etrog*. We're at the beginning of the month of Elul. I suggest that you save money from your allowance and from performing Psalms…With that money you should buy an *etrog*. Within a month and a half I gathered penny by penny, until the days just before Sukkot. I went with my savings bank to the Machane Yehudah market and bought an *etrog* in a closed and sealed box on which was written '*mehuddar*.'
>
> "My happiness knew no bounds, but when I arrived home and opened the box, I revealed that they [the sellers] had likely cheated me. The *etrog* was not particularly beautiful, but I did not know how to decide if I had bought, as it were, a cat in a sack. I simply did not know and was no expert in the *halakhot* of *etrogim*. I thus decided to go up to the home of Rabbi Mordechai Eliyahu who lived in our neighborhood to ask him if the *etrog* that I bought was *mehuddar*.
>
> "I arrived at the rabbi's house and gave him the *etrog*. The rabbi looked it over from all sides and said, 'Kosher.' I asked: 'Rabbi, but isn't it *mehuddar*?' The rabbi repeated and said: 'Kosher.' I kissed his hand and went out of the house, but my heart was heavy. Yet, before I could go down the steps, a boy from his household came out to me

and called: 'Excuse me, but the rabbi requests that you return to him.'

"I returned immediately to the rabbi. He looked at me with a smile and said: 'Come, let's do an exchange. Give me your *etrog*, the kosher one, and I will give you my *etrog*, which is *mehuddar*.'

"I was truly ashamed, overwhelmed. Tears came down my face and I didn't even stop to wipe them. I went out of the rabbi's house with an *etrog* worth more, perhaps, than a thousand shekels...

"The next day was the first day of Sukkot. I got up early to pray at sunrise. I went to pray with Rabbi Mordechai Eliyahu. I looked over at him when he took out the *etrog* and I did not believe it! I rubbed my eyes again and again, but it was not a mistake. My *etrog*, the 'just' kosher one, was in the *rabbi's* hands! He made the exchange with me a reality [by actually using the *etrog* that was kosher but not *mehuddar*]." [5]

That incident took place in the 1990s.[6] In that same period, Haym Soloveitchik published "Rupture and Reconstruction: The Transformation of Contemporary Orthodoxy,"[7] a pivotal article that sought to acknowledge and explain the historical and halakhic changes that had transformed Orthodox Judaism in the latter half of the 20th century. A renowned professor at the Hebrew University and Yeshiva University, Soloveitchik has also served as a dean and *rosh yeshiva*. Undeniably pertinent, Haym Soloveitchik

---

[5] My translation. There are at least two versions of this recollection. Though the wording is the same regarding the key events, some additional information appears in the version published in JDN. See לשכת הרב שמואל אליהו - בס"ד סיפור מדהים על קיום מצוות אתרוג ע"י מרן הרב מרדכי אליהו זצ"ל: Http://Bit.Ly/2kq0Hpu | Facebook, accessed April 12, 2021, https://m.facebook.com/permalink.php?story_fbid=1260070704108927&id=314191358696871&substory_index=0 and יעקב אבוביץ, עסקת החליפין והאתרוג המהודר של הגר"מ אליהו • סיפור מרגש, *JDN* - חדשות (blog), October 3, 2017, https://www.jdn.co.il/breakingnews/891380/.

[6] "אבוביץ, "עסקת החליפין והאתרוג המהודר של הגר"מ אליהו • סיפור מרגש.

[7] Haym Soloveitchik, "Rupture and Reconstruction: The Transformation of Contemporary Orthodoxy," *Tradition: A Journal of Orthodox Jewish Thought* 28, no. 4 (1994), 64–130.

(1937-) is the scion of one of the most eminent rabbinic families and the only son of Rabbi Joseph Ber Soloveitchik (1903-1993).

The elder Soloveitchik was the "preeminent spiritual leader of Modern Orthodoxy."[8] He ordained some 2,000 Orthodox rabbis as the paramount *rosh yeshiva* of Yeshiva University's Rabbi Isaac Elchanan Theological Seminary (RIETS).[9] He also framed many of the structures and boundaries of Modern Orthodox Judaism.

Haym Soloveitchik was the product of this development. Educated at the Maimonides School, New England's first Jewish day school, which his father had founded (1937); Harvard College; and the Hebrew University (Ph.D., 1972), Haym observed firsthand the challenges and development not only of Modern Orthodoxy, but of Orthodox Judaism in all its variations. He did so with a simultaneous and deep awareness of the cultural, ethical, and political realities of secular society.

From the outset of "Rupture and Reconstruction," he openly shares autobiographical observations that may seem jarring to those contemporary Orthodox Jews who have romanticized the past. He sets out to "understand the developments that have occurred within my lifetime in the community in which I live. The orthodoxy in which I, and other people my age, were raised scarcely exists anymore." In the immediate postwar era, two things primarily separated modern Orthodoxy from "ultra-" or haredi Orthodoxy: attitudes toward secular education and Zionism.[10] He argues that the changes he observed are not just "a swing to the Right" or the reflexive adoption of *humra* (stringency) in *halakhah*, but rather a new emphasis on the punctilious use of text rather than a transmission that is "mimetic, imbibed from parents and friends, and patterned on conduct regularly observed in home and street, synagogue and school."[11] He goes on: "the Ashkenazic community saw the law as manifesting itself in two forms: in the canonized written corpus (the Talmud and codes), and in the regnant practices of the people. Custom was a correlative datum of the halakhic system. And, on frequent occasions, the written word was reread in light of traditional behavior."[12] He

---

[8] Aaron Rothkoff and Dov Schwartz, "Soloveitchik, Joseph Baer," in *Encyclopaedia Judaica*, ed. Michael Berenbaum and Fred Skolnik, 2nd ed., vol. 18 (Detroit, MI: Macmillan Reference USA, 2007), 777–8.

[9] Ari L. Goldman, "Joseph D. Soloveitchik, 90, Orthodox Rabbi, Dies," *New York Times*, April 10, 1993.

[10] Soloveitchik, "Rupture and Reconstruction," 64.

[11] Soloveitchik, 66.

[12] Soloveitchik, 67.

shows that the mimetic practices held a formal place in halakhic decisions.[13]

More recently, however, accepted practices are based on text alone. For the Sabbath, Festivals, prayer, tefillin, etc., the *Mishnah Berurah*, the practical handbook and commentary on *Orach Chayim*,[14] written by the Chafetz Chayim (Rabbi Israel Meir Ha-Kohen Kagan [surname Poupko]; 1838–1933), has become the standard reference for observance in the Ashkenazi Orthodox community[15] or "enclave," as Soloveitchik calls it. For all its balance and erudition, the *Mishnah Berurah* is based on "the written literature alone." It does not consider the historic role of custom, *minhag*, despite the fact that there are longstanding cases where *minhag* supersedes *halakhah*.[16] The emphasis on the text alone has led to a power shift whereby laymen who historically wielded power within the Orthodox enclave now lack confidence in their own knowledge and have thus ceded their power to rabbinic authority. Yeshivot "produce great scholars now no less than in the past, and often successfully so, but cur-

---

[13] Soloveitchik, 66.

[14] Orach Chayim, (אורח חיים; "way of life") is one of the four sections of the *Shulkhan Arukh* (שולחן ערוך) that its compiler, Rabbi Yosef Karo (1488-1575) based on Rabbi Jacob ben Asher's (1269-1343) own compilation of *Halakhah*, *Arba'ah Turim*. *Orach Chayim* deals with daily rituals and calendrical events.

[15] The emphasis on text replacing mimetic tradition proposed in "Rupture and Reconstruction" has received further confirmation since the publication of the article in 1994. In yeshivot and similar venues, Rabbi Simcha Rabinowitz's commentary on the Mishnah *Berurah* itself, פסקי תשובות לפי סדר המשנה ברורה (6 vols. [Jerusalem, 1991-2019]), has become a commonly utilized compilation of supporting sources of the *Mishnah Berurah*. Thus, a new layer of text has been added to the process of understanding and observing Jewish law of *Orach Chayim*. This layer itself has been superseded by a new edition of the *Mishnah Berurah* published by Dirshu, an Orthodox educational organization founded in Toronto in 1997, which sponsors a variety of intensive halakhic lessons complete with optional exams. Dirshu is no small undertaking with hundreds of branches across five continents and some 150,000 people who have taken its exams (https://www.dirshu.co.il/%D7%90%D7%95%D7%93%D7%95%D7%AA-%D7%93%D7%A8%D7%A9%D7%95/). Dirshu has issued *Dirshu Mishnah Berurah* (New Edition; Jerusalem: Dirshu, 2016) and an index, *Sefer Hamafte'ach - Dirshu Mishnah Berurah* (Jerusalem: Dirshu, 2021). The Dirshu publication of *Mishnah Berurah* is becoming the preferred edition because of its inclusion of the following commentaries: *Musafim* (additional sources gathered from the Chafetz Chaim's other writings); *Bi'urim*, statements from the books of decisors (poskim) who came after the Chafetz Chaim, which clarify the Mishnah Berurah; *Piskei Halakhah*, pertinent halakhic decisions from contemporary poskim; and *Piskei Hazon 'Ish*, a compendium of the related positions of the Hazon Ish.

[16] Soloveitchik, "Rupture and Reconstruction," 69.

rently their major function is molding the cadres of the orthodox enclave."[17]

Soloveitchik illustrates the change from mimetic to text by citing the case of *shi'urim*, the minimal amounts or volumes necessary to fulfill a *mitzvah*. He notes that in the 18th century, scholars like the Noda Biyhudah (R. Ezekiel Landau, 1713-1793) and the Vilna Gaon (Elijah ben Solomon Zalman, 1720-1797) proposed changes in dry and liquid volumes, but their writing had little practical impact on observance until the 1950s when the Hazon Ish (Avraham Yeshaya Karelitz, 1878-1953) proposed increases in *shi'urim* that became standard within a generation.[18] The abrupt change in halakhic standards regarding the minimum volume of wine led to some paradoxical if not humorous consequences.

When the Hazon Ish was shown kiddush cups owned or given as gifts by leading, earlier halakhic authorities, he did not relent in his opinion. The acceptance of his position led to the ironic instance of the grandsons of the Chafetz Chayim refusing to use their grandfather's kiddush cup on Passover, because it was too small to hold the prescribed "amount (*shi'ur*) of the Hazon Ish." Their grandfather's authorship of the *Mishnah Berurah*, the very legal commentary that guides most of contemporary Ashkenazic Orthodox Jewry, did not change the grandsons' minds.[19] The recalcitrance of the Hazon Ish when confronted by historical evidence was thus mirrored a generation later when the grandchildren of the Chafetz Chayim proved as adamant even when confronted by the evidence of their grandfather's actual kiddush cup.

This state of affairs takes on additional irony in light of the *Mishnah Berurah*'s methodological dependence on text rather than mimetic tradition. Indeed, for Soloveitchik, the *Mishnah Berurah* is the very epitome of the text-based code (though, as he notes, it is technically a commentary on a code).[20] He suggests that the reason for the *Mishnah Berurah*'s adherence to text versus the mimetic tradition was that the Chafetz Chayim saw the challenges of the Enlightenment, Socialism, Zionism, and the decline of the mimetic tradition that had passed as standard Jewish practice from one generation to the next.

Ira Robinson adds to our understanding of the *Mishnah Berurah*'s tex-

---

[17] Soloveitchik, 89.

[18] Soloveitchik, 69.

[19] Menachem Friedman, "The Lost Kiddush Cup: Changes in Ashkenazi Haredi Culture—A Tradition in Crisis," pp. 175-186 in Jack Wertheimer, ed., *The Uses of Tradition: Jewish Continuity in the Modern Era* (New York: Jewish Theological Seminary, 1992), 181.

[20] Soloveitchik, "Rupture and Reconstruction," 106–7, n. 6.

tual commitment, its origin, and rationale. He suggests that the *Mishnah Berurah* was the crowning opus of a project that the Chafetz Chayim undertook by writing two prototypes, *Mahane Yisrael* ("The Camp of Israel," 1881) and *Nidhei Yisrael* ("The Dispersed of Israel," 1893), which he published, respectively, as handbooks of Jewish observance for 1) Jewish soldiers in the Russian army and 2) Jewish emigrants to the U.S., South America, and other lands that lacked a rabbinic superstructure. The Chafetz Chayim saw that realities of these new environments led to breakdowns in sexual mores, lack of Jewish education, social pressure from other Jews not to observe Jewish rituals (e.g., *tefillin* in public), and the abandonment of the laws of family purity. As Robinson points out, the Chafetz Chayim's response to these challenges was "to create an halakhic guide that was accessible and authoritative."[21] The publication of the *Mishnah Berurah* in six volumes (1893-1907) represented the fulfillment of this plan.

In a long, vital note, Soloveitchik contrasts the *Mishnah Berurah* with the contemporaneously published *Arukh Ha-Shulkhan* (published from 1884-1907). Written by Rabbi Yechiel Mechel Halevi Epstein (1829-1908) who penned it as a handbook, the *Arukh Ha-Shulkhan* differed from *Mishnah Berurah* in outlook and audience. While the *Mishnah Berurah* frequently relies on the Vilna Gaon, it does not use his methodology. The *Arukh Ha-Shulkhan* does, but it is not alone:

> "The crux of the Gaon's approach both to Torah study and *pesak* was its independence of precedent. A problem was to be approached in terms of the text of the Talmud mediated by the *rishonim*[22] (and in the Gaon's case even that mediation was occasionally dispensed with). What subsequent commentators say about this issue, was, with few exceptions (e.g. Magen Avraham, Shakh[23]), irrelevant. This approach is writ large on every page of *Biur ha-Gra*,[24] further

---

[21] Ira Robinson, "Introduction," pp. xiii-xxii in Simcha Fishbane, *The Boldness of a Halakhist: An Analysis of the Writings of Rabbi Yechiel Mechel Halevi Epstein's the Arukh Hashulhan* (Boston: Academic Studies Press, 2008), xiii-xxii.

[22] "First ones." rabbis and *poskim* who lived from the 11th to 15th centuries before the composition of the *Shulkhan Aruch*.

[23] Standard commentaries published with the *Shulkhan Aruch*: *Magen Avraham* by Rabbi Abraham Gombiner of Kalisz, Poland (c. 1637-1683); *Shakh* (Hebrew: ש"ך) stands for *Siftei Kohen*, by Shabbatai HaKohen (1621-1662).

[24] Glosses on the Babylonian Talmud and *Shulkhan Aruch* by the Vilna Gaon.

embodied in the *Hayyei Adam*[25] and the *Arukh ha-Shulhan*, and has continued on to our day in the works of such Lithuanian *posekim*, as the Hazon Ish and R. Mosheh [sic] Feinstein. *Mishnah Berurah* rejects *de facto* this approach and returns to the world of precedent and string citation."[26]

Recent scholarship has further documented such independence of precedent, particularly regarding the Vilna Gaon.[27] In the case of the *Arukh Hashulkhan*, that principle allowed for often lenient rulings as a matter of halakhic methodology. Indeed, its author, Rabbi Epstein, told a student: "When any problem in connection with the prohibitions of the Torah comes before you, you must first presume it is permitted, and only after you have carefully studied the rishonim and can find no possibility of leniency are you obliged to rule that it is forbidden" (Maimon, Sarei ha-Me'ah, p. 112)."[28]

Soloveitchik posits reasons for changes in Orthodox Judaism, especially exposure to secular society and its concomitant challenges. He suggests "the perception of God as a daily, natural force is no longer present to a significant degree in any sector of modern Jewry."[29] He acknowledges the sharp climb in intermarriage rates beginning in the 1950s after decades when it had been "extraordinarily low and stable" (4%-6%). By the publication of "Rupture and Reconstruction," he noted, the intermarriage rate was approaching 50%.[30] However, he discounts the impact of *ba'alei teshuvah*.[31]

"Rupture and Reconstruction" did not meet with universal affirmation. For example, the lack of God as a natural force in contemporary Judaism faced strong criticism.[32] Nevertheless, Soloveitchik's central thesis remains intact. As one of his critics summarized it, that thesis is: "(i) the tendency to

---

[25] A still popular digest of the laws in *Orach Chayim* by Avraham Danzig, 1748-1820.

[26] Soloveitchik, "Rupture and Reconstruction," 110–12, n. 20.

[27] Eliyahu Stern, *The Genius: Elijah of Vilna and the Making of Modern Judaism* (New Haven: Yale University Press, 2013), 76, 121–23.

[28] Quoted in Yehoshua Horowitz, "Epstein, Jehiel Michal Ben Aaron Isaac Ha-Levi," in *Encyclopaedia Judaica*, ed. Michael Berenbaum and Fred Skolnik, 2nd ed., vol. 6 (Detroit: Macmillan Reference USA, 2007), 47.

[29] Soloveitchik, "Rupture and Reconstruction," 102.

[30] Soloveitchik, 72 and 117, n. 42.

[31] Soloveitchik, 110, n. 19.

[32] H. Goldberg, "Responding to 'Rupture and Reconstruction' + R. Haym Soloveitchik's Transformation of Contemporary Jewish Orthodoxy," *Tradition-a Journal of Orthodox Jewish Thought* 31, no. 2 (Winter 1997), 31.

punctilious observance delineated in the books on the Halakhah (and, for the uninitiated, halakhic handbooks), and to convert humrot in the Law to normative positions of the Law, and (ii) a shift in religious authority from the family and local rabbinate to the academic, institutional masters of the book, the *rashei yeshivah*."[33] That critic, Isaac Chavel, refines, elucidates, and expands on "Rupture and Reconstruction" (regarding, e.g., the vitality of Modern Orthodoxy into the 1970s, a more significant influence of *baʿalei teshuvah*, the conscious agenda of *haredi yeshivot* to oppose Modern Orthodoxy and Yeshiva University in particular, and the willingness of some *haredi* leaders to ignore and even rewrite historical facts), but he does not undermine Soloveitchik's basic conclusions.

More than a quarter century after its appearance, "Rupture and Reconstruction" has held its place in the corpus of Jewish communal discussion. The editors of the journal in which it was published have recently described it as "one of the most significant items ever published in *Tradition*."[34] A cursory survey in Google Scholar[35] yields 710 citations in peer-reviewed academic journals, books, and the like. This number does not include popular magazines[36] and newspapers, social media, and blogs.[37] The article has appeared among dozens of other works in a proposed modern "Jewish canon."[38] Yet among the most convincing attestations of its impact is the symposium presented and published by the editors of *Tradition* to mark the 25th anniversary of its appearance in print.[39]

---

[33] Isaac Chavel, "On Haym Soloveitchik's 'Rupture and Reconstruction: The Transformation of Contemporary Orthodox Society': A Response," *The Torah U-Madda Journal* 7 (1997), 123.

[34] "(20+) Tradition Journal - Posts | Facebook," accessed April 22, 2021, https://www.facebook.com/TraditionJournal/posts/undoubtedly-one-of-the-most-significant-items-ever-published-in-tradition-was-pr/2384071578533894/.

[35] Soloveitchik, "Rupture and Reconstruction." The 710-item survey is at https://scholar.google.com/scholar?hl=en&as_sdt=0%2C39&q=rupture+and+reconstruction+soloveitchik&oq=%22Rupture+and+Reconstruction.

[36] "Thoughts on 'Rupture and Reconstruction'—Twenty-Five Years Later," *Jewish Action*, June 20, 2019, https://jewishaction.com/religion/jewish-thought/thoughts-on-rupture-and-reconstruction-twenty-five-years-later/.

[37] Micha Berger, "Rupture and Reconstruction at 25 Years," *Torah Musings* (blog), August 23, 2019, https://www.torahmusings.com/2019/08/rupture-and-reconstruction-at-25-years/.

[38] Yehuda Kurtzer and Claire E. Sufrin, eds., *The New Jewish Canon: Ideas & Debates 1980-2015*, Emunot: Jewish Philosophy and Kabbalah (Boston: Academic Studies Press, 2020).

[39] *Tradition* 51, no. 4 (2019) includes 18 articles based on "Rupture and Reconstruction."

Like any good theory, Soloveitchik's proposal that the "rupture" in the chain of mimetic transmission led to the need to "reconstruct" Orthodox Judaism based on text should be tested in the real world. Indeed, as previously noted, he cited illustrations (e.g., *shiurim*). However, many works inspired by his "Rupture and Reconstruction" concentrate on its sociological, theological, or historical implications. Applying its conclusions to actual halakhic cases may confirm or refine its conclusions. The subject of *kashrut* constitutes a concrete and accessible area where principles can be tested.

Chalav Yisrael versus Chalav Stam: A Test Case

The reconstructed emphasis on text has brought real-world changes in Orthodox Jewish practice. Observances previously viewed as unnecessary, excessive, or adopted to go beyond and "beautify" the basic halakhic requirement (*hiddur mitzvah*) have increasingly been presented as the accepted standard. "Rupture and Reconstruction" summarized this trend: "What had been a stringency peculiar to the Right…had become…a widespread practice in modern orthodox circles, and among its younger members, an axiomatic one."[40] The reality is clear: "There is currently a very strong tendency in both lay and rabbinic circles towards stringency (*humra*)."[41]

The case of milk or, more precisely, *chalav Yisrael* vs *chalav stam*, exemplifies this phenomenon. *Chalav Yisrael* is milk that was milked by a Jew or under a Jew's supervision. The modern term, *chalav stam*, is milk that did not have Jewish supervision, but is not *chalav akum* ("the milk milked by a non-Jew"), which is prohibited.

The Mishnah, Avodah Zara 2:6 forbids "milk that was milked by a non-Jew and a Jew did not see him (do the milking)." The Gemara (Avodah Zara 35b) explains that this rabbinic prohibition, actually a *gezerah*,[42] is due to the concern that the Gentile might mix in non-kosher milk. The *Shulkhan Aruch* (*Yoreh Deah* 115:1-3, esp. 115:1) forbids *chalav akum*, but immediately lists exceptions regarding cases when a Jew does not directly see the milking but where the milk is permitted. The Rama[43] reinforces and provides further detail, citing a number of Rishonim (e.g., Rabbi Meir of Rotenberg; the Mordechai; Rabbenu Peretz [Rabbi Perez ben Elijah of

---

[40] Soloveitchik, "Rupture and Reconstruction," 64–65.

[41] Soloveitchik, 72.

[42] A rabbinical enactment, typically a prohibition, issued as a preventive measure.

[43] The glosses on the *Shulkhan Arukh* by Rabbi Moses Isserles (1530-1572) that provide the Ashkenazic variations on Rabbi Joseph Karo's text.

Corbeil, died ca. 1298]). Rashi (Sh"t Rashi 152[44]) concurs.[45]

A minority opinion among Rishonim appears to take a more lenient position. *Chut Hameshulash*,[46] the commentary on *Tashbetz*,[47] states (4:32) that if there is no non-kosher animal in the non-Jew's flock and there are no non-kosher animals in the vicinity (courtyard) the milk is kosher.[48] *Tashbetz*[49] adds that if the non-kosher milk such as camel milk is more expensive there is no concern that they might mix it into the cow milk. The Shach 115:4 and Taz[50] 115:3 accept that if there was a Jew walking in and out, that milk would be *chalav Yisrael*.

Among the early *Aharonim* who were lenient on the issue of *chalav Yisrael*, the *Pri Chadash* stands out.[51] Its author, Hezekiah ben David da

---

[44] "Hebrewbooks_org_1734_235.Pdf," accessed April 25, 2021, https://beta.hebrewbooks.org/pagefeed/hebrewbooks_org_1734_235.pdf#toolbar=1&navpanes=0&statusbar=0&view=FitH.

[45] For a detailed discussion on the sources and issues regarding *chalav Yisrael* and *chalav stam*, refer to the lectures on *Shulkhan Arukh, Yoreh Deah*, 115:1 by Rabbi Aryeh Lebowitz to RIETS semichah (ordination) students: https://www.yutorah.org/lectures/lecture.cfm/998968/rabbi-aryeh-lebowitz/yoreh-deah-shiur-97-siman-115-chalav-akum/; https://www.yutorah.org/lectures/lecture.cfm/999406/rabbi-aryeh-lebowitz/yoreh-deah-shiur-98-siman-115-chalav-akum/; https://www.yutorah.org/sidebar/lecture.cfm/999466/rabbi-aryeh-lebowitz/yoreh-deah-shiur-99-siman-115-chalav-akum/

[46] "HebrewBooks.Org Sefer Detail: חוט המשולש—דיואן, יהודה בן עמרם," accessed April 25, 2021, https://hebrewbooks.org/131.

[47] *Tashbetz* (תשב"ץ) is the work of R. Simeon ben Zemah Duran (1361–1444); the *Chut Hameshulash* (חוט המשולש) is a commentary on that work, which was written by the grandchildren of the Tashbetz.

[48] Quoted in "Kosher Milk - Halachipedia," accessed April 25, 2021, https://halachipedia.com/index.php?title=Kosher_Milk#cite_note-5.

[49] "HebrewBooks.Org Sefer Detail: תשב"ץ—שמשון בן צדוק - לוריא, משה בצלאל בן שרגא פיבוש," accessed April 25, 2021, https://hebrewbooks.org/59358.

[50] Taz (ט"ז) is the abbreviation of *Turei Zahav* by David ha-Levi Segal (c. 1586—1667) and for Shakh, see above. The Taz and the Shach are major commentaries on the *Shulkhan Arukh* and are traditionally published immediately surrounding the texts by Yosef Karo and Moses Isserles.

[51] The fullest recent summary of the life, works, and halakhic approach of the Pri Chadash is Gavin Michal, "(161) The Ban, the Repeal, and the Censoring of the Pri Chadash," *Kotzk Blog* (blog), January 28, 2018, https://www.kotzkblog.com/2018/01/161-ban-repeal-and-censoring-of-pri.html; Abraham David, "Hezekiah Ben David Da Silva," in *Encyclopaedia Judaica*, ed. Michael Berenbaum and Fred Skolnik, 2nd ed., vol. 9 (Detroit: Macmillan Reference USA, 2007), 91–92; "Hezekiah Da Silva," in *Wikipedia*, April 25, 2021, https://en.wikipedia.org/w/index.php?title=Hezekiah_da_

Silva (1659-1698), gained acceptance as a rabbi and *posek* by the age of 30 when he was offered the Sephardic rabbinic leadership of Amsterdam. In the seventeenth century, with the independence of the Netherlands from Spain, Amsterdam had become a major center of refuge for Jews and conversos whose forbears had fled the Inquisition and expulsions from Spain and Portugal.[52] In Amsterdam, they publicly espoused Judaism, but such freedom led to divisions in the community between stringent and lenient groups. Da Silva thus chose to reject Amsterdam's invitation and instead became the head of a yeshiva in Jerusalem. The *Pri Chadash*'s lenient opinions initially created an outcry among rabbis in Egypt who banned them. Eventually, however, it became a standard commentary on the *Shulkhan Arukh*, but only after some of its more contentious positions had been excised.[53]

Withal, the *Pri Chadash*'s ruling on milk survived. In concert with the *Tashbetz* and the *Chut Hameshulash*, the *Pri Chadash* rules that if no non-kosher animals are in the vicinity or if milk from non-kosher animals is more expensive than the kosher milk, then milk milked by a non-Jew is permissible.[54]

Not so accepting, later *poskim* opposed any leniency. R. Moses Schreiber (1762–1839), better known as the Chatam Sofer, exemplified this trend. A prolific writer and renowned *posek*, he was rabbi of Pressburg (today Bratislava, Slovakia) for 33 years. There he established a yeshiva and trained dozens of eminent Hungarian and Central European rabbis.[55] He wrote responsa in the atmosphere of new social factors that challenged the traditional rabbinic structure of what would be called Orthodox Judaism.[56]

Silva&oldid=1019807827.

[52] J. C. H. Blom, R. G. Fuks-Mansfeld, and Ivo Schöffer, eds., *The History of the Jews in the Netherlands*, Littman Library of Jewish Civilization (Oxford; Portland, OR: The Littman Library of Jewish Civilization, 2002); Daniel Swetschinski, *Reluctant Cosmopolitans: The Portuguese Jews of Seventeenth-Century Amsterdam* / (London; Littman Library of Jewish Civilization, 2000).

[53] Michal, "(161) The Ban, the Repeal, and the Censoring of the Pri Chadash."

[54] "HebrewBooks.Org Sefer Detail: -1656 פרי חדש - יורה דעה—סילבה, חזקיה בן דוד די, 34–233, 1695, pp. 233-234; *Pri Chadash* 115:6 on *Shulkhan Arukh*, *Yoreh Deah*, 115, 1; accessed April 25, 2021, https://hebrewbooks.org/41539.

[55] For a representative list of leading students of the Pressburg yeshiva, see "Moses Sofer," in *Wikipedia*, February 18, 2021, https://en.wikipedia.org/w/index.php?title=Moses_Sofer&oldid=1007442256.

[56] Miriam Walfish, "Rabbi Moses Sofer and His Response to Religious Reform," Unpublished M.A. Thesis (Montreal, McGill University, 1989).

He ruled stringently on *chalav Yisrael*.⁵⁷

Judaism's confrontation with the Enlightenment had begun and the simultaneous prominence of Moses Mendelssohn in German and Jewish culture heralded more substantive change. The Chatam Sofer evinced genuine respect for Mendelssohn, who was an observant Jew. He even referred to Mendelssohn with a rabbinic acronym, רמ"ד (for Rabbi Moshe of Dessau).⁵⁸ Though Reform Judaism would see Mendelssohn as a prototypical inspiration, the Chatam Sofer denied any connection between the halakhically committed רמ"ד and the new movement that increasingly rejected the traditionally defining central principle of divinely given Jewish law (Torah). The Chatam Sofer thus vehemently opposed the nascent Reform movement. These factors may have strengthened his resolve to rule stringently on topics where leniency could inadvertently supply license for the new and radical Reform movement to diverge from traditional observance. Nevertheless, in the generations that followed the Chatam Sofer, his decision continued to receive official if not always operational acceptance in many quarters.

In 1803, three years before Chatam Sofer established his yeshiva at Pressburg, Chaim ben Yitzchak of Volozhin (1749-1821), popularly known as "Reb Chaim Volozhiner," the leading disciple of the Vilna Gaon established a yeshiva at Volozhin (now Valozhyn, Belarus). Throughout most of the 19th century (1803-1892), the Volozhin yeshiva was the preeminent institution of Eastern European rabbinic learning. Its students became the rabbinic leaders of European Jewish communities and, eventually, many occupied similar roles in America. Others founded or led yeshivot that became renowned in their own right.

In May 1902, 59 European-trained rabbis from 30 American cities, Montreal, and Toronto met to establish the Union of Orthodox Rabbis of the United States and Canada (UOR), or Agudath Harabonim. All *dayyanim* (qualified rabbinic judges), many of them had studied at the Volozhin Yeshiva. One of the UOR's central goals was the establishment of strict and uncorrupted standards for kashrut, yet the primary emphasis lay in establishing effective supervision of ritual slaughter (*shekhitah*) and oversight of the subsequent preparation and sale of meat and poultry.⁵⁹

---

⁵⁷ "Responsa Chatam Sofer," *Yoreh Deah*, 107, accessed April 25, 2021, https://www.sefaria.org/Responsa_Chatam_Sofer.

⁵⁸ Meir Hildesheimer, "The Attitude of the Hatam Sofer toward Moses Mendelssohn," *Proceedings of the American Academy for Jewish Research* 60 (1994), 141-187, esp., 143-145, https://doi.org/10.2307/3622572.

⁵⁹ Jeffrey S. Gurock, *Orthodox Jews in America* (Bloomington: Indiana University

Milk production did not seem to constitute an area for concern.

The pitfalls of supervising ritual slaughterers and butchers had taxed and perhaps expended the energies of Rabbi Jacob Joseph (1848[60]?-1902[61]). Rabbi Joseph, a renowned Volozhin-trained scholar, had come to the U.S. to serve as chief rabbi of New York (actually New York's Association of American Orthodox Hebrew Congregations) in 1888.[62] Though he did successfully institute a number of rigorous standards, butchers, patrons, and even some colleagues pressured him constantly. His funeral took place coincidently on or just before the day of the UOR's first organizing meeting.

In 1903, in Ozone Park, Queens, Isaac Balsam (1880-1945) is said to have established the first *chalav Yisrael* dairy in the Unites States. Eventually, the Balsam farm had 300 cows.[63] In 1900, New York City had a Jewish population of some 598,000.[64] Even presuming a small percentage of that number followed the Chatam Sofer, Balsam's farm would have proven inadequate to supply them. Those among the 59 founding members of the UOR who lived in smaller American cities may have had direct access to farmers and thus the ability to oversee the production of *chalav Yisrael*, but mass supervision of *chalav Yisrael* does not seem to have been been a priority. In any case, we know for certain that in Lithuanian yeshivot, *chalav Yisrael* was not the standard. No less a witness than Rabbi Menachem Genack, the longtime CEO of the Orthodox Union's kosher division, attests to that fact. He recollects that in the Lakewood Yeshiva (Beth Medrash Govoha), Rabbi Aaron Kotler (1891-1962), the yeshiva's founder and *rosh yeshiva*, did not regard *chalav Yisrael* as necessary:

"When Rav Aharon Kotler started Lakewood, he wasn't makpid ["punctilious"] on chalav Yisrael. The famous story that's told is that when he was finally convinced to switch to chalav Yisrael it came in a big canister, which

---

Press, 2009), 118–19, http://ebookcentral.proquest.com/lib/upenn-ebooks/detail.action?docID=437620.

[60] Abraham J. Karp, "New York Chooses a Chief Rabbi," *Publications of the American Jewish Historical Society* 44, no. 3 (March 1955): 129, photo caption.

[61] Sources differ on Rabbi Joseph's age at death: 59 or 51. Compare Jeffrey S. Gurock, "Resisters and Accommodators: Varieties of Orthodox Rabbis in America, 1886-1983," *American Jewish Archives* 35, no. 2 (November 1, 1983): 100; Gurock, *Orthodox Jews in America*.

[62] Karp, "New York Chooses a Chief Rabbi."

[63] "Isaac Balsam," in *Wikipedia*, October 28, 2020, https://en.wikipedia.org/w/index.php?title=Isaac_Balsam&oldid=985920198.

[64] "Berman Jewish DataBank," accessed April 29, 2021, https://www.jewishdatabank.org/databank/search-results/study/511.

overturned, and he was very upset about the entire switch."⁶⁵

The status of the principals is significant: Rabbi Kotler founded the Lakewood Yeshiva in 1943. Today it is the second largest yeshiva in the world. As of 2018, there were 6,715 students, 2,748 regular and 3,967 in Kollel status⁶⁶ with an estimated Orthodox population of 66,000 in Lakewood.⁶⁷ The Orthodox Union's kosher division that Rabbi Genack leads certifies over 1,000,000 products in more than 8,500 plants around the world and is "by far the world's largest kosher certification and kosher supervision agency."⁶⁸

In June of 1954, Rabbi Moshe Feinstein (1895-1986) penned the first of three responsa (*Igros Moshe, Yoreh Deah*, 1:47-48) permitting what he called "*chalav ha-companies she-be-medinatenu*" (חלב הקאמפאניעס שבמדינתנו, milk of the companies that are in our country). Reb Moshe, as he was often known, was the preeminent decisor of Jewish law in America⁶⁹ and, regarded by many as the *posek ha-dor* (the leading halakhic decisor of his generation). He had immigrated to the United States in 1937 and soon became the rosh yeshiva of Mesivtha Tifereth Jerusalem in New York. He was president of the UOR, chaired the Moetzes Gedolei HaTorah (the council of rabbinic sages) of Agudath Israel of America from the 1960s until his death, and decided the halakhah of contemporary medical questions for the Association of Orthodox Jewish Scientists.⁷⁰ Beginning in 1959, he published his responsa in his multi-volume work, *Igros Moshe*.⁷¹ Reb Moshe unflinchingly

---

⁶⁵ Yitzchok Frankfurter, "Rabbi Menachem Genack, CEO of OU Kosher," OU Kosher Certification, November 24, 2014, https://oukosher.org/blog/consumer-kosher/ami-magazine-interview-rabbi-menachem-genack/.

⁶⁶ "Enr2018.Pdf," accessed April 29, 2021, https://www.state.nj.us/highereducation/documents/pdf/statistics/fiscal/Enr2018.pdf; Kareem Fahim, "As Orthodox Population Grows, So Do Tensions," *The New York Times*, December 10, 2007, sec. New York, https://www.nytimes.com/2007/12/10/nyregion/10lakewood.html; "Lakewood's Orthodox Population Keeps Growing. We Talk to a Rabbi about Why, and What It Means. - Nj.Com," accessed April 29, 2021, https://www.nj.com/news/erry-2018/11/2bd79bf32a6683/lakewoods-orthodox-population.html.

⁶⁷ Landes, David, "How Lakewood, N.J., Is Redefining What It Means To Be Orthodox in America," *Tablet Magazine*, June 5, 2013, https://www.tabletmag.com/sections/community/articles/lakewood-redefining-orthodoxy.

⁶⁸ "OU Kosher Certification Agency. Kosher Supervision by Orthodox Union," OU Kosher Certification, accessed April 29, 2021, https://oukosher.org/.

⁶⁹ Gurock, *Orthodox Jews in America*, 187.

⁷⁰ Fred Rosner, "Rabbi Moshe Feinstein's Influence on Medical Halacha," *Journal of Halacha and Contemporary Society* 20 (1990), 47–75.

⁷¹ Moshe Feinstein, *HebrewBooks.Org Sefer Detail:* אגרות משה - חלק א—פיינשטיין, משה בן.

took on complex and varied questions[72] generated by modern discoveries and circumstances that often were charged with controversy.[73]

Reb Moshe's decision on "*chalav ha-companies*," (now commonly called *chalav stam*, "just milk") rules that such milk is permissible because U.S. governmental inspection verifies that commercially produced milk is not adulterated by milk from non-kosher animals. As such, the governmental inspection establishes the purity of the milk as a generally accepted fact to which the halakhic rule of *anan sahadei* אנן סהדי (Aramaic "we [i.e., the whole community] are witnesses"[74])—that we are all virtual witnesses to the fact—pertains, and it is as if there is actual visual supervision by the Jewish community of the milk in domestic dairies (*Igros Moshe, Yoreh Deah*, 1:47). To those who were concerned about the conditions in farms and transport before the milk is processed, Reb Moshe states that the rabbinic prohibition (*gezerah*) does not apply until the final point of possession of milk prior to its transfer to a Jewish consumer (see also, *Igros Moshe, Yoreh Deah*, 3:17).

By 2008, the government had changed its procedures and no longer checks milk at dairies to determine which species produced it. This development would invalidate Reb Moshe's rationale. However, government inspectors do inspect the farms themselves. One aspect of the farm inspection is certifying that only cows are producing the milk. On the basis of the new procedures, the Orthodox Union (OU) continues to supervise *chalav stam*, though as the OU notes, this is a "total reverse of Reb Moshe's heter [permission]: Reb Moshe was mattir [permitted] cholov stam based on dairy plants being inspected by the government…Now, in contradistinction, government inspection of farms plays the central role…."[75] In more recent

---

דוד, 8 vols. (Brooklyn: Moriah Offset Company, 1959), https://hebrewbooks.org/916.

[72] There is a useful index to topics in *Igros Moshe*: Daniel Eidensohn, יד משה: מפתח לכל ח׳ חלקים של שו״ת אגרות משה מאת משה פיינשטיין (Brooklyn: D. Eidensohn), 1999.

[73] For a selection of Rabbi Feinstein's most significant responsa, see "Moshe Feinstein - Biography—JewAge," accessed April 28, 2021, https://www.jewage.org/wiki/en/Article:Moshe_Feinstein_-_Biography.

[74] A systematic explanation of the concept of *anan sahadei* complete with definitions and examples appears in "אנן סהדי - ויקישיבה," accessed April 29, 2021, https://www.yeshiva.org.il/wiki/index.php/%D7%90%D7%A0%D7%9F_%D7%A1%D7%94%D7%93%D7%99.

[75] Avrohom Gordimer, "Rav Moshe Zt"l's Heter of Cholov Stam Revisited," accessed April 29, 2021, https://www.kashrut.com/articles/CholovStamHeter/; "Rav Moshe Zt"l's Heter of Cholov Stam Revisited," OU Kosher Certification, December 22, 2008, https://oukosher.org/blog/consumer-kosher/rav-moshe-ztls-heter-of-cholov-stam-revisited/. Though these articles are virtually identical, the first provides the name of the

years, technology has further strengthened the oversight. A system of milk samples linked to specific farms and barcoding links the farms to the dairies where the milk is processed.[76]

Rabbi Feinstein was not alone in his conclusions. In his commentary on *Yoreh Deah*, the Hazon Ish provides at least theoretical support for Rabbi Feinstein's position (*Hazon Ish, Yoreh Deah,* 41:4).[77] The Chazon Ish was typically aligned with more stringent halakhic positions and continues to be seen as a key authority in *Haredi* circles. Finally, Rabbi Joseph B. Soloveitchik provided three reasons to accept what was later called *chalav stam*: "if there are no non-Kosher animals found in the herd of animals that is being milked—אין בעדרו טמא—many opinions rule leniently. Second, we may rely on the government (USDA) supervision and inspections to ensure that the milk we consume is from cows. Number three, technically the rabbinic edict forbidding drinking milk from an animal that was milked by a non-Jew does not apply since today the cows are milked by machines."[78] In sum, preeminent rabbinic authorities of the last generation, chief among them the leading *posek* of his generation, and the OU permit *chalav stam*.

The practical applications of this conclusion have changed and shaped kashrut in America. There are four generally accepted national kosher supervisory agencies in the United States: the OU (Orthodox Union, New York); OK Kosher Certification (Brooklyn, NY); Star-K (Baltimore); and Kof-K (Teaneck, NJ). Each of them supervises products that are *chalav stam*. Indeed, supervisors at OU and Kof-K[79] state that "99%" of the dairy products their agencies oversee are *chalav stam*. The Star-K has a slightly different structure. "The STAR-K symbol on dairy products is ALWAYS cholov Yisroel." However, a separate division of Star-K, called Star-D is "administered by STAR-K personnel. All standards of STAR-K are em-

---

author, Rabbi Avrohom Gordimer—OU Rabbinic Coordinator for Dairy rather than designating him as OU Kosher Staff. The omission on the OU website is somewhat strange since the article is written in the first person.

[76] Avrohom Gordimer, interview by author, April 29, 2021.

[77] "HebrewBooks.Org Sefer Detail: 1878- ישעיהו, אברהם—קרליץ, חזון איש - יורה דעה 1953," accessed April 26, 2021, https://hebrewbooks.org/14334.

[78] "Chalav Yisrael—Part I Rav Soloveitchik's View by Rabbi Chaim Jachter," Kol Torah, accessed April 26, 2021, https://www.koltorah.org/halachah/chalav-yisrael-rabbi-soloveitchiks-view-by-rabbi-howard-jachter?rq=chalav%20yisrael. Rabbi Joseph B. Soloveitchik permitted cheese products that would not be seen as acceptable today, but a discussion of cheese is beyond the scope of this article.

[79] Rabbi Avrohom Gordimer, the supervisor for dairy products of the OU and Rabbi Yehudah Rosenbaum of Kof-K, separate telephone interviews, April 28, 2021.

ployed in Star-D certifications except for the fact that Star-D products are cholov stam."⁸⁰ The OK cites the various halakhic arguments and strongly encourages the use of *chalav Yisrael*, but says that "most [OK] dairy certified products are Cholov Stam."⁸¹

The proliferation of *chalav stam* products has meant that kosher dairy products can be found even in small or rural American communities, where supermarkets typically carry milk, cottage cheese, cream cheese, ice cream, and sour cream bearing the insignia of the most respected and largest kashrut agencies. In addition, though kashrut agencies are private, religious enterprises and their books are thus not open to the public, the proportion of dairy products that are *chalav stam* provides prima facie evidence that such products supply a significant portion of their revenue. In concert with technological advancements, *chalav stam* has also made possible the mass production of kosher cheese, a topic beyond the scope of this article.⁸²

The ubiquitous permissibility and availability of *chalav stam* products provides a useful test case for the proposals espoused in "Rupture and Reconstruction" and the simple point made by Rabbi Mordechai Eliyahu. Text has in fact replaced the mimetic observance that characterized an earlier generation of European-born Orthodox Jews. The problem is that even the text can be ignored in favor of the stringent. It is understandable when Hasidic Jews with a long tradition of *chalav Yisrael* reject the opinions of Lithuanian-trained *poskim*. However, in *Haredi* and even modern Orthodox environments, *chalav Yisrael* has become the creeping standard. Despite the fact that *rashei yeshiva* and many if not all of the communal chief rabbis of past generations did not require *chalav Yisrael*, their successors often do.

Communal unity and commercial success can converge. Thus, dairy restaurants tend to adopt *chalav Yisrael* to attract more customers. In 2019 an elegant, upscale kosher dairy restaurant opened in the Philadelphia suburbs. It served both *chalav Yisrael* and *chalav stam* and had separate kitchens and supervision.⁸³ Six months later, the owners decided to serve only *chalav stam*,

---

⁸⁰ "Star-D: STAR-K," accessed April 29, 2021, https://www.star-k.org/star-d.

⁸¹ "What's the Deal with Dairy - Kosher Spirit," OK Kosher Certification, accessed May 10, 2021, https://www.ok.org/article/whats-deal-dairy/.

⁸² Avrohom Gordimer, ‏חלב עכו"ם, השגחה על חליבה ועשיית גבינה ע"י ויאו‎ *Mesorah_27*. Pdf," 92-105; accessed April 26, 2021, https://oukosher.org/content/uploads/2012/12/Mesorah_27.pdf.

⁸³ "Zagafen Opens With Kosher Pizza and Italian-Inspired Fare in Bala Cynwyd," *Philadelphia Magazine* (blog), August 30, 2019, https://www.phillymag.com/foobooz/2019/08/30/zagafen-kosher-pizza-italian-restaurant-bala-cynwyd-philadelphia/.

but a few months thereafter, factors of quality, feasibility and customer appeal led to another revision, this time to all *chalav Yisrael*.[84] To accomplish that final conversion and assuage concerns by those who eschew *chalav stam*, all utensils that could be kashered were kashered while those that could not be kashered were discarded and new utensils purchased in their place. The OU, the restaurant's supervisory agency, did not consider the kashering halakhically necessary, but countenanced it to promote acceptance by those who actually regard *chalav stam* as not kosher, specifically members of the Hasidic community.[85]

The move to all *chalav Yisrael* made economic sense, but if doing so denied the kashrut of *chalav stam*, a clearly kosher food as documented above, then the halakhic system itself faces challenge from texts that generate gratuitous stringencies. "Rupture and Reconstruction" was originally developed through a scholarly project on fundamentalism.[86] The denial of the very validity of decisions permitting *chalav stam* suggests not only the triumph of text but a literalism that challenges the central role of *poskim* and the historic halakhic process. As Rabbi Mordechai Eliyahu demonstrated by his actions: Kosher but not *mehuddar* is still kosher.

---

[84] Andy Gotlieb, "Community Briefs: Zagafen Regains Cholov Yisroel Designation," *Jewish Exponent* (blog), October 15, 2020, https://www.jewishexponent.com/2020/10/15/community-briefs-cemetery-quotes-himmler-in-calendar/.

[85] Michael Kittell, the OU *mashgiach* for Zagafen dairy restaurant (370 Montgomery Ave, Merion Station, PA 19066), telephone communication, May 10, 2021.

[86] Haym Soloveitchik, "Migration, Acculturation, and the New Role of Texts in the Haredi World," in Martin E. Marty, R. Scott Appleby, and American Academy of Arts and Sciences, eds., *Accounting for Fundamentalisms: The Dynamic Character of Movements*, The Fundamentalism Project, v. 4 (Chicago: University of Chicago Press, 1994), 197–235.

Finding the Button and the Buttonhole

Eric George Tosi

> "Hear, O Israel: The Lord our God, the Lord is one! You shall love the Lord your God with all your heart, with all your soul, and with all your strength. And these words which I command you today shall be in your heart. You shall teach them diligently to your children, and shall talk of them when you sit in your house, when you walk by the way, when you lie down, and when you rise up. You shall bind them as a sign on your hand, and they shall be as frontlets between your eyes. You shall write them on the doorposts of your house and on your gates."
> —Deuteronomy 6:4-9

I first met Ora at JFK airport after a long flight back from Japan with her husband, Rabbi Joseph Prouser. We had been chaplains for the Boy Scouts at various national and international Jamborees (and roommates as well). We were bleary-eyed, exhausted and frankly tired of the constant whine of the engines for close to 19 hours. Yet when Ora and I first met and talked, I knew immediately that here was a kindred spirit whose love for God and for her family was acutely apparent. Her joy at seeing her husband was palpable yet that did not preclude her from warmly greeting me and my wife (who had come to pick me up as well). Through my many long-standing connections with her husband, I had come to know Ora in spirit, but only now did I have the opportunity to get to know her in person.

This led to a most unusual request (at least it seemed so at first) for me to come and speak at her seminary... on the topic of evangelism. Why is this unusual? Well, on two counts. First, I am a priest in the Orthodox Church who specializes in evangelism and mission from an Orthodox Christian perspective. Second, what would I have to say to a group of rabbinical students, totally out of my context, on how to do Jewish mission? Yet the more I thought about it, the more I believed that I did have something to say on the matter. My long, late-night discussions over the years with her husband had discovered an intersection of thought and practice. And perhaps an ecumenical *anknüpfungspunkt* (entry point, or, to be more linguistically precise.... where the button goes through the buttonhole), so that we may find some common ground in how we bring people to God.[1] So how do we get

---
[1] For a more precise examination into the concept of *anknüpfungspunkt* see Bowen, John

that button through the buttonhole in this matter?

First, We Have to Find the Button

The Book of Deuteronomy (*Devarim* in Hebrew) is seminal to the understanding of Judaism and Christianity. It contains the instructions for how to follow God and His commandments, and an exhortation on what that means for all people. From a Jewish perspective, the giving of the Commandments, the regulation of worship and communal behaviors, as well as the warnings of being faithful to God, form the basis of so much in Judaism (even if the practical implications are contested to this day). From an Orthodox Christian perspective, where there is so much in common on these matters, it informs the most central of all teachings, as found in the Gospel of Mark (12:28-30) when Christ was asked what was the greatest commandment. He repeated Deuteronomy 6:5 as to loving God with all your heart, all your soul and all your strength. *The Lord our God, the Lord is one! You shall love the Lord your God with all your heart, with all your soul, and with all your strength.*

This was the button. Loving God with all that you have so that you can find and serve God. This is the central tenet for all people of Faith: how do we truly love God above all else? I am reminded of a story of the first American Orthodox Saint, Herman of Alaska, who died in 1837 on Spruce Island, Alaska (a small island off of Kodiak). He was canonized by the Orthodox Church in 1970. As was common in his later life, he was exiled to Spruce Island by the Russian American Company for his support of the native Alaskans (Alaska was part of Russia at the time). Ships would stop by Spruce Island, allowing passengers and crew to meet and talk with this holy man. He once asked a group of Russian Naval Officers what they love best, what was dearest to them. They each replied by asking for a ship of their own, a good wife, wealth, etc. Fr. Herman then asked in response, "What about God?" Each one again replied, "Of course God. We need to love God." Fr. Herman then said, "And I, a poor sinner, have been trying these forty years to learn how to love God, and I cannot say I even now love Him properly, for if we love someone, we think of them always, we try to please them day and night, our heart and mind are full of the object of our love.... so then, gentlemen, do you love God? Do you turn to Him often? Do you remember Him always, pray always to Him, and do His will, according to the Scriptures? ....For our good, for our happiness let us vow that from this

---

P., *Evangelism for "Normal" People: Good News for Those Looking for a Fresh Approach* (Augsburg Fortress: Minneapolis, MN: 2002), Chapter 8.

day, from this hour, from this very minute, we should try to love God above all else and carry out his teachings!"[2]

Loving God is the key to any endeavor, particularly in understanding evangelism. If we love God, truly love God, then we naturally want to be with Him, talk about Him, follow Him and His Will. We then learn to pass that love on to others: our family, friends, those whom God has placed before us on a daily basis. Deuteronomy 6 urges us in the next sentences after the Great Commandment, *"And these words which I command you today shall be in your heart. You shall teach them diligently to your children, and shall talk of them when you sit in your house, when you walk by the way, when you lie down, and when you rise up.* If we were to find any common ground between us, it would need to rest on the love for God. So perhaps the separation between a Jewish Rabbinical School and an Orthodox Seminary on the topic of evangelism was not so very wide. Clearly, the goal was how to teach the love of God and how to live that love out in the world.

Now the Buttonhole

This was going to be a bit difficult, as it would seem the culture, the two religious communities' respective liturgical lives and theological presuppositions would preclude finding a common buttonhole. From an Orthodox Christian perspective, we owe our liturgical foundations to Jewish worship. The order of the Liturgy, the prayers that form the skeleton of the services (based primarily on the Book of Psalms), as well as certain communal disciplines such as fasting and prayers are quite familiar to one another. The services are chanted with no musical instruments. Even the structure and set-up of an Orthodox Christian Temple is in line with the Jewish people's Temple in Jerusalem. So, there is much that is familiar. There is also much that is different or has evolved as Judaism and Orthodox Christianity developed over the centuries. Nonetheless, this commonality of worship is certainly a starting point.[3]

I am reminded of the great 20th century Orthodox scholar, Protopresbyter Alexander Schmemann and what he wrote in his seminal work, *For the Life of the World*:

---

[2] For a look at the story of St. Herman, Wonderworker of Alaska, see Oleksa, Michael, *Alaskan Mission Spirituality* (St. Vladimir's Seminary Press: Crestwood, NY: 2010), Chapter 1.

[3] For an interesting examination into the Jewish basis for Orthodox Christian worship see Schmemann, Alexander, *Introduction to Liturgical Theology* (St. Vladimir's Seminary Press: Crestwood, NY: 1986), Chapter 2.

> "And in the Bible to bless God is not a 'religious' or 'cultic' act, but the *very way of life*. God blessed the world, blessed man, blessed the seventh day (that is, time), and this means that He filled all that exists with His love and goodness, made all of this 'very good.' So the only *natural* (and not supernatural) reaction of man, to whom God gave this blessed and sanctified world, is to bless God in return, to thank Him, to *see* the world as God sees it and—in this act of gratitude and adoration—to know, name and possess the world. All rational, spiritual and other qualities of man, distinguishing him from other creatures, have their focus and ultimate fulfillment in this capacity to bless God, to know, so to speak, the meaning of the thirst and hunger that constitutes his life. '*Homo sapiens*', '*homo faber*'...yes, but first of all, '*homo adorans.*' The first and basic definition of man is that he is the priest. He stands at the center of the world and unifies it in his act of blessing God, of both receiving the world from God and offering it to God..."[4]

This is the buttonhole, so to speak, as our first and primary vocation as a person is to worship God, to offer Him that which is already His. In the Orthodox Liturgy there is a primary moment in which the priest elevates the gifts and exclaims, "Thine Own of Thine Own, We Offer unto Thee on Behalf of All and For All." These are the words which each of us should be saying with every breath and action we take. Offer to God that which He offered to us in praise and worship. A human, after all, is principally a worshipping creature. This is the buttonhole we seek.

It is this commonality of the centrality of worship and our common vision of humanity offering that worship which allows us to have a common ground. Because once we recognize the centrality of worship which is part of one's very deepest essence as a human, all things will follow in close order. How we see ourselves, how we see the world, how we approach the greatest if not the most difficult of questions lie in that basic worldview. Even if we strongly disagree on approaches and even outcomes, the very basic fact of being a worshipping creature allows us to overcome them.

If we identify the button as the abiding love for God and the buttonhole as the love for God manifested in worship, then we can approach the world with a vision that remains in stark contrast to what is, sadly, too often pre-

---

[4] Schmemann, Alexander, *For the Life of the World* (St. Vladimir's Seminary Press: Crestwood, NY: 1973), p. 15.

sented to us: division, confusion, cynicism and despair. We must love God and worship God in order to find any sense in this fallen and confused world.

The Different Buttons and Buttonholes

But let us not be so Pollyannaish as to think that differences do not exist. There are some major theological and liturgical differences that are very apparent even in the most cursory of discussions. This is not the place to discuss those, nor to come to any grand conclusion. The purpose is first and foremost to acknowledge the most basic of commonalities, that is, that there is a button and buttonhole that we can agree on. Let us just keep that in its central place.

There are, of course, other buttonholes between us. One thing that became apparently clear in my many late-night discussions with Rabbi Joseph is how we shared a very similar culture. Many of our people came from the same regions in Eastern Europe, though divided by culture and religion and, yes, a sometimes violent history between the two groups. Yet there was another thing we shared in that common history: we both shared a history of violence against our people. The Jews have been violently and disgustingly persecuted for the longest of periods of history. There is simply no excuse for this. The Orthodox have similarly been violently and disgustingly persecuted for a long period of history. Most recently, the 20th century has seen the largest oppression of Orthodox by communists in Eastern Europe and by Muslims in the Middle East. In some places, even to this day they have been almost totally eliminated. We are people who know the effects of violence and oppression and so our people have lived with that violence and oppression. This is not to outdo each other as to "who suffered more," but rather simply to acknowledge the fact that we understand each other in these matters. That should be a major buttonhole in any discussion, because we sought refuge in precisely the same place, our faith and our worship, again confirming the centrality of us as worshipping creatures.

St. Nikolai Velimirovich, a 20th century Serbian Orthodox saint who was sent to Dachau for his support of the Jewish people (he survived but refused to return to Serbia, settling in America at one of our monasteries), wrote:

> "What does it mean to take up your cross? It means the willing acceptance, at the hand of Providence, of every means of healing, bitter though it may be, that is offered. Do great catastrophes fall on you? Be obedient to God's will, as Noah was. Is sacrifice demanded of you? Give yourself into God's hands with the same faith as Abram

had when he went to sacrifice his son. Is your property ruined? Do your children die suddenly? Suffer it all with patience, cleaving to God in your heart, as Job did. Do your friends forsake you, and you find yourself surrounded by enemies? Bear it all without grumbling, and with faith that God's help is at hand, as the apostles did."[5]

We all know of what he speaks.

Conclusion

To circle back to the verses from Deuteronomy, we come to the conclusion of the text: *"You shall bind them as a sign on your hand, and they shall be as frontlets between your eyes. You shall write them on the doorposts of your house and on your gates."* We go from loving God, to serving and teaching of God, to worshipping God and, in conclusion, we must witness to that God. We are not called to hide these things as a *"lamp under a bushel"* (Matthew 5:14-15, Mark 4:21-25, Luke 8:16-18), but rather to shine before the world the light of God and God's love. We need to make our mark on the doorposts of our house, so to speak, because it is only through this that our true love for God can be placed before the world.

We honor Dr. Ora Horn Prouser because she has done precisely this. She has been that light for the world to see, honoring God, teaching about God, worshipping God, and, ultimately, loving God. If we need anything right now, it is precisely this. We can find a way to put that button through the buttonhole because we have found that we share the same button and the same buttonhole. That is of great comfort. As Psalm 36:9 states, *"For with Thee is the fountain of life, in Thy light shall we see light."*

---

[5] Velimirovich, Nikolai, *Homilies: Volume 1* (Lazarica Press, Birmingham UK: 1996), p. 177.

"A TOrah Line"

Amy Roth

A brief novella based on the music of "A Chorus Line"

Our story begins with a family in suburban New Jersey, whose middle child had a three letter first name and the middle name Susan. In honor of Ora Susan Horn Prouser's sixtieth birthday, (and because Broadway theaters are shut due to the pandemic) I have gathered several Tony award winners, to help celebrate the big 6-**O**. "We" have come up with a musical look at Ora's life: through the music (re-written) of "A Chorus Line." Since our sixty-year-old celebrant is an expert at both Bible AND "A Chorus Line, " I call this piece , "A T**Ora**h Line."

* * *

Once upon a time, the Horns of Summit had three children. The middle child, Ora, was well-known for standing up for the injustices in the world (and at Solomon Schechter). She grew up in a home where Hebrew and Judaism were part of the daily vocabulary. Ora, a gentle and sensitive soul, is warm, creative and extremely kind. And she is a loyal and dedicated friend—a most unique person. Here is where we meet Ora…..her interests, her personality, the beginnings of her journey through life.

* * *

Musical Piece #1: O!

To the tune of "ONE"

O! from Summit, New Jersey, middle child of the Horns
O! early Torah reader, for girls it was not the norm!
O's style so understated we never knew
Just how much Ugaritic was much ado!
O! Everyone expected her to make a big shpiel
O! Winning an election - an office of Hagalil!
O's habits changed from being carn-ivore
Eating veggies and tofu she'd not known before!

O! Hard to read her writing, of her typing we are glad,
O! Starsky and Hutch not on—sure to make her mad!
Or maybe time to take a Quan-tum Leap….
For O the learning curve is never steep!

O! PhD by thirty all as Eema of three!
O! Scholar and mentor—a pro-fessor she would be!
O and Joe! Such a lear-ned zug,
Good thing Joe can make the food,
She's our O!!!!!

* * *

Back to our story ~
When Ora was fourteen, she decided that she wanted to leave Summit and live on a bus, with a bunch of other Jewish teenagers. That summer, Ora's world was broadened as she travelled for six weeks on the cross-country trip of a lifetime.

* * *

Musical Piece #2: Ode to Tiyul Gimmel

To the tune of "What I did for Love"

Nineteen seventy-five
The bus was Tiyul Gimmel
Elko, Rawlins and North Platte
Helped to set the scene
Ora was fourteen
When we went on Wheels!
Grand Canyon Tisha B'Av
Yosemite on Shabbos
Public venues everywhere
Davening outside, we sure did take pride
In our Jewish selves
(refrain)
Bus, singing on the bus
Sleeping on the bus
Bonding like not ever

Friends from all around
Even on Long Island:)!
Clapping, singing
Standing on chairs! (oops)
Finding her own way
As a young adult, as a good friend
(refrain)
Bus, singing on the bus
Noshing on the bus
Writing lots of letters
New York to LA
And many southern counties
Only Jews in Old Tucson
Salt Lake City and Las Vegas too
Hoover Dam in view!
(refrain)
Friends
Lot of new friends
Want summer not to end
Wheels we'll all remember
Nineteen seventy-five
I became good friends with Ora
Tiyul Gimmel in our hearts!
Won't forget, can't regret
What we learned on Wheels!

* * *

Back to our story

Ora graduated high school with distinction and as an officer of Hagalil USY. She entered the hallowed halls of JTS and Columbia University. Many vegetarian Shabbat meals in Mathilde Schechter and years later, it was time for Ora to choose a major and career path. As such a talented student, many avenues were open to her; all she needed to do was choose! But how does one choose an area of focus when working so hard to finish TWO college degrees simultaneously while also falling in love with her bashert?

* * *

Musical Piece #3: Psych or Bible

To the tune of "Dance: Ten; Looks: Three"

Psych or Bible
Study brains or Ugaritic
Ancient texts or analytic
Oh I don't know, Oh I don't know!

Psych or Bible
People's problems all day to listen
Or Teaching text until I glisten
Oh I don't know, Oh I don't know!
Psych or Bible
I have to choose a path
How will I decide what is next?
Psych or Bible, I flip a coin
It's HEADS! I go with TEXT

* * *

Back to our story
And so, a biblicist was born! Ora focused on the Bible and ancient languages, and especially how all of it illuminated (Ora does mean "light" after all) understanding and meaning of ancient texts. She found herself a writer, teacher, mother and partner. And then…..Ora arrived at AJR (how fortuitous for them) and proceeded to innovatively design the next generation of Jewish leaders. Ora's approach is both spiritual and with academic integrity—hence her doctoral dissertation, "The Phenomenology of the Lie in Biblical Narrative."

* * *

Musical Piece #4: Yom Huledet Sameach to Ora

To the tune of "I Hope I Get it!"

5-6-7-8
Ora's turning 60
She's turning 60
She's always been my younger friend!

Look at all that she's done
At AJR and
In the world biblical!
On the march for women
And in her writing
She's been a role model

(refrain : "I really need this job")
She's Ayal's circus mom
Won a seat for Hamilton!
Is Eitan's groupie, biggest fan
It goes to show
At sixty years, we know she will still grow

Savta at the births
Matan and Noam
How much more special can it be?

* * *

Close babysitter
So that the fun does never end
(refrain: "I really need this job")
And Ora married Joe
More shrewd you'll never know
Dynamic duo
Writers, Layners, creators
Brings spirituality
Advocate for diversity
Expert at lying in the Bible
And yet,
A more upright person
You've not met!

* * *

(Epilogue)
As you know, Ora's story continues. What will she be like AFTER turning sixty? Stay tuned for further adventures in Savta-hood, acrobatics (will she ever learn the trapeze?), biblical jewels, and sensitive interactions with her parents and friends. She might also be overheard apologizing for some-

thing unrelated to her at all, or ordering take-out from Veggie Heaven. May 2021 is a cause for celebration: Kol Ha Kavod to Rabbi Bill and Dena Horn for raising such an exceptional human! And although it is easy to laugh with Ora, she is also a wise, sympathetic listener; she offers valuable counsel, and insights into life. We are all fortunate to know and to celebrate Ora, and most of all, to share this journey through life with her.

Happy 60th, my friend!

Selected Bibliography: Dr. Ora Horn Prouser

Doctoral Dissertation, Jewish Theological Seminary: "The Phenomenology of the Lie in Biblical Narrative," 1991.

Esau's Blessing: How the Bible Embraces Those with Special Needs (Ben Yehuda Press), 2012.

Circus Texts/Sacred Arts, Ora Horn Prouser, Michael Kasper, and Ayal Prouser, eds., Ben Yehuda Press (forthcoming).

"Awe-tism and the Biblical God," *V'Ed Ya'aleh: Festschrift in Honor of Dr. Edward L. Greenstein* (SBL Press), Peter Machinist, Robert Harris, Joshua Berman, Nili Samet, and Noga Ayali-Darshan, eds. (forthcoming).

"Active Sitting in the Round: How the Body Can Learn Sacred Texts Through Circus Arts" *AJS Prespectives: The Body Issue*, Fall 2019.

"A Certain Time: An Intertextual Reading of Havdalah and Esther," in *Havdalah* (Mesorah Matrix), Martin Cohen, ed., 2017.

"Living Pluralism at AJR," in *Studies in Judaism and Pluralism Honoring the 60th Anniversary of the Academy for Jewish Religion* (Ben Yehuda Press), Leonard Levin, ed., 2016.

"Rabbinic Education: More than an Academic Exercise," in *Keeping Faith in Rabbis*, Hayim Herring and Elie Roscher, eds., 2014.

"The Case for 'True Pluralism,'" op-ed in *The Jewish Week* 8/20/14.

"Staying Abraham's Hand: On Withholding Disturbing Biblical Texts," in *HaYidion*, RAVSAK, Summer 2012.

The Ziegler School of Rabbinic Studies, American Jewish University, *Walking With History*, Unit Two: The Biblical Period, 2012.

"Probing Communal Views on Patrilineal Descent," op-ed in *The Jewish Week* 3/13/12.

"Scents and Sensuality from the Temple to Today: Review of Books," *Lilith* 36 (2011-2012), pp. 43-44.

"Vaetchanan: Main Commentary," *The Torah: A Women's Commentary*, Tamara Cohn Eskenazi and Andrea Weiss, eds., URJ Press, 2007.

"Chukat: Another View," *The Torah: A Women's Commentary*, Tamara Cohn Eskenazi and Andrea Weiss, eds., URJ Press, 2007.

"Eschewing Footwear: The Call of Moses as Biblical Archetype," *Jews and Shoes*, Edna Nahshon, ed., Berg Publishers, 2007.

Contributed to *Open Hearts, Open Minds, Open Doors: Creating Access and Inclusion in Worship*, Pathways Awareness Foundation, Chicago.

The Abayudaya Torah, edited a Hebrew-Luganda translation of the Torah for the Jewish Community of Uganda, 2005.

Parashat Yitro, Chancellor's Parashah Commentary, 2/14/98 http://www.jtsa.edu/PreBuilt/ParahsahArchives/5758/yitro.shtml

"Agents of the Divine Plan," *Sh'ma: A Journal of Jewish Responsibility*. Jewish Family & Life (JFL Media), December 1999, pp. 11-12.

"The Hebrew Bible," in *Lectures in Jewish History and Literature* (Russian), Burton Visotzky & David Fishman, eds., Moscow State University, 1999. Adaptation for English edition, *From Mesopotamia to Modernity: Ten Introductions to Jewish History and Literature*, Westview Press, 1999.

"Striking Images in Hosea," *Jewish Education News* 18:2 (1997), pp. 16-17.

"Suited to the Throne: The Symbolic Use of Clothing in David and Saul Narratives," *Journal for the Study of the Old Testament* 71 (1996), pp. 27-37. Abridged in *Bible Review* 14 (1998), pp. 22-27.

Review of *Narrative Art in the Hebrew Bible* by David Gunn and Danna Nolan Fewell, *AJS Review: The Journal of the Association of Jewish Studies* 21 (1996), pp. 127-129.

"Living in Transition," *Lifecycles, Volume II*, Debra Orenstein, Jane Rachel Litman, eds., Jewish Lights Publishing, 1996.

Contributed to *The Bible Through the Ages*, Robert V. Huber, ed., Reader's Digest, 1996.

"The Truth About Women and Lying," *Journal for the Study of the Old Testament*, 61 (1994), pp. 15-28.

Divrei Torah
(interpretations of the weekly Torah portion) in The Jewish Week:

"Hearing From Jews With Disabilities," 4/9/19.
Thinking about those with disabilities in the Bible from their own perspective.
"The Bones of Joseph," 1/15/19.
The hopeful statement involved in bringing Joseph's bones as part of the Exodus.
"Imagining Moses," 1/23/18
Moses' need to rely on others as a model for leadership and vulnerability.
"A Kind Word for Esau," 11/14/17.
The reconciliation of Jacob and Esau as a model of communication with "the other."
"Esau, Beautiful and Misunderstood," 11/24/15.
Esau as a model of living life free of guilt, blame, and regret.
"Echoes of the Scapegoat," 4/28/15.
An intertextual reading of the scapegoat narrative and Genesis 21-22.
"A Tale of Two Brothers," 2/11/14.
The Moses-Aaron relationship as the first truly successful biblical sibling relationship.

"When a Donkey Sees What a Prophet Won't," 7/3/12.
The importance of being changed by spiritually heightened experiences.
"Moses Finds His Voice," 8/2/11.
The growth in Moses as he learns to trust his own speech.
"The Inevitability of Revelation," 8/13/08.
An intertextual reading of Moses' final speech and the Book of Esther.
"The Plot Thickens," 11/12/08.
How an intertextual reading of the narratives of Jacob and Esau and Joab and David helps us understand the laws of Exodus.

Contributors

Rabbi Dr. Bradley Shavit Artson holds the Abner and Roslyn Goldstine Dean's Chair of the Ziegler School of Rabbinic Studies and is Vice President of American Jewish University in Los Angeles. Rabbi Artson has long been a passionate advocate for social justice, human dignity, diversity and inclusion. He wrote a book on Jewish teachings on war, peace and nuclear annihilation in the late 80s, became a leading voice advocating for LGBT marriage and ordination in the 90s, and has published and spoken widely on environmental ethics, special needs inclusion, racial and economic justice, cultural and religious dialogue and cooperation, and working for a just and secure peace for Israel and the Middle East. A member of the Philosophy Department, he is particularly interested in theology, ethics, and the integration of science and religion. He mentors Camp Ramah in California in Ojai and Ramah of Northern California in the Bay Area. He is also dean of the Zacharias Frankel College in Potsdam, Germany, ordaining Conservative rabbis for Europe. A frequent contributor for the Huffington Post, the Times of Israel, and a Contributing Writer for the Jewish Journal of Greater Los Angeles, he has a public figure Facebook page with over 70,000 likes. Rabbi Artson is the author of 12 books and over 250 articles, most recently *Renewing the Process of Creation: A Jewish Integration of Science and Spirit*. Married to Elana Artson, they are the proud parents of twins, Jacob and Shira.

Rabbi Elliot N. Dorff, Ph.D., is Rector and Distinguished Service Professor of Philosophy at American Jewish University and Visiting Professor at UCLA School of Law. He has served on three federal commissions and one State of California commission on issues in medical ethics. Since 2007 he has chaired the Conservative Movement's Committee on Jewish Law and Standards, which approved the responsum included in this volume by a vote of 21 in favor, one opposed, and three abstaining on May 13, 2020. He has written 14 books and over 200 articles on Jewish thought, law, and ethics, and has edited or co-edited an additional 14 books on those topics. Chapter Twelve of his book, *Matters of Life and Death: A Jewish Approach to Modern Medical Ethics,* is especially relevant to understanding the background of the essay included here.

Rabbi Nancy Fuchs Kreimer, Ph.D., is Associate Professor of Religious Studies and the founding Director of the Department of Multifaith Studies and Initiatives at the Reconstructionist Rabbinical College where she was ordained in 1982. She also holds a master's degree from Yale Divinity School and a doctorate from Temple University. With support from the Henry Luce Foundation, Nancy has pioneered innovative community-based learning opportunities for rabbinical students and their peers of other faiths. Her projects include: "Dialogue Retreats for Emerging Muslim and Jewish Leaders;" "Cultivating Character: A Conversation across Communities;" and "Campus Chaplaincy for a Multifaith World." Nancy is a past president of the Reconstructionist Rabbinical Association and a founding board member of the Interfaith Center of Philadelphia, Shoulder-to-Shoulder of the Islamic Society of North America (where she now serves on the Executive Committee), and the Sisterhood of Salaam Shalom (where she continues to serve on the board). She recently co-edited *Chapters of the Heart: Jewish Women Sharing the Torah of our Lives (*Wipf and Stock, 2013) and co-authored *Strangers, Neighbors, Friends: Muslim-Christian-Jewish Reflections on Compassion and Peace (*Wipf and Stock, 2018). In Spring, 2021, Nancy has had the honor of teaching "Deep Ecumenism" to 20 students in the Aleph Ordination Program.

Rabbi Matthew Goldstone is the Assistant Academic Dean at the Academy for Jewish Religion, where he teaches courses in Talmud and Halakhah. He is the author of *The Dangerous Duty of Rebuke* and co-author of *Binding Fragments of Tractate Temurah and the Problem of* Lishana 'Acharina.

Rabbi Prof. David Golinkin is the President of the Schechter Institutes, Inc., and a Professor of Talmud and Halakhah at the Schechter Institute of Jewish Studies in Jerusalem. He is the author or editor of sixty books in the fields of Halakhah, Midrash and other areas of Jewish Studies.

Dr. Edward L. Greenstein is Professor Emeritus of Bible at Bar-Ilan University. Prior to that he was Professor of Bible at Tel Aviv University and at the Jewish Theological Seminary in New York. He has also taught at Columbia, Yale, Princeton, and other institutions of higher learning and has lectured widely. An expert in ancient Semitic studies as well as Bible, Greenstein has edited the *Journal of the Ancient Near Eastern Society* since 1974 and has published hundreds of articles, essays, and reviews. He has been writing commentaries on Job, Lamentations, and Ruth, as well as other books. He has received many distinguished research fellowships and grants in the U.S. and in Israel. Bar-Ilan University awarded him a prize for innovative research. His much-acclaimed annotated translation of the Book of Job was published in 2019 by Yale University Press. In 2020 Greenstein was awarded the EMET Prize ("Israel's Nobel") for the area of Humanities in the field of Biblical Studies.

Debra E. Guston, Esq. is an attorney in New Jersey and a Visiting Lecturer at Rutgers School of Law where she teaches Family Law. Deb graduated cum laude from Mount Holyoke College, holds an M.A. from Emerson College and received her J.D. from Cardozo School of Law. Deb's practice focuses on family formation through adoption and assisted reproduction and family protection through estate planning, estate litigation and administration and guardianships for seniors and special needs children. She also represents non-profit organizations in formation and governance issues. Deb is a Past President of the Academy of Adoption & Assisted Reproduction Attorneys and currently serves as its Adoption Director, guiding adoption policy and advocacy. Deb serves as the Chair of the Bergen County LGBTQ Advisory Committee and is a Past President and current Trustee of ACLU-NJ.

Rabbi Jill Hackell, M.D. is Rabbi of West Clarkstown Jewish Center, a small, non-affiliated congregation in Rockland County, New York. She received her ordination from the Academy for Jewish Religion (AJR), along with an MA in Judaic Studies from Gratz College. She received a BS from Tufts University and an MD plus pediatric residency training at Johns Hopkins, practicing general pediatrics before going on to a career in the pharmaceutical industry in clinical research on new vaccines. She has combined these two paths through an interest in bioethics, teaching this subject on the graduate level, including at AJR. She also teaches subjects of general Jewish interest at the Jewish Federation of Rockland County. She serves on the AJR board as the alumni liaison to the Association of Rabbis and Cantors (ARC).

Rabbi Jill Hammer, Ph.D. is the Director of Spiritual Education at the Academy for Jewish Religion, and co-founder of the Kohenet Hebrew Priestess Institute. Her most recent book is titled *Return to the Place: The Magic, Meditation, and Mystery of Sefer Yetzirah*, and her forthcoming book is titled *Undertorah: An Earth-Based Jewish Kabbalah of Dreams*. Rabbi Hammer is also the author of other books including *The Hebrew Priestess: Ancient and New Visions of Jewish Women's Spiritual Leadership* (with Taya Shere), *The Jewish Book of Days: A Companion for all Seasons*, *Sisters at Sinai: New Tales of Biblical Women*, and *The Book of Earth and Other Mysteries*. She is the translator of *The Romemu Siddur* and *Siddur haKohanot: A Hebrew Priestess Prayerbook*.

Rabbi Jeffrey Hoffman holds a Doctorate in Jewish Literature (D.H.L.) in the field of Liturgy, rabbinic ordination, and an M.A. from The Jewish

Theological Seminary of America. He earned a B.A. with a double major in Judaic Studies/Hebrew from The State University of New York at Albany. He also engaged in undergraduate and graduate studies at The Hebrew University of Jerusalem and talmudic studies at Yeshivat HaMivtar in Jerusalem. He is the author of *Karov L'Chol Korav, For All Who Call: A Manual For Enhancing the Teaching of Prayer*, editor of *Siddur Tisha B'Av* for The Rabbinical Assembly, author of many articles and reviews, and author of a forthcoming book-length commentary on the *siddur*. He has served as a faculty member at The Jewish Theological Seminary and continues to teach at The Academy for Jewish Religion which he has served in various roles for over thirty years. He served for three years as assistant rabbi of Congregation Beth Israel in Vancouver, British Columbia and for twenty years as rabbi of Congregation Sons of Israel in Nyack, New York. He continues to love rock 'n roll, especially the music of the Grateful Dead, and has played guitar in various rock and folk bands over many years.

Rabbi Peter E. Hyman is the spiritual leader of Temple B'nai Israel in Easton, Maryland. A native of Connecticut, Rabbi Hyman came to Easton after serving congregations in Pennsylvania, Texas and Florida. Rabbi Hyman graduated from the Hebrew Union College Jewish Institute of Religion in Cincinnati, Ohio and was ordained in 1980. In 2005, he received an honorary Doctor of Divinity from the Hebrew Union College. Involved with all aspects of synagogue life and community relations, Rabbi Hyman has a passion for teaching and a commitment to share the wisdom and beauty of Judaism with all those he encounters. Rabbi Hyman has received many awards from religious and community groups, including the Union for Reform Judaism's Belin Award for Outreach Program Excellence, the Silver Buffalo Distinguished Service Award from the Boy Scouts of America, and the Bronze Wolf from the World Organization of the Scout Movement. He is the proud father of two sons, Daniel and Ari Hyman, grandfather to Ayla Reese Hyman, and a longtime friend of Dr. Ora Horn Prouser and Rabbi Joseph Prouser.

Hazzan Michael Kasper was born in Newark and raised in West Orange, New Jersey. He moved to New York in 1974 after graduation from the George Washington University and winning first prize in a National Society of Arts and Letters choreographer's competition. He apprenticed with Twyla Tharp and went on to direct and choreograph for his own company, the Michael Kasper Dance Company. He has taught and performed throughout the United States and Israel. He received an M.S.W. in 1985 and graduated from the New York Center for Psychoanalytic Training in

1992, eventually teaching there as well. More recently he taught in Hunter College's Post Master's Program in Clinical Social Work and is published in the book *Controversies On Countertransference*. For many years he was an ice-skating instructor at the Westchester Skating Academy specializing in his work with autistic and special needs children. More recently, Hazzan Kasper retired from the pulpit at Congregation Sons of Israel (Nyack, New York), which he held for ten years, before leaving in order to devote himself full-time to the Academy for Jewish Religion, where he is the Dean of Cantorial Studies and Director of Student Life and Placement.

Rabbi Dov Linzer is President and Rosh HaYeshiva of Yeshivat Chovevei Torah Rabbinical School. An acclaimed Torah and halakhic scholar, Rabbi Linzer serves as religious guide to the yeshiva's current rabbinical students and its over 150 rabbis serving in the field. Rabbi Linzer became YCT's president in 2019, assuming the institutional leadership of YCT in addition to its Torah leadership. Rabbi Linzer has been a leading rabbinic voice in the Modern Orthodox community for over 25 years. He has published over 100 teshuvot (responsa) and scholarly Torah articles, and answers hundreds of questions each year from rabbis in the field. He hosts a number of highly popular podcasts and videocasts, including "Joy of Text" and "Iggros Moshe A to Z," in addition to his daf yomi podcast covering all of shas. In 2012, he was the convener of a Modern Orthodox Siyyum HaShas.

Rev. Dr. Barbara Horkoff Mutch is the Senior Director of Accreditation for the Association of Theological Schools in the United States and Canada. For 34 years she served the Canadian Baptists of Western Canada, first as the Associate Pastor of First Baptist Church (Regina, Saskatchewan) and then as the Charles Bentall Professor of Pastoral Studies and Academic Vice President of Carey Theological College (Vancouver, British Columbia). Her Doctor of Ministry degree is from Princeton Theological Seminary. Barbara admires Ora Horn Prouser, is a fan of the Academy of Jewish Religion, and is both grateful and honored for the opportunity to contribute to this volume.

Rabbi Joseph H. Prouser, who edited this volume, is Rabbi of Temple Emanuel of North Jersey, in Franklin Lakes, New Jersey. He is a Mesader Gittin (scribe and adjudicator of Jewish divorce), and has served on the Rabbinical Assembly's Committee on Jewish Law and Standards, as a member of the Joint Bet Din of the Conservative Movement, and as the Rabbinical Assembly Liaison to the U.S. Department of Health and Human Services. He was a Daniel Jeremy Silver Fellow at Harvard University's Center for Jewish Studies, and the National Jewish Chaplain of the Boy Scouts of America. Rabbi Prouser holds a BA in Religious Studies from Columbia, as well as BA, MA, Rabbinic Ordination, and honorary Doctor of Divinity degrees from the Jewish Theological Seminary of America. He is married to Dr. Ora Horn Prouser (cf. Proverbs 18:22).

Rabbi Jonathan Rosenbaum, Ph.D., is President Emeritus and Professor Emeritus of Jewish Studies at Gratz College. Since 2009, he has also been a Visiting Scholar at the University of Pennsylvania. Rosenbaum previously received academic tenure at three institutions and held an endowed professorship. He possesses the unusual distinction of having served congregations and been recognized as a rabbi in the Reform, Conservative, and Orthodox streams of Judaism.

Rabbi Amy Roth is Director of Congregational Schools at Temple Israel of Great Neck. She was ordained at the Jewish Theological Seminary, and received a BA from Barnard College. Prior to joining the staff at Temple Israel, Rabbi Roth spent eleven years as the Associate Director of Camp Ramah in the Berkshires, where her four children grew up (one of whom was almost born there). She has served as Adult B'nai Mitzvah coordinator at New City Jewish Center, and was the Jewish Enrichment Educator at the YJCC of Bergen County. Rabbi Roth has also served as a faculty member of the Passover Retreat at Camp Ramah Darom in Clayton, Georgia. In addition, Rabbi Roth has taught adult education mini-courses at a variety of synagogues and churches in the New York metropolitan area. Amy grew up in Bloomfield, New Jersey, is an alumna of Hagalil USY, and is married to Rabbi Noam Marans. She is privileged to have had Ora Horn Prouser in her life since their early USY days!

Dr. Shuly Rubin Schwartz, Irving Lehrman Research Professor of American Jewish History, is the eighth chancellor of The Jewish Theological Seminary. She is the first woman to serve in this role in its 135-year history. Chancellor Schwartz is devoted to building on JTS's unique strengths as a Jewish institution of higher learning that trains future leaders through deep study—with both head and heart—of Jewish texts, ideas and history. In JTS's thriving community, students develop the creative ability to imbue others with the intellectual, cultural, and religious sustenance that our tradition offers, and they enrich every community of which they are a part. Previously, Dr. Schwartz played a central role in shaping and strengthening JTS's academic programs while teaching and mentoring countless students. From 1993 to 2018, she served as dean of the Albert A. List College of

Jewish Studies, JTS's undergraduate dual-degree program with Columbia University and Barnard College. In 2010, she was also named dean of the Gershon Kekst Graduate School. In 2018, she assumed the provostship, while continuing as dean of the Kekst School. Chancellor Schwartz was one of the first women on the JTS faculty and played an instrumental role in introducing Jewish gender studies into the curriculum. As a scholar, she brings to light previously overlooked contributions of women to Jewish life and culture over the centuries and continually expands our understanding of American Judaism. Among her publications is the award-winning book, *The Rabbi's Wife*, a penetrating examination of the role of rabbis' wives in the development of American Jewish life.

Archpriest Eric George Tosi is the Rector of St. Gregory the Theologian Orthodox Church in Wappingers Falls, New York, and Assistant Professor of Pastoral Theology at St. Vladimir's Orthodox Theological Seminary in Crestwood, New York. He served for twelve years as the Secretary of the Orthodox Church in America before returning to parish ministry. He has served parishes in Montana, Nevada and New Jersey. Prior to entering the priesthood, he served as a Cavalry Officer in the US Army. Father Tosi was a chaplain and chief chaplain for the Boy Scouts of America at both national and world Jamborees. He is the former Chair of the Department of Evangelization of the OCA and currently leads the Commission on Missions and Evangelism for the Diocese of New York and New Jersey. He has a BA in Economics and History from Fordham University, an MA in European History from Fordham University, an MDiv from St. Vladimir's Seminary, and a Doctor of Ministry from the University of Toronto (Trinity). He is married with two children.

www.ingramcontent.com/pod-product-compliance
Lightning Source LLC
Chambersburg PA
CBHW070551160426
43199CB00014B/2454